Kaplan Publishing are constantly finding new ways to make a difference to your studies and our exciting online resources really do offer something different to students looking for exam success.

This book comes with free MyKaplan online resources so that you can study anytime, anywhere. **This free online resource is not sold separately and is included in the price of the book.**

Having purchased this book, you have access to the following online study materials:

CONTENT	AAT	
	Text	Kit
Electronic version of the book	✓	✓
Progress tests with instant answers	✓	
Mock assessments online	✓	✓
Material updates	✓	✓

How to access your online resources

Kaplan Financial students will already have a MyKaplan account and these extra resources will be available to you online. You do not need to register again, as this process was completed when you enrolled. If you are having problems accessing online materials, please ask your course administrator.

If you are not studying with Kaplan and did not purchase your book via a Kaplan website, to unlock your extra online resources please go to www.mykaplan.co.uk/addabook (even if you have set up an account and registered books previously). You will then need to enter the ISBN number (on the title page and back cover) and the unique pass key number contained in the scratch panel below to gain access. You will also be required to enter additional information during this process to set up or confirm your account details.

If you purchased through Kaplan Flexible Learning or via the Kaplan Publishing website you will automatically receive an e-mail invitation to MyKaplan. Please register your details using this email to gain access to your content. If you do not receive the e-mail or book content, please contact Kaplan Publishing.

Your Code and Information

This code can only be used once for the registration of one book online. This registration and your online content will expire when the final sittings for the examinations covered by this book have taken place. Please allow one hour from the time you submit your book details for us to process your request.

Please scratch the film to access your MyKaplan code.

Please be aware that this code is case-sensitive and you will need to include the dashes within the passcode, but not when entering the ISBN. For further technical support, please visit www.MyKaplan.co.uk

AAT

AQ2016

Management Accounting: Decision and Control

EXAM KIT

This Exam Kit supports study for the following AAT qualifications:
AAT Professional Diploma in Accounting – Level 4
AAT Level 4 Diploma in Business Skills
AAT Professional Diploma in Accounting at SCQF Level 8

British Library Cataloguing-in-Publication Data

A catalogue record for this book is available from the British Library.

Published by:

Kaplan Publishing UK

Unit 2 The Business Centre

Molly Millar's Lane

Wokingham

Berkshire

RG41 2QZ

ISBN: 978-1-78740-534-9

Printed and bound in Great Britain

CONTENTS

Features in this exam kit

In addition to providing a wide ranging bank of real exam style questions, we have also included in this kit:

- unit-specific information and advice on exam technique
- our recommended approach to make your revision for this particular unit as effective as possible.

You will find a wealth of other resources to help you with your studies on the AAT website:

www.aat.org.uk/

Quality and accuracy are of the utmost importance to us so if you spot an error in any of our products, please send an email to mykaplanreporting@kaplan.com with full details, or follow the link to the feedback form in MyKaplan.

Our Quality Co-ordinator will work with our technical team to verify the error and take action to ensure it is corrected in future editions.

UNIT-SPECIFIC INFORMATION

THE EXAM

FORMAT OF THE ASSESSMENT

The assessment will comprise eight independent tasks. Students will be assessed by computer-based assessment.

In any one assessment, students may not be assessed on all content, or on the full depth or breadth of a piece of content. The content assessed may change over time to ensure validity of assessment, but all assessment criteria will be tested over time.

The learning outcomes for this unit are as follows:

	Learning outcome	Weighting
1	Analyse a range of costing techniques to support the management accounting function of an organisation	10%
2	Calculate and use the standard costing to improve performance	40%
3	Demonstrate a range of statistical techniques to analyse business information	10%
4	Use appropriate financial and non-financial performance techniques to aid decision making	30%
5	Evaluate a range of cost management techniques to enhance value and aid decision making	10%
	Total	100%

Time allowed

2 hours 30 minutes

PASS MARK

The pass mark for all AAT CBAs is 70%.

 **Always keep your eye on the clock and make sure you attempt all questions!**

DETAILED SYLLABUS

The detailed syllabus and study guide written by the AAT can be found at:

www.aat.org.uk/

INDEX TO QUESTIONS AND ANSWERS

EXAM TECHNIQUE

- **Do not skip any of the material** in the syllabus.
- **Read each question** *very* carefully.
- **Double-check your answer** before committing yourself to it.
- Answer **every** question – if you do not know an answer to a multiple choice question or true/false question, you don't lose anything by guessing. Think carefully before you **guess.**
- If you are answering a multiple-choice question, **eliminate first those answers that you know are wrong.** Then choose the most appropriate answer from those that are left.
- **Don't panic** if you realise you've answered a question incorrectly. Getting one question wrong will not mean the difference between passing and failing.

Computer-based exams – tips

- Do not attempt a CBA until you have **completed all study material** relating to it.
- On the AAT website there is a CBA demonstration. It is **ESSENTIAL** that you attempt this before your real CBA. You will become familiar with how to move around the CBA screens and the way that questions are formatted, increasing your confidence and speed in the actual exam.
- Be sure you understand how to use the **software** before you start the exam. If in doubt, ask the assessment centre staff to explain it to you.
- Questions are **displayed on the screen** and answers are entered using keyboard and mouse. At the end of the exam, you are given a certificate showing the result you have achieved.
- In addition to the traditional multiple-choice question type, CBAs will also contain **other types of questions**, such as number entry questions, drag and drop, true/false, pick lists or drop down menus or hybrids of these.
- In some CBAs you will have to type in complete computations or written answers.
- You need to be sure you **know how to answer questions** of this type before you sit the exam, through practice.

KAPLAN'S RECOMMENDED REVISION APPROACH

QUESTION PRACTICE IS THE KEY TO SUCCESS

Success in professional examinations relies upon you acquiring a firm grasp of the required knowledge at the tuition phase. In order to be able to do the questions, knowledge is essential.

However, the difference between success and failure often hinges on your exam technique on the day and making the most of the revision phase of your studies.

The **Kaplan Study Text** is the starting point, designed to provide the underpinning knowledge to tackle all questions. However, in the revision phase, poring over text books is not the answer.

Kaplan Pocket Notes are designed to help you quickly revise a topic area; however you then need to practise questions. There is a need to progress to exam style questions as soon as possible, and to tie your exam technique and technical knowledge together.

The importance of question practice cannot be over-emphasised.

The recommended approach below is designed by expert tutors in the field, in conjunction with their knowledge of the examiner and the specimen assessment.

You need to practise as many questions as possible in the time you have left.

OUR AIM

Our aim is to get you to the stage where you can attempt exam questions confidently, to time, in a closed book environment, with no supplementary help (i.e. to simulate the real examination experience).

Practising your exam technique is also vitally important for you to assess your progress and identify areas of weakness that may need more attention in the final run up to the examination.

In order to achieve this we recognise that initially you may feel the need to practice some questions with open book help.

Good exam technique is vital.

THE KAPLAN REVISION PLAN

Stage 1: Assess areas of strengths and weaknesses

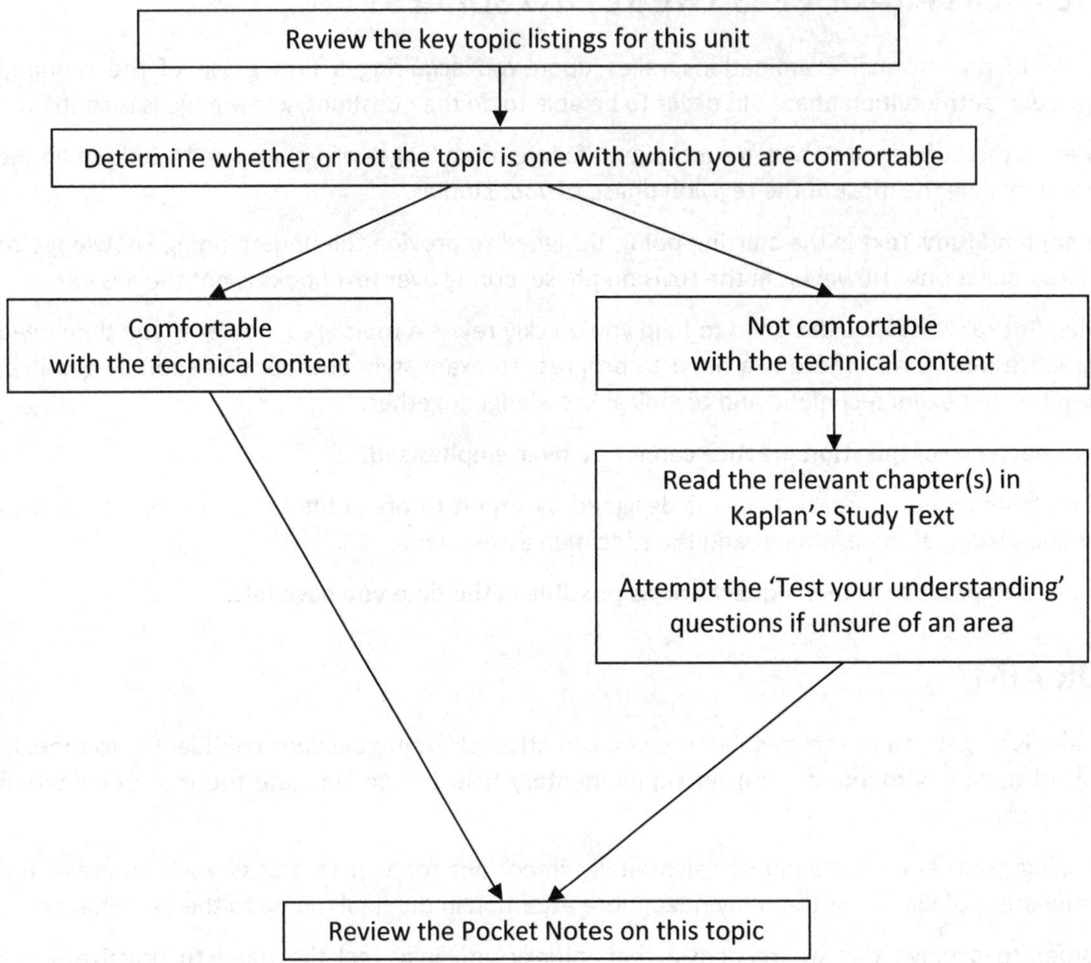

Stage 2: Practice questions

Follow the order of revision of topics as presented in this Kit and attempt the questions in the order suggested.

Try to avoid referring to Study Texts and your notes and the model answer until you have completed your attempt.

Review your attempt with the model answer and assess how much of the answer you achieved.

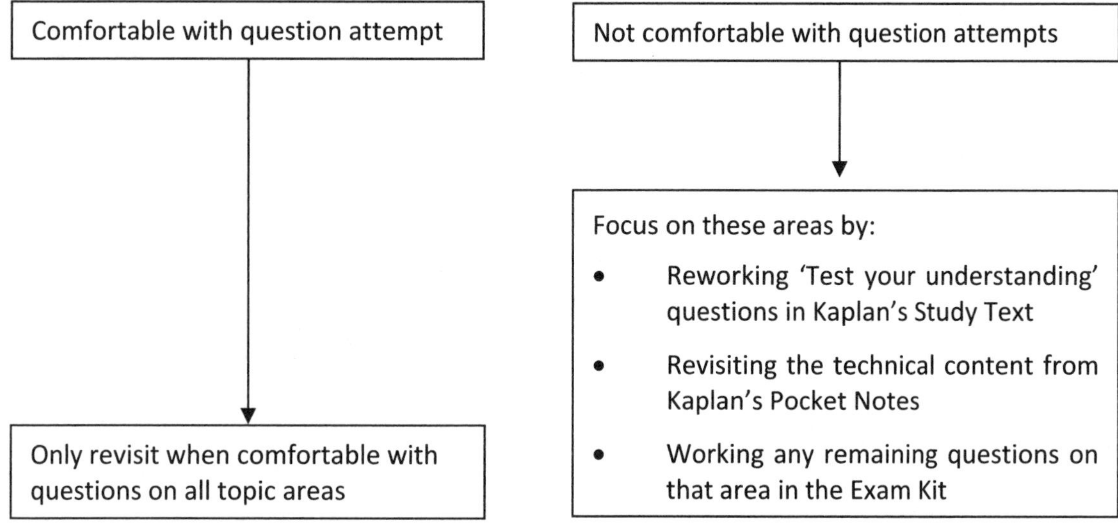

Stage 3: Final pre-exam revision

We recommend that you **attempt at least one mock examination** containing a set of previously unseen exam-standard questions.

Attempt the mock CBA online in timed, closed book conditions to simulate the real exam experience.

Section 1

PRACTICE QUESTIONS

COLLECTION OF COST INFORMATION

1 HIGH – LOW

X has recorded their units of production and their total costs for the past six months.

	Production units	*Total costs*
Jan	11,150	£60,000
Feb	12,345	£66,000
Mar	11,766	£63,080
Apr	13,055	£69,500
May	12,678	£67,500
Jun	13,100	£69,750

The management of X wish to know the total fixed cost and variable cost per unit.

Variable cost per unit is £ [ ]

Fixed costs in total are £ [ ]

2 HILOW

Y has recorded their units of production and their total costs for the past six months.

	Production units	*Total costs £*
Jan	420	4,600
Feb	450	4,965
Mar	430	4,750
Apr	460	5,000
May	440	4,900
Jun	410	4,500

The management of Y wish to know the total fixed cost and variable cost per unit.

Variable cost per unit is £ [ ]

Fixed costs in total are £ [ ]

3 STEPPED

A company has achieved the following output levels and total costs:

Volume of production (units)	25,000	29,000
Total cost	£418,750	£458,750

Total cost includes a fixed element which steps up by £25,000 at an activity level of 27,000 units.

The variable cost per unit is constant.

The variable cost per unit is £ [ ]

4 STEEPLE

A company has achieved the following output levels and total costs:

Volume of production (units)	2,000	2,400
Total cost	£15,000	£21,000

Total cost includes a fixed element which steps up by £5,000 at an activity level of 2,100 units.

The variable cost per unit is constant.

The variable cost per unit is £ [ ]

5 PEN

A company has achieved the following output levels and total costs:

Volume of production (units)	20,000	23,400
Total cost	£150,000	£192,000

Total cost includes a fixed element which steps up by £25,000 at an activity level of 21,100 units.

The variable cost per unit is constant.

The variable cost per unit is £ [ ]

6 POPPY

A company has achieved the following output levels and total costs:

Volume of production (units)	28,000	34,000
Total cost	£38,750	£48,750

Total cost includes a fixed element which steps up by £2,500 at an activity level of 30,000 units.

The variable cost per unit is constant.

The variable cost per unit is £ [ ]

7 LAPEL

Lapel Ltd has produced three forecasts of activity levels for the next period for one of its bins. The original budget involved producing 50,000 bins, but sales and production levels of between 60,000 and 70,000 bins are now more likely.

Complete the table below to estimate the production cost per bin (to 3 decimal places) at the three different activity levels.

Bins made	50,000	60,000	70,000
Costs:	£	£	£
Variable costs:			
Direct materials	5,250		
Direct labour	2,250		
Overheads	11,100		
Fixed costs:			
Indirect labour	9,200		
Overheads	15,600		
Total cost	43,400		
Cost per bin	0.868		

The following budgeted annual sales and cost information relates to bin types A and B:

Product	*A*	*B*
Units made and sold	300,000	500,000
Machine hours required	60,000	40,000
Sales revenue (£)	450,000	600,000
Direct materials (£)	60,000	125,000
Direct labour (£)	36,000	70,000
Variable overheads (£)	45,000	95,000

Total fixed costs attributable to A and B are budgeted to be £264,020.

Complete the table below (to 2 decimal places) to show the budgeted contribution per unit of A and B sold, and the company's budgeted profit or loss for the year from these two products.

	A (£)	*B* (£)	*Total* (£)
Selling price per unit			
Less: variable costs per unit			
Direct materials			
Direct labour			
Variable overheads			
Contribution per unit			
Sales volume (units)			
Total contribution			
Less: fixed costs			
Budgeted profit or loss			

8 SLUSH

A company has produced three forecasts of demand levels for the next quarter. The original budget was to produce 10,000 litres per quarter, but demand levels of 14,000 litres and 18,000 litres are also now feasible.

Complete the table below to estimate the production cost per litre at the three different demand levels.

Litres made	10,000	14,000	18,000
Costs:	£	£	£
Variable costs:			
Direct materials	1,200		
Direct labour	1,000		
Overheads	1,600		
Fixed costs:			
Indirect labour	700		
Overheads	1,600		
Total cost	6,100		
Cost per litre (to 2 d.p.)	0.61		

9 THREE MONTHS

The following production and total cost information relates to a single product organisation for the last three months:

Month	Production units	Total cost £
1	1,200	66,600
2	900	58,200
3	1,400	68,200

The variable cost per unit is constant up to a production level of 2,000 units per month but a step up of £6,000 in the monthly total fixed cost occurs when production reaches 1,100 units per month.

What is the total cost for a month when 1,000 units are produced?

10 EASTERN BUS COMPANY

Eastern Bus Company (EBC) has produced three forecasts of miles to be driven during the next three months for a particular contract. The original contract is for journeys totalling 10,000 miles. It now seems likely, however, that the total journeys involved will increase to either 12,000 or 14,000 miles.

Notes:

- The rate charged by EBC per mile will stay the same irrespective of the total mileage.
- Drivers on this contract are paid entirely on a per mile driven basis.

Complete the table below in order to estimate the profit per mile (in pounds, to 3 decimal places) of this contract for the three likely mileages.

Likely miles	10,000	12,000	14,000
	£	£	£
Sales revenue	100,000		
Variable costs:			
Fuel	8,000		
Drivers' wages and associated costs	5,000		
Overheads	6,000		
Fixed costs:			
Indirect labour	10,600		
Overheads	25,850		
Total cost	55,450		
Total profit	44,550		
Profit per mile to 3 d.p.	4.455		

ACCOUNTING FOR OVERHEADS

11 PRODUCT R

The following information relates to product R during the month of October 2014.

	£	Units
Direct materials cost per unit	22.50	
Direct labour cost per unit	17.50	
Total variable overheads cost	20,000	
Total fixed overheads cost	50,000	
Number of units sold		750
Number of units produced		1,000

Note: There were no opening inventories.

Calculate the cost per unit of product R under:

Variable (marginal) costing

	£
Material	
Labour	
Variable overhead	
Variable cost	

Full absorption costing

	£
Material	
Labour	
Variable overhead	
Fixed overhead	
Total absorption cost	

State how much the difference in the closing inventory valuation and the reported profit for October would be under the two costing principles.

	Working	£
Change in inventory × fixed production overhead		

12 PRODUCT D

The following information relates to the manufacture of product D during the month of April:

Direct materials per unit	£10.60
Direct labour per unit	£16.40
Total variable overheads	£60,000
Total fixed overheads	£80,000
Number of units produced	10,000

Calculate the cost per unit of product D under:

Variable (marginal) costing

	£
Material	
Labour	
Variable overhead	
Variable cost	

Full absorption costing

	£
Material	
Labour	
Variable overhead	
Fixed overhead	
Total absorption cost	

13 UNDER/OVER ABSORPTION

Total direct labour hours worked in June	26,500 hours
Budgeted fixed overhead absorption rate per direct labour hour	£2.50 per hour
Actual fixed overhead for June	£66,300

(a) **The total fixed overhead absorbed for June is £** [ ]

(b) **The amount of fixed overhead under or over absorbed for June is £** [ ]

(c) **This will be recorded in the income statement for June as a** [ ]

(Choose from DEBIT or CREDIT.)

14 BRANDED/OWN LABEL

Branded products and Own label products profit centres absorb (recover) their overheads on a machine hour basis.

Branded products has budgeted overheads of £5,997,232 while Own label products has budgeted overheads of £2,844,968.

The budgeted number of machine hours for Quarter 1 are:

Branded products	187,414
Own label products	118,540

The overhead absorption rates for both profit centres (to the nearest whole pound) are:

	Branded products	*Own label products*
Rate per machine hour		

Assume that at the end of Quarter 1 the actual overheads incurred in the Branded products profit centre were £1,506,000, and the actual machine hours operated were 48,000 hours.

The under/over absorption for Quarter 1 was:

		£
Overhead absorbed		
Overhead incurred		
Absorption	OVER/UNDER *(Delete as appropriate.)*	

Complete the following table to show the journal entries for the absorption of overheads in Quarter 1.

	Debit (£)	*Credit* (£)
Overhead absorbed		
Under/over absorption		
Overhead control account		

15 MIXING AND CANNING

The Ingredients mixing department is largely automated and budgeted its fixed overheads to be £465,820. The Canning department is largely labour intensive and budgeted that its fixed overheads would be £326,180.

The budgeted machine and labour hours for these two departments for the next quarter (to 30 September) are:

	Ingredients mixing department	*Canning department*
Budgeted machine	7,400	4,800
Budgeted direct labour	4,500	10,200

The budgeted overhead recovery (absorption) rate for EACH department, using the most appropriate basis is: *(round your answer to the nearest penny).*

	Ingredients mixing	*Canning*
Overhead recovery rate £		

At the end of the quarter (to 30 September) the actual overheads incurred in the Ingredients mixing department were found to be £450,060, and the actual machine hours operated were 6,800 hours.

The under/over absorption for the quarter (to 30 September) are:

Ingredients mixing		£
Overhead absorbed		
Overhead incurred		
Absorption	UNDER/OVER (delete as appropriate.)	

Complete the following table to show the journal entries for the absorption of overheads in the quarter (to 30 September).

	Debit (£)	*Credit* (£)
Overhead absorbed		
Under/over absorption		
Overhead control account		

16 AIRCRAFT

During the first week of December 2008 the actual number of miles flown by a charter flight aircraft was 6,890 miles and the actual overheads incurred were £2,079,000.

The budgeted overhead was £300 per mile.

The actual overhead absorbed by the aircraft in the first week of December 2008 (to the nearest whole £) was £ ______

The ______ ***(choose from UNDER or OVER)*** **absorbed overheads for the week were £** ______

The under/over absorbed overheads will be recorded in the company's income statement in December as a ______ ***(Choose from DEBIT or CREDIT.)***

17 GARY

Production information for one unit is given below.

Complete the table:	*Quantity*	Per unit	*Total* £
Material	3 kg	£5	
Direct labour	2 hrs	£4	
Variable overhead	2 hrs	£2	
Fixed overhead			£120,000
Budgeted production	10,000 units		

Fixed overhead absorption rate per hour is £ [ ]

Marginal cost of one unit is £ [ ]

Total absorption cost of one unit is £ [ ]

If budgeted sales are 9,000 units at £50/unit, calculate the budgeted profit using marginal costing and absorption costing:

	Marginal cost		*Absorption cost*	
	£	£	£	£
Sales				
Material				
Direct labour				
Variable costs				
Fixed costs				
Closing inventory				
	______		______	
		______		______
Contribution/Profit				
Fixed costs				
		______		______
Profit				
		______		______

Reconcile the difference between these two profit figures.

	Working	£
MAC profit		
Change in inventory × fixed production overhead		
TAC profit		

18 CPL

CPL is considering what the effect would be of costing its products under marginal costing (MAC) principles, instead of under full absorption costing (FAC) principles that it currently follows.

The following information relates to one of the company's products:

Selling price per unit	£12
Prime cost per unit	£4
Variable production overhead per unit	£3
Budgeted fixed production overhead	£30,000 per month
Budgeted production	15,000 units per month
Budgeted sales	12,000 units per month
Opening inventory	2,000 units

Calculate the contribution per unit (on a MAC basis):

	£
Selling price	
Variable production cost	
Contribution per unit	

Calculate the profit per unit (on a FAC basis):

	£
Selling price	
Marginal cost	
Fixed production cost	
Full absorption cost	
Profit/unit	

Complete the table below to produce an income statement for the product for the month under marginal costing (MAC) principles.

	£	£
Sales		
Opening inventory		
Variable production costs		
Closing inventory		
Cost of sales (MAC basis)		
Contribution		
Fixed costs		
Profit		

Complete the table below to produce an income statement for the product for the month under full absorption costing (FAC) principles.

	£	£
Sales		
Opening inventory		
Production costs		
Closing inventory		
Cost of sales (FAC basis)		
Profit		

Reconcile the profit figures:

	Working	£
MAC profit		
Change in inventory × fixed production overhead		
FAC profit		

19 TRICKY (I)

Tricky Plc have bought a factory, it is their first month of operation and they have decided to use the factory to produce a single product, the unpredictable. Overheads are absorbed on a budgeted production basis. Inventory is valued on a FIFO basis.

	Month 1	Month 2	Month 3
Selling price (£)	28	26	25
Production (units)	8,000	8,000	8,000
Sales (units)	7,500	7,900	8,400
Direct materials (£ per unit)	7	7	7
Direct labour (£ per unit)	5	5	5
Other variable production costs (£)	24,000	24,000	20,000
Fixed production costs (£)	64,000	64,000	64,000

(a) Complete the table below. If any answer is zero, enter "0" into the relevant cell.

For sales to fixed overhead rows, use positive number only (do not use minus signs). For the final row, record any loss figure with a minus sign.

	Absorption costing			**Marginal costing**		
	Month 1 (£)	**Month 2 (£)**	**Month 3 (£)**	**Month 1 (£)**	**Month 2 (£)**	**Month 3 (£)**
Sales						
Opening inventory						
Production costs						
Closing inventory						
Cost of sales						
Fixed overheads						
Profit/(Loss)						

(b) Reconcile the differences between the profit figures:

	Month 1			**£**	**Month 2**			**£**
MAC profit								
Change in inventory × fixed production overhead recovery rate per unit.	units		ORR		units		ORR	
		×				×		
TAC profit								

	Month 3			**£**
MAC profit				
Change in inventory × fixed production overhead recovery rate per unit.	units		ORR	
		×		
TAC profit				

Tricky miscalculated at the start of the period and the actual fixed overheads were £65,000 each month, actual sales of the unpredictable were in line with budget, but production was 5% higher than expected in month 1, then 3% lower in month 2 and as expected in month 3.

(c)What is the under/over recovery for each month:

Month 1: £................ under/ over recovered.

Month 2: £................ under/ over recovered.

Month 3: £................ under/ over recovered.

20 HAIRWORKS

Hairworks, a company that makes a hairdryer, has the following sales and production information:

Sales price		£100 per unit
Variable production costs	(materials, labour, etc.)	£40 per unit
Fixed production overheads	(rent, etc.)	£400,000
Fixed selling and admin costs		£150,000

Production was 12,500 units but sales were only 10,000.

Complete the following tables.

Marginal Costing Income statement		
	£000	£000
Sales		
Cost of sales		
Production costs		
Less closing inventory		
CONTRIBUTION		
Less		
Fixed production costs		
Fixed selling and admin costs		
Profit for period		

Absorption Costing Income statement		
	£000	£000
Sales		
Cost of sales		
Production costs		
Less closing inventory		
GROSS PROFIT		
Less		
Fixed selling and admin costs		
Profit for period		

	Working	£000
Marginal costing profit		
Change in inventory × fixed production overhead		
Absorption costing profit		

21 RH

RH makes and sells one product, the standard production cost of which is as follows for one unit:

		£
Direct labour	3 hours at £6 per hour	18
Direct materials	4 kilograms at £7 per kg	28
Production overhead	Variable	3
	Fixed	20
		—
Standard production cost		69
		—

Costs relating to selling, distribution and administration are:

Variable 20% of sales value

Fixed £180,000 per annum.

There are no units in finished goods inventory at 1 October 20X2. The fixed overhead expenditure is spread evenly throughout the year. The selling price per unit is £140.

For the two six-monthly periods detailed below, the number of units to be produced and sold are budgeted as:

	Six months ending	*Six months ending*
	31 Mar 20X3	30 Sept 20X3
Production	8,500	7,000
Sales	7,000	8,000

Prepare statements for management showing sales, costs and profits for each of the six-monthly periods, using:

Marginal costing

	Six months ending		*Six months ending*	
	31 March 20X3		*30 September 20X3*	
	£000	£000	£000	£000
Sales				
Variable cost of sales				
opening inventory				
production cost				
8,500 units				
7,000 units				
	———		———	
less closing inventory				
	———		———	
		———		———
Variable selling costs				
		———		———
Contribution				
Fixed production costs				
Fixed selling costs				
	———		———	
		———		———
Profit				
		———		———

Absorption costing

	Six months ending		*Six months ending*	
	31 March 20X3		*30 September 20X3*	
	£000	£000	£000	£000
Sales				
Cost of sales				
opening inventory				
8,500 units				
7,000 units				
	———		———	
less closing inventory				
	———		———	
		———		———
absorption				
		———		———
Gross profit				
selling, etc. costs				
variable				
fixed				
	———		———	
		———		———
Profit				
		———		———

Reconcile the difference in profit:

	First six months	*Second six months*
	£000	£000
Marginal costing profit		
Change in inventory × fixed production overhead		
	———	———
Absorption costing profit		
	———	———

ACTIVITY BASED COSTING

22 CAT

Details of four products and relevant information are given below for one period:

Product	*A*	*B*	*C*	*D*
Output in units	120	100	80	120
Costs per unit	£	£	£	£
Direct material	40	50	30	60
Direct labour	28	21	14	21
Machine hours (per unit)	4	3	2	3

The four products are similar and are usually produced in production runs of 20 units and sold in batches of 10 units.

The production overhead is currently absorbed by using a machine hour rate, and the total of the production overhead for the period has been analysed as follows:

	£
Machine department costs (rent, business rates, depreciation and supervision)	10,430
Set up costs	5,250
Stores receiving	3,600
Inspection/quality control	2,100
Materials handling and dispatch	4,620
Total	26,000

You have ascertained that the 'cost drivers' to be used are as listed below for the overhead costs shown:

Cost	*Cost driver*
Set up costs	Number of production runs
Stores receiving	Requisitions raised
Inspection/quality control	Number of production runs
Materials handling and dispatch	Orders executed

The number of requisitions raised on the stores was 20 for each product and the number of orders executed was 42, each order being for a batch of 10 of a product.

The machine hour absorption rate and total costs for each product if all overhead costs are absorbed on a machine hour basis are:

(W1) Machine hour absorption rate = £ [ ] per machine hour

The cost per unit and total cost per product using absorption costing are:

Per unit	*A*	*B*	*C*	*D*
	£	£	£	£
Direct materials				
Direct labour				
Production overhead				
	——	——	——	——
Per unit				
	——	——	——	——
Total cost				

The total costs for each product, using activity based costing are:

Total costs	*A*	*B*	*C*	*D*
	£	£	£	£
Direct materials				
Direct labour				
Machine dept costs				
Set up costs				
Stores receiving				
Inspection/quality control				
Materials handling despatch				
	——	——	——	——
Total cost				
	——	——	——	——

Workings

Cost driver rates:

Machine dept costs (m/c hour basis)

Set up costs

Stores receiving

Inspection/quality control

Material handling despatch

23 SMASH-HIT

Smash-Hit manufactures tennis and squash racquets. Until recently it has recovered its production overhead in a conventional way by using a series of recovery rates based on direct labour hours for each producing costs centre.

The following relates to its budget for quarter ended 30 June 20X3:

Cost centre	*Machining*	*Finishing*	*Packing*
Production and other overhead	£160,000	£65,000	£35,000
Direct labour hours	25,000	12,500	6,500

One of its products the 'Heman 3' has the following specifications (per unit):

Direct material	£38	
Direct labour		
Machining	1.5 hours	
Finishing	1.0 hour	Labour rate per hour £7
Packing	0.2 hours	

In determining the selling price of the product it is company policy to add 15% to cover selling distribution and administration costs and a further 10% to cover profit.

The accounting technician and the production manager have been considering the use of activity based costing as an alternative method of dealing with overheads.

After examining the 'value adding activities' across the business they have prepared the following schedule:

Budget quarter ended 30 June 20X3

Activity	*Cost pool*	*Cost driver volume*
	£	
Process set up	80,000	200 set-ups
Material procurement	20,000	100 purchase orders
Maintenance	25,000	20 maintenance plans
Material handling	50,000	4,000 movements
Quality control	45,000	500 inspections
Order processing	40,000	600 customers
	———	
	260,000	
	———	

A production batch of 'Heman 3' equates to 750 units of output, requiring the following:

- 6 set-ups
- 6 purchase orders
- 2 standard maintenance plans
- 150 material movements
- 75 inspections
- 10 sales customers

Using a traditional absorption costing method based on labour hours for the period:

Determine overhead recovery rates for each cost centre.

Cost centre	*Machining*	*Finishing*	*Packing*
Production overhead			
Direct labour hours			
Recovery rate per labour hour			

Calculate the production cost for one unit of output of 'Heman 3'.

	£
Direct labour	
Direct material	
Production overhead	
Machining	
Finishing	
Packing	
	——
Production cost	
	——

Calculate the selling price ex VAT for one unit of 'Heman 3'.

	£
Production cost	
Add: 15% for selling, admin and distribution	
	——
Add: 10% to cover profit	
	——
Selling price	
	——

Using an activity-based costing method calculate the cost driver rates for the period.

Activity	*Cost pool*	*Cost driver volume*	*Cost driver rate*
Process set up			
Material procurement			
Maintenance			
Material handing			
Quality control			
Order processing			

Calculate the overhead chargeable to the batch of units of 'Heman 3'.

	£
Set up	
Order	
Plan	
Material movement	
Inspection	
Customer	
	____
	____

Calculate the production cost of one unit of 'Heman 3'.

	£
Direct labour	
Direct material	
Production and other overhead	
	____
Production cost	
	____

24 ABC LTD

ABC Limited manufactures two products, the DEF and the GHI.

It takes 5 hours of labour to make a DEF and 7 hours of labour to make a GHI.

The overhead activities for these, machine set ups and special parts handling, have budgets of £80,000 and £40,000 respectively.

Other information about the DEF and GHI is below.

	DEF	*GHI*
Direct materials – £ per unit	8	12
Direct labour – £ per unit	25	35
Number of special parts	300	100
Number of machine set ups	150	50
Budgeted production units	1,000	5,000

(a) Calculate the fixed overheads assuming they are absorbed on a budgeted labour hour basis.

	DEF (£)	*GHI* (£)
Fixed overheads		

(b) Complete the table below using Activity Based Costing (ABC) principles.

	£	*DEF* (£)	*GHI* (£)
Cost driver rate – special parts handling			
Cost driver rate – machine set ups			
Total special parts			
Total machine set ups			

(c) Using the information from (a) and (b) calculate the total cost per unit using traditional absorption costing and using ABC. Give your answers to two decimal places.

	DEF	*GHI*
Total unit cost – Absorption costing		
Total unit cost – ABC		

25 FOUR LIONS LTD

Four Lions Limited manufactures two products, the Lion and the Pride.

The overhead activities for these, material movements and quality control, have budgets of £180,000 and £140,000 respectively.

It takes 3 hours of machine time to make a Lion and 4 hours of machine time to make a Pride.

Other information about the Lion and Pride is below.

	Lion	*Pride*
Direct materials – £ per unit	12	20
Direct labour – £ per unit	16	24
Material movements	2,000	500
Quality inspections	15	85
Budgeted production units	20,000	10,000

(a) Calculate the fixed overheads assuming they are absorbed on a budgeted machine hour basis.

	Lion (£)	*Pride* (£)
Fixed overheads		

(b) Complete the table below using Activity Based Costing (ABC) principles.

	£	*Lion* (£)	*Pride* (£)
Cost driver rate – material movements			
Cost driver rate – quality control			
Total material movements			
Total quality control			

(c) Using the information from (a) and (b) calculate the total cost per unit using traditional absorption costing and using ABC. Give you answers to two decimal places.

	Lion	*Pride*
Total unit cost – Absorption costing		
Total unit cost – ABC		

(d) Discuss how Activity Based Costing could help improve decision making at Four Lions Ltd.

26 RVI

RVI is a private hospital carrying out 2 procedures, A and B.

The overhead costs for these, nursing costs and remedial visits, have budgets of £300,000 and £500,000 respectively.

It takes 2 hours of surgeon time to carry out a procedure A and 1.5 hours of surgeon time to carry out a procedure B.

Other information about the procedures is below.

	A	*B*
Surgeon cost – £ per unit	275	235
Total nursing hours	2,000	4,000
Total remedial visits	2,000	3,000
Budgeted procedures	1,000	2,000

(a) Calculate the fixed overheads assuming they are absorbed on a budgeted surgeon hour basis.

	A (£)	B (£)
Fixed overheads		

(b) Complete the table below using Activity Based Costing (ABC) principles.

	£	*A* (£)	*B* (£)
Cost driver rate – nurse costs			
Cost driver rate – remedial costs			
Total nursing costs			
Total remedial costs			

(c) Using the information from (a) and (b) calculate the total cost per procedure using traditional absorption costing and using ABC. Give you answers to two decimal places.

	A	*B*
Total procedure cost – Absorption costing		
Total procedure cost – ABC		

(d) Explain the difficulties that RVI could have switching from traditional absorption costing to Activity Based Costing.

27 ABC STATEMENTS (I)

Complete the following statements:

A cost [ ] is any factor that causes a change in the cost of an activity.

driver/pool/rate/unit

VPS manufactures touchscreens, the most likely cost driver for the cost pool called 'quality control' is number of [ ]

machine hrs/batches/special parts/inspections

28 ABC STATEMENTS (II)

Complete the following statements:

A cost [ ] is an activity which consumes resources and for which overhead costs are identified and allocated.

driver/pool/rate/unit

F supplies pharmaceutical drugs, the most likely cost driver for the cost pool 'invoice processing costs' is the number of [ ]

orders/deliveries/inspections/invoices processed

STANDARD COSTING

29 BUDGIE

The budgeted and actual results for the month of January 20X1 are as follows:

		Budget		*Actual*
Production (units of A)		3,500		3,600
Direct materials	7,000 litres	£17,500	6,950 litres	£18,070
Direct labour	1,750 hours	£15,750	1,800 hours	£16,020
Fixed overheads (absorbed on a unit basis)		£35,000		£34,500
Total		£68,250		£68,590

Complete the following sentences:

(a) The standard quantity of labour per unit is [ ] minutes.

(b) The budgeted quantity of materials needed to produce 3,000 units of A is [ ] litres.

(c) The budgeted labour hours to produce 3,600 units of A is [ ] hours.

(d) The budgeted labour cost to produce 3,600 units of A is £ [ ]

(e) The budgeted overhead absorption rate is £ [ ]

In February the company budgeted to produce 4,000 units with fixed production overheads of £43,500. The actual volume produced was 4,200 units and the actual fixed overheads were £44,000.

(f) The fixed overheads were (Insert: under or over absorbed) [ ] **by £** [ ]

30 CARROT

The budgeted and actual results for the month of March 20X1 are as follows:

		Budget		*Actual*
Production (units of B)		10,000		9,950
Direct materials	4,000 kg	£10,000	3,900 kg	£9,900
Direct labour	250 hours	£2,500	245 hours	£2,695
Fixed overheads (absorbed on a unit basis)		£3,000		£3,100
Total		£15,500		£15,695

Complete the following sentences:

(a) The standard quantity of labour per unit is [ ] **minutes.**

(b) The budgeted quantity of materials needed to produce 9,950 units of B is [ ] **kg.**

(c) The budgeted labour hours to produce 9,950 units of B is [ ] **hours.**

(d) The budgeted labour cost to produce 9,950 units of B is £ [ ]

(e) The budgeted overhead absorption rate is £ [ ]

In April the company budgeted to produce 9,000 units with fixed production overheads of £2,900. The actual volume produced was 10,200 units and the actual fixed overheads were £3,000.

(f) The fixed overheads were (insert: under or over absorbed) [ ] **by £** [ ]

31 RABBIT

The budgeted and actual results for the month of January 20X1 are as follows:

		Budget		*Actual*
Production (units of A)		12,500		12,600
Direct materials	25,000 litres	£100,000	26,950 litres	£108,070
Direct labour	12,500 hours	£125,000	13,100 hours	£116,020
Fixed overheads (absorbed on a unit basis)		£75,000		£74,500
Total		£300,000		£298,590

Complete the following sentences:

(a) The standard quantity of labour per unit is ☐ minutes.

(b) The budgeted quantity of materials needed to produce 12,000 units of A is ☐ litres.

(c) The budgeted labour hours to produce 12,600 units of A is ☐ hours.

(d) The budgeted labour cost to produce 12,600 units of A is £ ☐

(e) The budgeted overhead absorption rate is £ ☐

In February the company budgeted to produce 13,000 units with fixed production overheads of £78,000. The actual volume produced was 12,800 units and the actual fixed overheads were £74,000.

(f) The fixed overheads were (insert: under or over absorbed) ☐ by £ ☐

32 BELLS

The following information has been calculated for the production of 1 box of Bells.

- Each box will require 16 kilograms of material at a cost of £1.50 per kilogram.
- Each box will require 3 hours of labour at a total cost of £27.
- Fixed overheads total £324,000 and the estimated output will be 5,400 boxes.

Complete the standard cost card below:

1 box of Bells	*Quantity*	*Cost per unit £*	*Total cost £*
Material			
Labour			
Fixed overheads			
Total			

33 TEA BAGS

The bagging division operates a standard costing system in which:

- purchases of materials are recorded at standard cost
- direct material costs and direct labour costs are variable
- production overheads are fixed

The standard cost card for the coming months is being prepared and you have been provided with the following information:

- Loose tea is expected to cost £5 per kilogram
- 1,000 tea bags require 3 kilograms of loose tea
- Tea bags cost 0.6 pence per bag
- One machine can package 5,000 bags per hour and requires one operator who costs £10 per hour
- Budgeted labour hours are 4,000 per month
- Fixed production overheads are £200,000 per month
- Budgeted production is 20,000 batches of 1,000 tea bags per month
- Fixed production overheads are absorbed on the basis of direct labour hours

Complete the standard cost card for the production of 1,000 tea bags.

1,000 tea bags		*Quantity (Units)*	*Unit price £*	*Total cost £*
Loose tea	Kilograms			
Tea bags	Bags			
Direct labour	Hours			
Fixed production overheads	Hours			

34 GEM

The following information has been calculated for the production of 1 unit of Gem.

- Each unit will require 5.25 litres of material at a cost of £7.00 per litre.
- Each unit will require 3.5 hours of labour at a cost of £3 per hour.
- Fixed overheads, absorbed on a labour hour basis, total £525,000. The expected output of Gem is 10,000 units.

Complete the standard cost card below.

1 unit of Gem	*Quantity*	*Cost per unit*	*Total cost*
Material			
Labour			
Fixed overheads			
Total			

It takes a manufacturing department 750,000 hours to produce 250,000 units of Gem. What are the standard hours per unit? [ ]

35 BESPOKE SUIT

The following information has been calculated for the production of 1 bespoke suit:

- Each suit will require 4.5 metres of fabric at a cost of £48 per metre
- Each suit will require 40 hours of labour at a total cost of £600
- Fixed overheads total £240,000 and the estimated output for the year will be 600 suits. Fixed overheads are absorbed using direct labour hours.

Complete the standard cost card below.

1 bespoke suit	*Quantity*	*Cost per unit*	*Total cost*
Material			
Labour			
Fixed overheads			
Total			

36 GARDEN SHEDS

The following information has been calculated for the production of garden sheds:

- Each shed will require 90 kilograms of material at a cost of £6.50 per kilogram
- Each unit will require 5 hours of labour at a total cost of £50
- Fixed overheads total £500,000 and the estimated output is 5,000 sheds. Fixed overheads are absorbed using direct labour hours.

Complete the standard cost card below.

1 Shed	*Quantity*	*Cost per unit*	*Total cost*
Material			
Labour			
Fixed overheads			
Total			

37 PERFORMANCE

Performance Limited makes car bulbs. The following information has been calculated for the production of a batch of 1,000 bulbs.

- Each batch will require 40 kilograms of material at a total cost of £200
- Each batch will require 2 hours of labour at an hourly cost of £7 per hour.
- Fixed overheads total £240,000 and the estimated output will be 8,000 batches. Fixed overheads are absorbed using direct labour hours.

Complete the standard cost card below.

1000 bulbs	*Quantity*	*Cost per unit*	*Total cost*
Material			
Labour			
Fixed overheads			
Total			

Performance uses 1,500 kilograms of material to manufacture a batch of 1,000 bulbs. The standard quantity in each bulb is [ ]

38 DISCO

A disc grinder expects to use 25,000 machine hours to manufacture 5,000 discs in a month.

The standard machine time required for a disc is [ ] **hours.**

39 HARRY

A manufacturer expects to use 2,000 labour hours to manufacture 500 units in a month.

The standard labour time required for a unit is [ ] **hours.**

40 OSCAR

A widget manufacturer expects to use 5,000 machine hours to manufacture 2,000,000 widgets in a month.

The standard machine time required for a widget is [ ] **hours.**

41 PIZZA

A pizza chain expects to use 300,000 kilograms of flour to manufacture 1,500,000 pizzas per month.

The standard quantity of flour for a pizza is [ ] **kilograms**

MATERIAL VARIANCES

42 MAT (1)

A company bought 1,000 kilograms of material paying £5 per kilogram. It managed to make 200 units whilst the budget had been for 220 units. The standard quantity of material allowed for in the budget was 6 kilograms per unit, and the budgeted price per kilogram was £5.50.

Complete the following table.

			£
Standard cost of materials for actual production			
Variances	**Favourable**	**Adverse**	
Direct materials price			
Direct materials usage			
Total variance			
Actual cost of materials for actual production			

43 MAT (2)

A company bought 12,000 kilograms of material paying £4 per kilogram. It managed to make 2,000 units whilst the budget had been for 1,900 units. The standard quantity of material allowed for in the budget was 5 kilograms per unit, and the budgeted price per kilogram was £4.50.

Complete the following table.

			£
Standard cost of materials for actual production			
Variances	**Favourable**	**Adverse**	
Direct materials price			
Direct materials usage			
Total variance			
Actual cost of materials for actual production			

44 SMITH

Smith budgets to produce 10,000 units. Each unit requires 3kg. Production does not go as planned and only 9,800 units are produced, using 29,000 kg of materials with a total cost of £8,000. The budgeted cost per kg was £0.27.

What is the material usage variance? £__________ __.

45 ORANGINA

Orangina Limited had direct material costs relating to last month as follows:

- Standard kilograms used for actual production 3,100 kg
- Standard cost of material per kilo £0.50
- Material price variance £338A
- Material usage variance £152A

What is the actual materials cost per kilo? Give your answer to 3 decimal places. **£______.**

46 CUFF

Cuff Limited purchased 100 litres of solvent. The standard cost was £1 per litre. At the end of the period, there is an adverse price variance of £20.

What was the actual cost of the 100 litres purchased? £_______.

47 SAPPHIRE

A company expects to produce 140,000 units of Sapphire using 280,000 kg of material. The standard cost of material is £6/kg.

If the actual output is 145,000 units what is the total standard material usage? _______kg

48 MATERIAL

A company purchases 60,000 tonnes of material at a cost of £720,000. The standard cost per tonne is £11 and the standard quantity per unit is 10 tonnes.

What is the total material price variance? £________ __.

49 KILO

A company purchases and uses 8,000 kilograms of material at a cost of £24,000. The budgeted production was 2,000 units, which required 7,200 kilograms of material at a total standard cost of £20,160. The actual production was 1,800 units.

What is the material usage variance? £________ __.

50 MOUSE

A drinks manufacturer expects to produce 2,000,000 bottles of cola using 60,000 kilograms of sugar. The standard cost of sugar is £0.75 per kilogram.

If the actual output is 2,450,000 bottles, what is the total standard cost of sugar?

A £1,837,500

B £45,000

C £55,125

D £1,500,000

51 RAW MATERIALS

A product should require 2kg of raw material costing 75p per kg. In February, 2,500kg of raw materials were purchased at a cost of £2,250; 2,300kg of raw materials were issued to production and 1,200 products were produced.

If raw material inventory is valued at standard cost and there was no opening inventory of raw material, what was the materials usage variance for February?

A £375 A

B £150 A

C £75 A

D £75 F

52 ALPHA

A company purchases 10,000 kilograms of material at a cost of £55,000. The standard cost per kilogram is £5.

The total material price variance is

A £5,500 F

B £5,000 A

C £5,000 F

D £5,500 A

53 BETA

A company purchases 5,000 kilograms of material at a cost of £27,500. The standard cost per kilogram is £5.00.

The total material price variance is

A £2,750 A

B £2,500 F

C £2,500 A

D £2,750 F

54 CHARLIE

A company purchases 100,000 kilograms of material at a cost of £525,000, they use that material to make 42,000 units. The standard cost per kilogram is £4.50 and the standard quantity per unit is 2.5 kilograms.

The total material usage variance is

A £75,000 A

B £2,250 A

C £7,500 F

D £22,500 F

55 DELTA

A company purchases and uses 10,000 kilograms of material at a cost of £30,000. Budgeted production was 1,000 units, using 8,000 kg of material at a total standard cost of £28,000. Actual production was 1,000 units.

The total material usage variance is

A £7,000 A

B £7,000 F

C £2,000 A

D £2,000 F

56 EPSILON

A company has a total material variance which is £60 adverse. Budgeted production was 1,000 units, using 800 kg of material at a total standard cost of £2,800. Actual production was 1,050 units using 1,000 kg.

Complete the following table:

		£
Standard cost of materials for actual production		
Variances	**Favourable / adverse / no variance**	
Direct materials price		
Direct materials usage		
Actual cost of materials for actual production		

57 FLY

A company purchases and uses 15,000 kilograms of material, at an actual cost of £450,000. The budget included 20,000 kg of material at a total standard cost of £640,000. Actual production for the period was 14,000 units and the total material variance was £2,000 adverse.

Complete the following table:

		£
Standard cost of materials for actual production		
Variances	**Favourable / adverse / no variance**	
Direct materials price		
Direct materials usage		
Actual cost of materials for actual production		

LABOUR VARIANCES

58 LAB (1)

A company used 12,000 hours of labour paying £8 per hour. During this time it managed to make 2,000 units whilst the budget had been for only 1,900 units. The standard number of hours allowed was 5 per unit, and the budgeted rate per hour was £8.50.

Complete the following table.

			£
Standard cost of labour for actual production			
Variances	**Favourable**	**Adverse**	
Direct labour rate			
Direct labour efficiency			
Total variance			
Actual cost of labour for actual production			

59 LAB (2)

A company used 22,000 hours of labour paying £10 per hour. During this time it managed to make 21,000 units whilst the budget had been for 22,000 units. The standard number of hours allowed was one hour per unit, and the budgeted rate per hour was £9.80.

Complete the following table.

			£
Standard cost of labour for actual production			
Variances	**Favourable**	**Adverse**	
Direct labour rate			
Direct labour efficiency			
Total variance			
Actual cost of labour for actual production			

60 BEALE

Beale Limited makes cages. Each cage should take three standard hours to produce at £15 per labour hour. Total labour costs for the period were £5,440 and a total of 340 labour hours were used.

What is the labour rate variance? £_______ __.

61 MY

My company expects to produce 6,000 units of X using 3,000 labour hours. The standard cost of labour is £7 per hour. The actual output is 7,000 units.

What is the total standard labour cost? £________

62 MCQ

A company pays £52,800 for 12,000 labour hours. The standard rate per hour is £4.

What is the labour rate variance? £_______ __.

63 DIAMOND

Diamond Ltd takes 15,000 hours to complete their March production at a total cost of £150,000. The labour rate variance was £3,750 F and the efficiency variance was £5,000 A.

What was the standard labour rate per hour? £______.

64 JARVIS

Jarvis Ltd produced 24,000 units of product X in July using 18,000 labour hours. The standard cost of labour is £8 per hour. The labour rate variance is £7,600 adverse.

What was the actual cost of labour for July? £__________.

65 GOSSIP

G expects to produce 120,000 units of glug using 60,000 labour hours. The standard cost of labour is £14 per hour.

If actual output is 140,000 units, what is the total standard labour cost? £__________.

66 HIT

HIT expects to produce 10,000 units of glug using 8,000 labour hours. The standard cost of labour is £10 per hour.

If actual output is 11,000 units, what is the total standard labour cost? £__________.

67 JOY

J takes three standard hours to produce a unit at £15 per labour hour. Total labour costs for the period were £53,140 and a total of 3,400 labour hours were used. Units produced were 1,000.

The labour rate variance is

A £2,140 F

B £6,000 A

C £2,140 A

D £6,000 F

68 KAP

A company pays £55,800 for 10,000 actual labour hours. Actual output was 10,000 units and standard labour hours were 1.2 hours per unit. The standard rate per hour is £5.

The labour rate variance is

A £10,000 F

B £5,800 F

C £5,800 A

D £10,000 A

69 LEMON

A company pays £62,500 for 7,000 actual labour hours. Actual output was 1,000 units and standard labour hours were 6 hours per unit. The standard rate per hour is £9.

The labour efficiency variance is

A £1,800 F

B £1,800 A

C £9,000 F

D £9,000 A

70 MUFFIN

Actual output was 10,000 units in 16,000 hours at an actual rate of £10 per hour. Standard labour hours were estimated at 1.5 hours per unit. The standard rate per hour is £12.

The labour efficiency variance is

A £32,000 A

B £32,000 F

C £12,000 F

D £12,000 A

71 JAYRO

Jayro Ltd manufactures gas canisters for use in the medical industry.

The Gas Division operates a standard cost system in which:

- purchases of materials are recorded at standard cost
- direct material and direct labour costs are variable
- production overheads are fixed and absorbed on a per unit basis.

The budgeted activity and actual results for the month of August are as follows:

	Budget		*Actual*	
Production units		50,000		55,000
Direct materials	1,000 litres	£20,000	1,100 litres	£23,100
Direct labour	4,000 hours	£32,000	4,950 hours	£40,095
Fixed overheads		£100,0000		£120,000
Total cost		£152,000		£183,195

Calculate the following variances, if any, for August:

Variance		
	£	*A/F*
Direct material usage variance		
Direct material price variance		
Direct labour efficiency variance		

72 PICTURE PERFECT

Picture Perfect Ltd manufactures several types of picture frame and operates a standard costing system. Production overheads are absorbed based on expected output.

The budgeted activity and actual results for one of the company's bestselling frames "Look at Me" are as follows:

	Budget		*Actual*	
Production units		450,000		425,000
Direct materials (wood)	225,000 m^2	£675,000	250,000 m^2	£775,000
Direct material (glass)	90,000 m^2	£450,000	85,000 m^2	£415,000
Direct labour	112,500 hours	£450,000	100,000 hours	£390,000
Fixed production overheads		£1,000,000		£1,100,000
Total cost		£2,575,000		£2,680,000

Calculate the following variances, if any:

Variance	£	*A/F*
Direct material (wood) usage variance		
Direct labour rate variance		
Direct labour efficiency variance		

73 DIVISION

Division operates a standard costing system in which:

- purchases of materials are recorded at standard cost
- direct material and direct labour costs are variable.

The budgeted activity and actual results for the month of January are as follows:

	Budget	
Production units		5,000
	Cost per unit £	Budgeted cost £
Direct materials	2.00	10,000
Direct labour	4.00	20,000
Total cost		30,000

Actual production for the period was 6,000 units and the total variances incurred were as follows:

	Total Variance £
Direct materials	890 Favourable
Direct labour	1,000 Adverse

During the period the actual cost of material was £10.10 per litre and the standard quantity per unit was 0.2 litres.

4,500 actual hours were worked.

The standard time per unit was 0.8 hours per unit.

Complete the following table, for January:

Variance	£	*A/F*
Actual cost of materials		
Direct material price variance		
Direct material usage variance		
Standard material cost of production		
Actual cost of labour		
Direct labour rate variance		
Direct labour efficiency variance		
Standard labour cost of production		

74 NIGHT

N operates a standard cost system in which:

- purchases of materials are recorded at standard cost
- direct material and direct labour costs are variable.

The budgeted activity and actual results for the month of December are as follows:

	Budget	
Production units		1,000
	Cost per unit £	Budgeted cost £
Direct materials	20.00	20,000
Direct labour	40.00	40,000
Total cost		60,000

Actual production for the period was 900 units and the following variances were incurred:

	Variance *£*
Direct materials price	100 Adverse
Direct labour total	2,095 Adverse

During the period the actual amount of material used was 950 litres and the standard quantity per unit was 1 litre.

3,950 actual hours were worked.

The standard time per unit was 4 hours per unit.

Complete the following table, for December:

Variance	£	*A/F*
Actual cost of materials		
Direct material usage variance		
Direct material total variance		
Standard material cost of production		
Actual cost of labour		
Direct labour rate variance		
Direct labour efficiency variance		
Standard labour cost of production		

75 SETTING BUDGETS

A company uses standard costing to set budgets.

Which of the following would be useful for controlling costs?

A Actual results versus flexed budget

B Actual results versus original budget

C Seasonal variations versus original budget

D Seasonal variations versus actual results

76 HINDER

Hinder Limited is obliged to buy sub-standard material at lower than standard price as nothing else is available.

As a result, are the following variances likely to be adverse or favourable?

	Materials price	*Materials usage*
A	Adverse	Favourable
B	Adverse	No change
C	Favourable	Adverse
D	Favourable	No change

77 LABOUR VARIANCE RATIOS

During a period, the actual hours worked by professional staff totalled 3,471. Budgeted hours were 3,630. The standard hours for the work totalled 3,502. The total hours paid were 3710.

Calculate the: *(each to one decimal place)*

Labour Activity ratio = [ ] %

Labour Efficiency ratio = [ ] %

Idle time ratio = [ ] %

78 LAB VAR RATIOS

During a period, the actual hours worked by employees totalled 31,630. Budgeted hours were 29,470 hours. The standard hours for the work totalled 30,502. The total hours paid were 32,000.

Calculate the: *(each to one decimal place)*

Labour Activity ratio = [ ] %

Labour Efficiency ratio = [ ] %

Idle time ratio = [ ] %

79 LABOUR

One possible reason for a favourable labour efficiency variance is:

Better quality material used	
Lack of motivation in workers	
Supervisor off sick	

80 BASIC

A company uses the basic standard to set budgets.

Which of the following statements is correct?

A The basic standard reflects current conditions, and is therefore challenging for the staff.

B The basic standard is a tried and tested target, which should help motivate staff.

C The basic standard no longer reflects current prices and performance levels.

D The basic standard is set under perfect conditions and it is difficult to meet, which can be demotivating for staff.

81 STANDARD

Which of the following is NOT a characteristic of an ideal standard?

A It assumes that machines and employees will work with optimal efficiency.

B It assumes that no materials will be wasted in production.

C It leads to unachievable objectives being set.

D It leads to increased motivation to achieve challenging objectives.

82 TIDLE

Tidle expects to produce 40,000 pots of paint using 5,000 labour hours. The standard cost of labour is £7 per hour. Actual production was 41,000 pots and actual hours paid were 5,200 hours, of which 300 hours were idle due to a machine breakdown. The actual wage bill was £39,000.

The labour rate variance is £ [ ]

The idle time variance is £ [ ]

The labour efficiency variance is £ [ ]

The total labour variance is £ [ ]

83 BRIDLE

Bridle expects to produce 4,000 units using 5,000 labour hours. The standard cost of labour is £7 per hour. Actual production was 4,100 units and actual hours paid were 5,200 hours, due to a machine breakdown the idle time variance was £700 adverse. The actual wage bill was £36,000.

The labour rate variance is £ [ ]

The actual hours worked are [ ]

The labour efficiency variance is £ [ ]

84 SIDLE

Sidle expects to produce 10,000 pots of paint using 5,000 labour hours. The standard cost of labour is £10 per hour. Actual production was 9,000 pots; 200 hours were idle due to a machine breakdown. The actual rate of pay was £9.61 and the total labour variance is £4,011 adverse.

The actual hours worked are [ ]

Complete the following table

		£
Standard labour cost for actual production		
Variances	**Favourable / adverse / no variance**	
Labour rate variance		
Idle time variance		
Labour efficiency variance		
Actual labour cost from actual production		

VARIABLE OVERHEAD VARIANCES

85 VAR (1)

Workers worked 12,000 hours and their company variable overhead rate was £5 per hour. During this time they managed to make 2,000 units whilst the budget had been for only 1,900 units. The standard number of hours allowed was 5 per unit, and the budgeted variable overhead rate per hour was £5.50.

Complete the following table.

			£
Standard cost of variable overheads for actual production			
Variances	**Favourable**	**Adverse**	
Variable overhead expenditure			
Variable overhead efficiency			
Total variance			
Actual cost of variable overheads for actual production			

86 JIF

Jif takes three standard hours to produce one unit at a variable overhead rate of £15 per hour. Total variable overhead costs for the period were £53,140 and a total of 3,400 labour hours were worked. Units produced were 1,000.

What is the variable overhead expenditure variance? £________ __.

87 CALLUM

A company incurred variable overheads of £55,800 and 10,000 labour hours were worked. Actual output was 10,000 units and standard labour hours were 1.2 hours per unit. The standard variable overhead rate per hour was £5.

What is the variable overhead efficiency variance? £________ __.

88 VALERIE (1)

Valerie takes two standard hours to produce one unit at a variable overhead rate of £5 per hour. Total variable overhead costs for the period were £103,140 and a total of 23,400 labour hours were worked. Units produced were 11,000.

The variable overhead expenditure variance is:

A £13,860 F

B £13,860 A

C £7,000 A

D £7,000 F

89 VALERIE (2)

Valerie takes two standard hours to produce one unit at a variable overhead rate of £5 per hour. Total variable overhead costs for the period were £103,140 and a total of 23,400 labour hours were worked. Units produced were 11,000.

The variable overhead efficiency variance is:

A £13,860 F

B £13,860 A

C £7,000 A

D £7,000 F

90 SHIRLEY

A company incurred a total variable overhead variance of £6,300 adverse and 10,000 labour hours were worked. Actual output was 11,000 units and standard labour hours were 0.9 hours per unit. The standard variable overhead rate per hour was £5.

The actual variable overheads are £ [ ]

The variable overhead expenditure variance is: £ [ ] **F/A**

The variable overhead efficiency variance is: £ [ ] **F/A**

91 VAR (2)

The variable overhead efficiency variance was £8,500 adverse. The workers managed to make 21,000 units whilst the budget had been for 22,000 units. The standard number of hours allowed was one hour per unit, and the budgeted rate per hour was £8.50. The actual rate per hour was £8.

Complete the following table.

			£
Standard cost of variable overheads for actual production			
Variances	**Favourable**	**Adverse**	
Variable overhead expenditure			
Variable overhead efficiency		**8,500**	
Total variance			
Actual cost of variable overheads for actual production			

FIXED OVERHEAD VARIANCES

92 OVERHEAD

Budgeted overheads are £20,000

Budgeted output is 10,000 units

Actual output is 12,000 units

Actual overheads are £25,000

The fixed overhead volume variance is £ [ ] **A/F**

The fixed overhead expenditure variance is £ [ ] **A/F**

93 BUDGET

Budgeted overheads are £180,000

Budgeted output is 15,000 units

Actual output is 15,600 units using 220,000 labour hours

Actual overheads are £172,000

The fixed overhead expenditure variance is £ [ ] **A/F**

The fixed overhead volume variance is £ [ ] **A/F**

94 FRANK

Budgeted overheads are £800,000

Budgeted output is 40,000 units

Actual output is 42,000 units

Actual overheads are £900,000

The fixed overhead volume variance is £ [ ] **A/F**

The fixed overhead expenditure variance is £ [ ] **A/F**

95 FIXED OVERHEADS

Budgeted overheads are £540,000

Budgeted output is 6,000 units using 90,000 labour hours

Actual output is 7,000 units using 114,000 labour hours

Actual overheads are £600,000

The fixed overhead expenditure variance is £ [ ] **A/F**

The fixed overhead volume variance is £ [ ] **A/F**

96 TRUMPET

Budgeted production is based on 14,000 labour hours.

Actual fixed overheads are £209,000.

Actual output was 6,000 units and each unit took 2 hours to complete. The standard time allowed was 1.75 hours. The overhead is absorbed at £25 per unit

The budgeted production is [ ] **units**

The fixed overhead expenditure variance is £ [ ] **A/F**

The fixed overhead volume variance is £ [ ] **A/F**

97 FLOPPY

Budgeted production is 100,000 units

Standard labour time per unit is 2 hours

Overheads are absorbed at a rate of £15 per unit

Actual production of 110,000 units took 210,000 hours

Actual overheads were £1,750,000

The fixed overhead expenditure variance is £ [ ] **A/F**

The fixed overhead volume variance is £ [ ] **A/F**

98 TROMBONE

Budgeted overheads are £56,000

Budgeted output is 8,000 units

Actual output is 8,200 units

Total fixed overhead variance for the period was £1,640 adverse.

The overhead absorption rate is £ [ ] per unit.

The actual overheads for the period are £ [ ]

The fixed overhead volume variance is £ [ ] A/F

The fixed overhead expenditure variance is £ [ ] A/F

99 VIOLIN

Budgeted overheads are £66,000

Budgeted output is 10,000 units

Actual output is 10,200 units

The fixed overhead expenditure variance is £3,040 adverse.

The actual fixed production overheads are £ [ ]

The total fixed production overhead variance is £ [ ] A/F

100 HARP

Budgeted overheads are £52,000

Budgeted output is 5,000 units

Actual output is 5,200 units

Total fixed overhead variance for the period was £4,960 adverse.

The actual overheads for the period are £ [ ]

The fixed overhead volume variance is £ [ ] A/F

The fixed overhead expenditure variance is £ [ ] A/F

101 CYMBAL

Budgeted overheads are £46,000

Budgeted output is 18,000 units

Actual output is 17,800 units

The fixed overhead expenditure variance is £3,040 A

The fixed overhead volume variance is £ [ ] A/F

The actual fixed overheads are £ [ ]

102 PIANO

The overhead absorption rate is £25 per unit.

Actual output is 18,000 units, 20% higher than budget, using 957,000 labour hours

The total fixed overhead variance for the period is £50,000 F

The actual fixed overhead is £ [ ]

The budgeted fixed overhead is £ [ ]

The fixed overhead expenditure variance is £ [ ] **A/F**

The fixed overhead volume variance is £ [ ] **A/F**

103 ORGAN

Budgeted overheads are £54,000

Budgeted output is 600 units using 9,000 labour hours

Actual output is 700 units using 11,400 labour hours

The total fixed overhead variance for the period is £3,000 F

The fixed overhead expenditure variance is £ [ ] **A/F**

The fixed overhead volume variance is £ [ ] **A/F**

The actual fixed overhead incurred is £ [ ]

104 FIDDLE

Budgeted overheads are £270,000

Budgeted output is 3,000 units

Actual output is 3,500 units

The fixed overhead expenditure variance is £30,000 A.

Actual fixed production overheads are £ [ ]

Total fixed production overheads variance is £ [ ] **A/F**

The overhead absorption rate is £ [ ] **per unit**

The fixed production overhead volume variance is £ [ ] **A/F**

105 FIX (1)

A company has budgeted fixed overheads of £400,000 and budgeted output is 20,000 units.

Actual output was 21,000 units and actual overheads were £450,000.

Complete the following table.

			£
Budgeted/Standard fixed cost for actual production			
Variances	**Favourable**	**Adverse**	
Fixed overhead expenditure			
Fixed overhead volume			
Total variance			
Actual fixed cost for actual production			

106 FIX (2)

A company has budgeted fixed overheads of £250,000 and budgeted output is 2,000 units.

Actual output was 2,100 units and actual overheads were £245,000.

Complete the following table.

			£
Budgeted/Standard fixed cost for actual production			
Variances	**Favourable**	**Adverse**	
Fixed overhead expenditure			
Fixed overhead volume			
Total variance			
Actual fixed cost for actual production			

OPERATING STATEMENTS

107 GOGGLE

The following budgetary control report has been provided for Goggle Limited:

	Budget		*Actual*	
Production		14,700		13,500
Direct material	14,960 kgs	£24,436	13,500 kgs	£20,650
Direct labour	920 hrs	£4,238	890 hrs	£3,971
Variable overheads		£20,520		£20,000
Fixed overheads		£10,250		£9,600
Total cost		£59,444		£54,221

The following variances have been calculated:

Direct materials price	1,401F
Direct materials usage	390F
Direct labour rate	129F
Direct labour efficiency	208A
Variable overhead expenditure	149A
Variable overhead efficiency	1,006A
Fixed overhead expenditure	650F
Fixed overhead volume	837A

Complete this operating statement using absorption costing.

Budgeted/standard cost for actual production			
Variances	**Favourable**	**Adverse**	
Direct materials price			
Direct materials usage			
Direct labour rate			
Direct labour efficiency			
Variable overhead expenditure			
Variable overhead efficiency			
Fixed overhead expenditure			
Fixed overhead volume			
Total variance			
Actual cost of actual production			

Complete this operating statement using marginal costing.

Budgeted/standard variable cost for actual production			
Budgeted fixed costs			
Variances	**Favourable**	**Adverse**	
Direct materials price			
Direct materials usage			
Direct labour rate			
Direct labour efficiency			
Variable overhead expenditure			
Variable overhead efficiency			
Fixed overhead expenditure			
Total variance			
Actual cost of actual production			

108 PUG

The following budgetary control report has been provided for Pug Limited:

	Budget		*Actual*	
Production		13,000		14,300
Direct material	3,250 kgs	£19,500	3,640 kgs	£20,020
Direct labour	390 hrs	£3,471	420 hrs	£3,738
Variable overheads	390 hrs	£20,150	420 hrs	£23,936
Fixed overheads		£9,100		£9,750
Total cost		£52,221		£57,444

The following variances have been calculated:

Direct materials price	1,820 F
Direct materials usage	390 A
Direct labour rate	0
Direct labour efficiency	80 F
Variable overhead expenditure	2,236 A
Variable overhead efficiency	465 F
Fixed overhead expenditure	650 A
Fixed overhead volume	910 F

Complete this operating statement using absorption costing.

Budgeted/standard cost for actual production			
Variances	**Favourable**	**Adverse**	
Direct materials price			
Direct materials usage			
Direct labour rate			
Direct labour efficiency			
Variable overhead expenditure			
Variable overhead efficiency			
Fixed overhead expenditure			
Fixed overhead volume			
Total variance			
Actual cost of actual production			

Complete this operating statement using marginal costing.

Budgeted/standard variable cost for actual production			
Budgeted fixed costs			
Variances	**Favourable**	**Adverse**	
Direct materials price			
Direct materials usage			
Direct labour rate			
Direct labour efficiency			
Variable overhead expenditure			
Variable overhead efficiency			
Fixed overhead expenditure			
Total variance			
Actual cost of actual production			

109 TASKFORCE/OVUNABS

You work in the accounts department at Taskforce Ltd, your manager has had to go on an unexpected but urgent business trip and she has asked you to complete the budgetary report she was working on.

The work she has done is shown below and is so far correct.

	Budgeted quantity	Budget £	Actual quantity	Actual £
Production volume	40,000 units		41,250 units	
Direct materials	80,000 kg	240,000	86,625 kg	256,410
Direct labour	60,000 hours	156,000	61,875 hours	173,250
Variable Overheads	60,000 hours	84,000	61,875 hours	84,150
Fixed overheads		118,000		120,000
Total production costs		598,000		633,810

The company use absorption costing and absorb overheads on units.

Variances	£
Direct materials price variance	3,465.00
Total direct labour variance	12,375.00
Variable overheads rate variance	2,475.00
Total fixed overhead variance	1,687.50

Complete the operating statement below using absorption costing

If an answer is zero, enter 0. Use positive numbers only – do not use minus signs. Each numeric entry must be to 2 decimal places.

Identify whether each variance is favourable or adverse or whether there is no variance.

		£
Standard absorption cost of actual production		
Variance	**Favourable / Adverse / No variance**	
Material price		3,465.00
Material usage		
Direct labour rate	Adverse	
Direct labour efficiency		
Variable overhead rate		2,475.00
Variable overhead efficiency		
Fixed overheads: expenditure variance		
Fixed overheads: volume variance	Favourable	
Total actual cost of actual production		633,810.00

Another company, Ovunabs Co, also use absorption costing, and absorbs overheads based on units produced for the single product that they make.

One of the accounting technicians at Ovunabs has had a mishap, lost some of the papers she was working on and has requested help. She has found the following information on overheads:

Fixed overhead volume variance	£4,250 Favourable
Over/(under) absorption	£7,000
Actual overhead incurred	£180,000
Actual production	22,000 units

Complete the below table to help

Budgeted units	
Budgeted overhead (£)	
Overhead absorption rate (£ to 2DP)	

110 BUDGETARY CONTROL REPORT

The following report has been provided:

	Budget		*Actual*	
Production		4,000		4,200
Direct materials	2,000 litres	£50,000	2,300 litres	£59,800
Direct labour	8,000 hours	£56,000	8,800 hours	£59,840
Variable overheads	8,000 hours	£240,000	8,800 hours	£294,000
Fixed overheads		£240,000		£260,000
Total cost		£586,000		£673,640

The following variances have been calculated:

Direct materials price	£2,300 A
Direct materials usage	£5,000 A
Direct labour rate	£1,760 F
Direct labour efficiency	£2,800 A
Variable overhead expenditure	£30,000 A
Variable overhead efficiency	£12,000 A
Fixed overhead expenditure	£20,000 A
Fixed overhead volume	£12,000 F

Complete this operating statement using absorption costing.

Budgeted/Standard cost for actual production			
Variances	**Favourable**	**Adverse**	
Direct materials price			
Direct materials usage			
Direct labour rate			
Direct labour efficiency			
Variable overhead expenditure			
Variable overhead efficiency			
Fixed overhead expenditure			
Fixed overhead volume			
Total variance			
Actual cost of actual production			

111 BUDGET V ACTUAL

The following budgetary control report has been provided:

	Budget		*Actual*	
Production (barrels)		2,500		2,400
Material	12,500 litres	£106,250	11,520 litres	£99,072
Direct labour	10,000 hours	£60,000	10,080 hours	£61,488
Fixed overheads		£200,000		£185,808
Total cost		£366,250		£346,368

The following variances have been calculated:

Fixed overhead expenditure	£14,192 F
Direct materials price	£1,152 A
Direct materials usage	£4,080 F
Direct labour rate	£1,008 A
Direct labour efficiency	£2,880 A
Fixed overhead volume	£8,000 A

Complete this operating statement using absorption costing.

Standard cost for actual production			
Variances	**Favourable**	**Adverse**	
Direct materials price			
Direct materials usage			
Direct labour rate			
Direct labour efficiency			
Fixed overhead expenditure			
Fixed overhead volume			
Total variance			
Actual cost of actual production			

112 OPERATING STATEMENT

The following budgetary control report has been provided:

	Budget		*Actual*	
Production		35,000		33,000
Oranges	420,000	£84,000	320,000	£70,400
Cartons	35,000 units	£1,750	33,100 units	£1,660
Direct labour	8,750 hours	£26,250	9,000 hours	£26,100
Fixed overheads		£350,000		£365,000
Total cost		£462,000		£463,160

Complete this operating statement using marginal costing.

Budgeted/Standard variable cost for actual production (W1)			
Budgeted fixed costs			
Variances	**Favourable**	**Adverse**	
Direct materials price (oranges)			
Direct materials price (cartons)			
Direct materials usage (oranges)			
Direct materials usage (cartons)			
Direct labour rate			
Direct labour efficiency			
Fixed overhead expenditure			
Total variance			
Actual cost of actual production			

CONTROLLABLE AND UNCONTROLLABLE VARIANCES

113 BUGLE (1)

M Ltd produces and sells a single product, the Bugle. One Bugle uses 3 kg of direct materials, with a standard cost of £10 per kg.

During July, M Ltd's standard material price was revised to £9.50 per kg and actual results were:

Production: 1,000 Bugles

Direct materials: 3,500 kg purchased, cost £31,500

The controllable material price variance is:

A £1,750 A

B £1,750 F

C £3,500 F

D £3,500 A

114 BUGLE (2)

M Ltd produces and sells a single product, the Bugle. One Bugle uses 3 kg of direct materials, with a standard cost of £10 per kg.

During July, M Ltd's standard material price was revised to £9.50 per kg and actual results were:

Production: 1,000 Bugles

Direct materials: 3,500 kg purchased, cost £31,500

The uncontrollable material price variance is:

A £1,750 A

B £1,750 F

C £3,500 F

D £3,500 A

115 BUGLE (3)

M Ltd produces and sells a single product, the Bugle. One Bugle uses 3 kg of direct materials, with a standard cost of £10 per kg.

During July, M Ltd's standard material usage was revised to 3.2 kg and actual results were:

Production: 1,000 Bugles

Direct materials: 3,500 kg used, cost £31,500

The controllable material usage variance is:

A £3,000 A

B £500 F

C £5,000 A

D £2,000 A

116 BUGLE (4)

M Ltd produces and sells a single product, the Bugle. One Bugle uses 3 kg of direct materials, with a standard cost of £10 per kg.

During July, M Ltd's standard material usage was revised to 3.2 kg and actual results were:

Production: 1,000 Bugles

Direct materials: 3,500 kg used, cost £31,500

The uncontrollable material usage variance is:

A £2,000 A

B £500 F

C £5,000 A

D £3,000 A

117 BUST (1)

Bust produces and sells a single product, the Bumper. One Bumper uses 5 kg of direct materials, with a standard cost of £7 per kg.

During July, Bust's standard material price was revised to £6.95 per kg and actual results were:

Production: 10,000 Bumpers

Direct materials: 50,500 kg purchased, cost £350,000

The controllable material price variance is:

A £975 F

B £975 A

C £3,500A

D £3,500 F

118 BUST (2)

Bust produces and sells a single product, the Bumper. One Bumper uses 5 kg of direct materials, with a standard cost of £7 per kg.

During July, Bust's standard material price was revised to £6.95 per kg and actual results were:

Production: 10,000 Bumpers

Direct materials: 50,500 kg purchased, cost £350,000

The uncontrollable material price variance is:

A £975 F

B £975 A

C £2,525 A

D £2,525 F

119 BUST (3)

M Ltd produces and sells a single product, the Bumper. One Bumper uses 5 kg of direct materials, with a standard cost of £7 per kg.

During July, Bust's standard material usage was revised to 4.9 kg and actual results were:

Production: 10,000 Bumpers

Direct materials: 50,500 kg used, cost £350,000

The controllable material usage variance is:

A £7,000 F

B £3,500 A

C £10,500 A

D £3,500 F

120 BUST (4)

Bust produces and sells a single product, the Bumper. One Bumper uses 5 kg of direct materials, with a standard cost of £7 per kg.

During July, Bust's standard material usage was revised to 4.9 kg and actual results were:

Production: 10,000 Bumpers

Direct materials: 50,500 kg used, cost £350,000

The uncontrollable material usage variance is:

A £7,000 F

B £3,500 A

C £10,500 A

D £3,500 F

121 CONTROLLABLE

Index produces and sells a single product, the India.

One India should use 5 kg of direct materials. The quantity index was set many years ago when the index was 90.

The material has a standard cost of £7 per kg (set when the price index was 100).

During July, Index's standard material price per kg was revised due to the price index rising to 110. Its standard material usage was also revised as the quantity index had risen to 108.

Actual results were:

Production: 10,500 units

Direct materials: 50,250 kg purchased and used at a cost of £360,000

The controllable material price variance is £ [ ]

The uncontrollable material price variance is £ [ ]

The controllable material usage variance is £ [ ]

The uncontrollable material usage variance is £ [ ]

122 UNCONTROLLABLE

Indicator produces and sells a single product.

One product should use 8 kg of direct materials. The quantity index was set recently when the index was rebased to 100.

The material has a standard cost of £10 per kg (set when the price index was 100).

During June, the product's standard material price per kg was revised due to the price index rising to 115. Its standard material usage was also revised as the quantity index had risen to 105.

Actual results were:

Production: 1,000 units

Direct materials: 9,000 kg purchased and used at a cost of £107,900

The controllable material price variance is £ [ ]

The uncontrollable material price variance is £ [ ]

The controllable material usage variance is £ [ ]

The uncontrollable material usage variance is £ [ ]

TIMES SERIES, LINEAR REGRESSION AND INDEXING

123 TREND

The actual purchase price per tonne of materials, together with its estimated seasonal variation, is as below:

	Q1	*Q2*	*Q3*	*Q4*
Actual price	£30	£34	£54	£66
Seasonal variation	–£4	–£8	+£4	+£8

The trend in prices is an increase of [ ] **per quarter.**

124 RPI

A company has provided the following information:

	2008	*2009*	*2010*
Cost per kg of materials	£17.00	£18.60	£19.40
Retail price index	184	192	200

The percentage increase in purchase costs, after removing the effect of general inflation, between 2008 and 2010 was:

A 14.12%

B 8.70%

C 4.99%

D 24.04%

125 PRODUCT Z

The cost per unit of a product has decreased from £36 in October 20X7 to £32 in December 20X7. The cost per unit was £30 when the index was rebased to 100 in January 20X7.

A The cost index in December was 107 and the decrease from October to December is 11.11%

B The cost index in December was 89 and the decrease from October to December is 11.11%

C The cost index in December is 107 and the decrease from October to December is 12.5%

D The cost index in December is 89 and the decrease from October to December is 12.5%

126 TANZANITE

The table below contains the last three months cost per metre for product Tanzanite.

Jan	*Feb*	*Mar*
Actual price was £6.90	Actual price was £7.00	Actual price was £7.40
Seasonal variation was –10p	Seasonal variation was –15p	Seasonal variation was 10p

The trend in prices is an increase of £ [ ] **per month**

127 MARCH

A company has provided the following information:

	Jan	*Feb*	*March*
Total cost	£450,000	£500,000	£650,000
Total quantity purchased	20,000 m	25,000 m	27,500 m

The cost index for March, based upon January being the base period with an index of 100, is:

A 105

B 138

C 144

D 167

128 COST PER UNIT

The cost per unit of a product has increased from £52 in February to £56 in April. The cost per unit was £50 in January when the index was rebased to 100.

Which of the following statements is correct?

A The cost index in April was 112 and the increase from January to April is 12%

B The cost index in April was 112 and the increase from January to April is 8%

C The cost index in April was 108 and the increase from January to April is 12%

D The cost index in April was 108 and the increase from January to April is 8%

129 PRODUCT Y

The table below contains the last three months cost per kilogram for product Y

Apr	*May*	*Jun*
Actual price was £6.56	Actual price was £7.14	Actual price was £7.35
Seasonal variation was (£0.30)	Seasonal variation was £0.14	Seasonal variation was £0.21

The trend in prices is an increase of £ [ ] per month

130 A COMPANY

A company has provided the following information:

	Jan	*Feb*	*March*
Total cost	£100,000	£132,000	£127,000
Total quantity purchased	10,000 kgs	12,000 kgs	11,500 kgs

The cost index (to the nearest whole number) for March based upon January being the base period of 100 is:

A 120

B 110

C 127

D 115

131 PRODUCT X

The cost per unit of a product has increased from £46 in January to £52 in April. The cost per unit was £42 when the index was rebased to 100. (Assume an inflationary economy.)

A The cost index in April was 123.8 and the increase from January to April is 13.0%

B The cost index in April was 113 and the increase from January to April is 13.0%

C The cost index in April is 123.8 and the increase from January to April is 11.5%

D The cost index in April is 113 and the increase from January to April is 11.5%

132 INDEX

The cost per unit of a product has increased from £82 in May to £96 in July. The cost per unit was £70 when the index was 100. (Assume an inflationary economy.)

A The cost index in July is 137, and the increase from May to July is 17%

B The cost index in July is 127, and the increase from May to July is 17%

C The cost index in July is 137, and the increase from May to July is 15%

D The cost index in July is 127, and the increase from May to July is 15%

133 DEXTER

The cost per unit of a product has increased from £1,350 in June to £1,710 in September. The cost per unit was £1,080 when the index was rebased to 100.

A The cost index in September is 126 and the increase from June to September is 21.05%

B The cost index in September is 158 and the increase from June to September is 21.05%

C The cost index in September is 126 and the increase from June to September is 26.67%

D The cost index in September is 158 and the increase from June to September is 26.67%

134 WASTE

A company has provided the following information for kilograms of waste sent to landfill by Moody Co.

	Jan	*Feb*	*March*
Kgs	1000	1250	1100
Price per kilo	5	6	7
Total cost	£5000	£7500	£7700

The cost index for March based upon January being the base period of 100 is:

A 120

B 140

C 117

D 83

135 FIZZ

The table below contains the last three months cost per litre for Fizz.

Jan	*Feb*	*Mar*
Actual price was £550	Actual price was £675	Actual price was £650
Seasonal variation was –£50	Seasonal variation was +£50	Seasonal variation was Nil

The trend in prices is an increase of £ [ ] per month

136 ACRID

The table below contains the last three months cost per tonne for product Acrid.

Jan	*Feb*	*Mar*
Actual price was £50	Actual price was £50	Actual price was £65
Seasonal variation was £5	Seasonal variation was –£5	Seasonal variation was Nil

The trend in prices is an increase of £ [ ] per month.

137 PRODUCT J

The table below contains the last three months cost per litre for product J.

	April	*May*	*June*
Actual price	£7.20	£7.50	£6.90
Seasonal variation	£0.10	£0.20	(£0.60)

The trend in prices is an increase of £ [ ] per month.

138 ABCO

A company has provided the following information:

	October	*November*	*December*
Total cost	£1,250	£1,390	£1,610
Quantity purchased	1,000 kg	1,100 kg	1,200 kg

The cost index for December based upon October prices is:

A 101

B 107

C 125

D 134

139 SOAP

The soap industry maintains a price index for soap. The index for May was 105 and the actual price per tonne was £1,200. The forecast index for the three months ending November 2009 is shown below.

Month	*September*	*October*	*November*
Underlying trend in index	120	125	130
Seasonal variation in index	+6	–6	+3
Seasonally adjusted index	126	119	133

Calculate the expected cost of one tonne of soap for each of the three months.

September	£
October	£
November	£

140 ASPHALT

The Production Director has asked for your help. She has been given an equation and information to estimate the cost of asphalt for the coming three months.

The equation is Y = a + bX, where

X is the time period in months

the value for X in April is 24 and May is 25

Y is the cost of asphalt

The constant "a" is 125 and constant "b" is 2.

The cost of asphalt is set on the first day of each month and is not changed during the month. The cost of asphalt in May was £175 per tonne.

The expected price of asphalt per tonne for June is £ [ ] and for July is £ [ ]

Convert into index numbers (to 2 d.p.) the asphalt prices per tonne for June and July, using May as the base.

June	
July	

141 BEST FIT

You have calculated the line of best fit as y = 25.97 + 3.56x, where y is the cost per litre and x is the period. January 20X3 is period 21.

The forecast cost per litre, using the line of best fit, for June 20X3 is £ [ ]

142 LEAST

You have calculated the line of best fit as y = 105.97 + 12.56x, where y is the cost per kilogram and x is the period. March 20X1 is period 45.

The forecast cost per kilogram, using the line of best fit, for July 20X1 is £ [ ]

143 MOST

The Production Director has asked for your help. She has been given an equation and information to estimate the cost of a supply for the coming months.

The equation is Y = a + bX, where

X is the time period in months

the value for X in April 20X9 is 19 and May 20X9 is 20

Y is the cost of the supply

The constant "a" is 15 and constant "b" is 4.

The expected price of the supply for June 20X9 is £ [ ] and for July 20X9 is £ [ ]

Convert in to index numbers (to 2 d.p.) the supply prices for June and July, using May 20X9 as the base.

June	
July	

144 TEA

Tea is imported from India and the historical cost per kilogram is shown below.

	June X7 £	*July X7* £	*Aug X7* £	*Sept X7* £	*Oct X7* £	*Nov X7* £
Cost per kg of tea	4.95	4.97	4.99	5.05	5.08	5.10

Convert the costs per kilogram for June and November to index numbers using January 20X7 as the base year. The cost per kilogram in January 20X7 was £4.80.

	June X7 £	*Nov X7* £
Cost per kg of tea		
Base cost		
Index		

It is expected that the index number for tea for January 20X8 will be 108.25. The expected cost per kilogram for January 20X8 is £ [ ]

The percentage increase in the price of tea from January 20X7 to January 20X8 is: [ ] %.

145 FRUIT

The vitamin which is derived from soft fruit is either imported or purchased from UK farmers. The price of the vitamin fluctuates month by month depending on the time of year. The cost information for the 4 months ending August 20X6 is given below.

	May X6	*June X6*	*July X6*	*August X6*
Cost per 1,000 kg of vitamin	£1,000	£900	£700	£800

The underlying cost does not change during the period May to August. The change in cost over the 4 months is due only to the seasonal variations which are given below.

	May X6	*June X6*	*July X6*	*August X6*
Seasonal variations	£200	£100	(£100)	£0

Calculate the underlying cost per 1,000 kilograms for the period May to August 20X6.

	May X6	*Jun X6*	*Jul X6*	*Aug X6*
Cost per 1,000 kg				
Seasonal variation				
Trend				

Indications are that the underlying cost per 1,000 kilograms for the period May 20X7 to August 20X7 will be £850. The percentage increase in the underlying cost from 20X6 to 20X7 is [ ] %.

Calculate the forecast cost per 1,000 kilograms for the period May 20X7 to August 20X7 using the underlying cost and the seasonal variations given above.

	May X7	*June X7*	*July X7*	*Aug X7*
Trend				
Seasonal variation				
Cost per 1,000 kgs				

146 YANKEE (2)

The Sales Manager for Yankee Limited is reviewing the company's quarterly sales (shown below) for the last financial year. External information for the label printing market indicates average annual growth of 16%. The Sales Manager's analysis suggests Yankee's sales have increased by 18% over the last year. As this is better than the market average the Manager will be awarded a performance related bonus.

	Q1	*Q2*	*Q3*	*Q4*
Actual sales volume	224,000	196,000	215,000	265,000

Before the Sales Manager's bonus is calculated and paid you have been asked to verify his findings. Having carried out some research you have established the following seasonal variations.

	Q1	*Q2*	*Q3*	*Q4*
Seasonal variations	14,000	–24,000	–15,000	25,000

Calculate the seasonally adjusted sales volume for EACH of the FOUR quarters for Yankee Ltd.

Calculate the seasonally adjusted growth in sales volume from Quarter 1 to Quarter 4 for Yankee Ltd. Express your answer as a percentage, to the nearest whole %.

Should the Sales Manager be paid his bonus? YES/NO *(Delete as appropriate.)*

147 SEB

Seb uses product XYZ and has collected data from the last few months in order to forecast the cost per litre of XYZ in the next few months.

	Apr X3	May X3	Jun X3
Cost per litre of XYZ	£104.55	£107.70	£110.85

Complete the table below to forecast the expected price of product XYZ in July X3 and September X3.

	July X3	September X3
Cost per litre of XYZ		

148 TOAST

The Production Director at Toast has asked for your help. She has been given an equation and information to estimate the cost of a supply for the coming months.

The equation is Y = a + bX, where

X is the time period in quarters

the value for X in quarter 1 of 20X3 is 24 and quarter 2 of 20X3 is 25

Y is the underlying trend of the cost of the supply. The supply is of seasonal nature and can cost more at certain times of the year due to a shortage of supply or excessive demand.

Below are the actual prices paid in each quarter of 20X3 and the seasonal variations.

(a) Calculate the trend figures.

	20X3 Qtr 1	20X3 Qtr 2	20X3 Qtr 3	20X3 Qtr 4
Actual	£3,200	£3,020	£3,320	£3,060
Seasonal variation	+£200	-£80	+£120	-£240
Trend				

(b) From the above trend figures, determine the value of a and b in the equation Y = a + bX

	£
b	
a	

(c) Using the trend equation, calculate the trend for 20X7 quarter 1 and 3:

	Trend (£)
20X7 Qtr 1	
20X7 Qtr 3	

(d) Assuming the seasonal variation acts as in 20X3, calculate the forecast cost for 20X7 quarter 2 and 4.

	Forecast (£)
20X7 Qtr 2	
20X7 Qtr 4	

(e) If the forecast figures for quarter 1 and 2 of 20X8 are 5,200 and 5,020, express these as an index number with base Qtr 1 20X3.

	Index number (2DP)
20X8 Qtr 1	
20X8 Qtr 2	

149 COAST

The Production Director at Coast has asked for your help. She has been given an equation and information regarding historic costs to help forecast costs in the future.

The equation is Y = a + bX, where

X is the time period in quarters

the value for X in quarter 1 of 20X2 is 10 and quarter 2 of 20X2 is 11

Y is the underlying trend of the cost of the supply. The supply is of seasonal nature and can cost more at certain times of the year due to a shortage of supply or excessive demand.

The trend in prices is an increase of £0.50 per quarter.

Below is an incomplete table showing actual prices paid, amounts purchased, cost per kg and trend figures in each quarter of 20X2.

(a) Calculate missing figures:

	20X2 Qtr 1	20X2 Qtr 2	20X2 Qtr 3	20X2 Qtr 4
Actual paid (£)		418,500		791,000
Quantity purchased (kg)	10,000		11,000	
Cost per kg (£ to 2DP)	44.00			
Seasonal variation (£ to 2DP)	-5.00	-3.00	2.00	6.00
Trend (£ to 2DP)				

(b) If the price in 20X5 Qtr 1 is £50, what would be the index number if the base is 20X2 Qtr 1 to the nearest whole number?

150 STATATAC

Statatac Ltd use trend analysis to help their business plan for the future. They have provided the following information about sales volumes for the third quarter of20X6.

(a) Complete the table below by entering the missing figures. Use the minus signs for negative numbers.

20X6 volume of units ('000)	July	August	September
Trend			100
Seasonal variation	10	5	
Seasonally adjusted sales		100	92

(b) Assuming the trend of the seasonal variations continue as in (a) above, complete the table below to show the projected sales volumes for the last quarter of 20X7. Use minus signs for negative figures.

20X7 volume of units ('000)	October	November	December
Trend			
Seasonal variation	–10	–12	–15
Seasonally adjusted sales			

Flexi-Indexy paid £12 per kilogram (kg) for material in February 20X7, the base month. In October 20X7 the index is expected to be 112.

(c) Forecast the price per kg (to the nearest penny) in October 20X7.

£ [ ]

If in February 20X8 the price is now £14.50 per kilogram.

(d) What would the index (with base Feb 20X7) be to the nearest whole number?

[ ]

151 TEX-MEX-INDEX

Tex-Mex-Index Co started purchasing a material for use in the manufacture of their products in 20X1. The price in 20X1 (the base year) was 4.50 per kg. It is now 20X8, they have incomplete records regarding the prices paid and the price index for the material over the years.

(a) Complete the table below

Give index umbers to the nearest whole numbers and prices in £ to 2 decimal places.

Year	Index	Price per kg £
20X2	105	
20X3		4.87
20X4	110	
20X5		4.61
20X6		4.82
20X7	115	

Another company, Dexi's MR Ltd have a table showing the index of prices for a certain commodity over the last five years (base 20X1):

Year	20X3	20X4	20X5	20X6	20X7
Index	105	115	127	140	152

The price was £10 per kg in 20X5.

(b) Complete the following sentences (to 2 decimal places):

The percentage increase in price from 20X4 to 20X6 is [ ] %.

The price in 20X7 is £[ ] per kg.

Trendy Wendy Ltd is a chain of clothes store specialising in summer fashion. They use trend analysis and have forecast their quarterly sales. Unfortunately some of the data has been lost.

(c) Complete the below table

20X7 volume of units ('000)	Quarter 1	Quarter 2	Quarter 3	Quarter 4
Trend	100			
Seasonal variation	–50		+90	–60
Seasonally adjusted sales		130		70

VARIANCE ANALYSIS WRITTEN QUESTIONS

152 ARTETA

You have been provided with the following information for an organisation, which manufactures a product called Persie, for the month just ended:

	Budget		*Actual*	
Production (units)		10,000		11,000
Direct materials	15,000 kg	£30,000	16,000 kg	£33,500

The finance director has asked you to write a note to help in the training of a junior accounting technician. The note is to explain the calculation of the total direct material variance and how this variance can be split into a price variance and a usage variance.

Prepare a note explaining the total material variance and how it can be split into a price variance and a usage variance. Calculations should be used to illustrate your explanation.

To:	**Subject:**
From:	**Date:**

153 MERTESACKER

You have been provided with the following information for an organisation, which manufactures a product called Wilshere, for the month just ended:

	Budget		*Actual*	
Production (units)		100		95
Direct labour	1,500 hours	£30,000	1,600 hours	£31,500

The finance director has asked you to write a note to help in the training of a junior accounting technician. The note is to explain the calculation of the total direct labour variance and how this variance can be split into a rate variance and an efficiency variance.

Prepare a note explaining the total labour variance and how it can be split into a rate variance and an efficiency variance. Calculations should be used to illustrate your explanation.

To:	**Subject:**
From:	**Date:**

154 TOP DOG

The following budgetary control report has been provided:

	Budget		*Actual*	
Production (barrels)		2,500		2,400
Material	12,500 litres	£106,250	11,520 litres	£99,072
Direct labour	10,000 hours	£60,000	10,080 hours	£61,488
Fixed overheads		£200,000		£185,808
Total cost		£366,250		£346,368

The following variances have been calculated:

Direct materials price	£1,152
Direct materials usage	£4,080
Direct labour rate	£1,008
Direct labour efficiency	£2,880
Fixed overhead expenditure	£14,192
Fixed overhead volume	£8,000

Using this information, prepare a report to the Managing Director of Top dog to cover an analysis of each variance by

- **identifying the sign of the variances**
- **explaining what the variance means**
- **providing one possible reason for each variance**
- **explaining any links between the variances**
- **Providing an action which could have been taken.**

To:	**Subject:**
From:	**Date:**

Direct materials price variance

Direct materials usage variance

Labour rate variance   **Labour efficiency variance**   **Fixed overhead expenditure variance**   **Fixed overhead volume variance**

155 OPSTAT

The following budgetary control report has been provided:

	Budget		*Actual*	
Production		35,000		33,000
Oranges	420,000	£84,000	320,000	£70,400
Cartons	35,000 units	£1,750	33,100 units	£1,660
Direct labour	8,750 hours	£26,250	9,000 hours	£26,100
Fixed overheads		£350,000		£365,000
Total cost		£462,000		£463,160

The following variances have been calculated:

Direct materials (oranges) price	£6,400
Direct materials (oranges) usage	£15,200
Direct materials (cartons) price	£5
Direct materials (cartons) usage	£5
Direct labour rate	£900
Direct labour efficiency	£2,250
Fixed overhead expenditure	£15,000
Fixed overhead volume	£20,000

Using this information, prepare a report to the Managing Director of Opstat to cover an analysis of each variance by

- **identifying the sign of the variances**
- **explaining what the variance means**
- **providing one possible reason for each variance**
- **explaining any links between the variances**
- **providing an action which could have been taken.**

To:	**Subject:**
From:	**Date:**

Direct materials (oranges) price variance

Direct materials (oranges) usage variance

Direct materials (cartons) price variance

Direct materials (cartons) usage variance

Labour rate variance

Labour efficiency variance

Fixed overhead expenditure variance

Fixed overhead volume variance

156 DIXON

Dixon plc manufactures a range of products for use in the electrical industry. The company uses a standard absorption costing system with variances calculated monthly.

It is midway through month 7 of the current financial year and a number of events have occurred which may impact on the month-end variances for one particular product – the ELC.

The production director has asked for a report indicating the possible effects of the various events.

Notes for the production of the ELC

- The ELC uses a specialist industry material – TRI3
- Recent advances in the production of material TR13 have increased its availability which has led to a reduction in its price per metre by 10% in the last month. It is expected that the reduction in price will continue to the year end
- The standard price was set before the decrease in price occurred
- The quality control department has tested the latest batch of TR13 and reported that it is of higher quality than expected
- The company implemented a strict material usage policy at the beginning of the year to monitor levels of wastage. This was overseen by the quality control department and no additional payroll costs were incurred
- Employees usually receive an annual pay rise at the beginning of month 7 and this was included in the standard cost. Due to the current economic climate this pay rise has been suspended indefinitely
- The budgeted production for the month is 1,500 units
- An order for 500 units to be produced in month 7 was cancelled. The company has been unable to replace this order and the actual production for month 7 will only be 1,000 units
- The production machinery settings needed to be altered to deal with the higher quality TR13. In addition, one of the machines was found to be defective and required a complete overhaul. These costs are to be included in the month's fixed production overheads

Complete the report for the production director covering the possible impact of the above events on the TR13 price and usage variances, the labour efficiency variance and the fixed overhead expenditure and volume variances. The report should:

- **Identify whether each variance is likely to be favourable or adverse at the end of the month**
- **Explain what each variance means**
- **Provide one possible reason why each variance is likely to be adverse or favourable at the end of the month**
- **Identify possible links between variances**

You are not required to perform any calculations.

To:	**Subject:**
From:	**Date:**

TR13 price variance

TR13 usage variance

Labour efficiency variance

Fixed overhead expenditure variance

Fixed overhead volume variance

157 GRIPPIT (2)

Grippit Ltd processes old tyres into a product called Crumb. Crumb is used in a variety of applications from road surfaces to brake linings. Grippit Ltd processes the tyres in the Crumbing Division and then either sells Crumb to other companies or uses Crumb in the manufacture of rubberised asphalt in the Road Division.

You work as an Accounting Technician reporting to the Finance Director.

The Crumbing Division operates a standard cost system in which

- purchases of material are recorded at nil cost, as they are delivered free of charge from major tyre companies
- direct labour costs are variable
- production overheads are fixed and absorbed on a unit basis.

The budgeted activity and actual results for the month of May 2008 are as follows:

		Budget		*Actual*
Production (tonnes)		200		210
Direct labour	600 hours	£4,800	600 hours	£5,100
Fixed overheads		£90,000		£95,000
Total cost		£94,800		£100,100

(a) Calculate the following for May:

(i) Standard labour rate per hour	
(ii) Standard labour hours for actual production	
(iii) Budgeted cost per tonne of Crumb	
(iv) Budgeted overhead absorption rate per tonne	
(v) Overheads absorbed into actual production	
(vi) Total standard cost of actual production	

(b) Calculate the following variances for May:

	£	*F/A*
(i) Direct labour rate variance		
(ii) Direct labour efficiency variance		
(iii) Fixed overhead expenditure variance		
(iv) Fixed overhead volume variance		

(c) Using the variances you have calculated, complete the operating statement for May which reconciles the standard cost of total actual production with the actual cost of total actual production.

Budgeted/Standard cost for actual production			
Variances	**Favourable**	**Adverse**	
Direct labour rate			
Direct labour efficiency			
Fixed overhead expenditure			
Fixed overhead volume			
Total variance			
Actual cost of actual production			

The Production Director has reviewed the variances and has given you the following information.

- A pay rise of 25p per hour was awarded after the standard had been set.
- A software upgrade was purchased for the production machinery which cost £120,000 for a 2-year licence. The cost is being amortised (depreciated) on a straight line basis.
- The software upgrade should increase labour efficiency by 10%, reducing the standard labour time to 2.7 hours per tonne.

Using the information provided by the Production Director, draft a report for the Finance Director explaining the variances you calculated above.

To:	**Subject:**
From:	**Date:**
(i) Direct labour rate variance	
(ii) Direct labour efficiency variance	

(iii) Fixed overhead expenditure variance

(iv) Fixed overhead volume variance

158 VARIANCE ETHICS

Below are some of the results for one of the divisions of Variance Ltd for the last month.

Variances	£
Materials price	6,000 adverse
Materials usage	10,000 adverse
Labour rate	2,000 favourable
Labour usage	3,000 favourable

The production managers at Variance Ltd receives a bonus based on labour variances. The bonus is paid if the overall labour variance is favourable.

Explain the ethical issues and any issues with goal congruence.

Ethical issues

Goal congruence issues

159 WOODEN SPOON

Wooden Spoon Ltd manufacture and sell handmade kitchen utensils from rolling pins to porridge stirrers, from chopping boards to wooden spoons.

They use standard costing, and below is an extract from their system:

Standard direct cost of one wooden spoon	£
Wood	3.45
Treatment	0.46
Labour	4.80
Variable overhead	2.40
	11.11

The amount of wood required and treatment used in a wooden spoon was set many years ago and the design has changed in line with fashions from big and bulky to a more streamlined design. They have found that a batch of wood can manufacture around 15% more wooden spoons than from the initial designs.

The labour cost is based on no stoppages or idle time in the production process. Month on month non-productive time has ranged from 3% to 8% and over the last year the average was 4%. The labour rate is also based on the wages that the workers were paid when the company first set up. It is estimated that wages are now 10% higher.

(a) Write a memo to your manager in which you evaluate the consequences of Wooden Spoon Ltd.'s approach to standard setting. You should:

(i) Explain the types of standard being used for the different materials and labour,

(ii) Explain the behavioural implications of those standards and the consequences for variances analysis,

(iii) Calculate appropriately revised standards based on the information provided and justify your revised standards.

To: Manager	**Subject:** Standard setting at Wooden Spoon
From: Accounting Technician	**Date:** 24/3/20X7

(i) Types of standard

(ii) Behavioural implications

(iii) Revised standards and justification

Wooden Spoon Ltd's Floor manager will receive a bonus if the net cost variance for the period is favourable. Based on current forecasts the variances will be net adverse. The manager has decided to delay the maintenance of the factory to try to overturn the adverse variance in the current period.

(b) Briefly explain the ethical and goal congruence issues that may arise as a result of this behaviour.

160 FOODRINK

Foodrink Ltd manufactures and distributes nutritional supplements. One of its main products is IQ, a special vitamin supplement which claims to increase the concentration levels of individuals and helps them think carefully, especially when taking an exam. The supplement makes students read questions very carefully and show all their workings.

You work as an Accounting Technician reporting to the Finance Director.

The company operates an integrated standard cost system in which:

- purchases of materials are recorded at standard cost
- direct material costs and direct labour costs are variable
- production overheads are fixed and absorbed on a unit basis.

The budgeted activity and actual results for May are as follows:

		Budget		*Actual*
Production (units)		9,000		9,900
Direct materials	450 kgs	£5,400	594 kgs	£6,534
Direct labour	300 hours	£4,500	325 hours	£4,225
Fixed overheads		£18,000		£19,000
Total cost		£27,900		£29,759

(a) Calculate the following for May:

(i)	Standard price of materials per kilogram	
(ii)	Standard usage of materials for actual production	
(ii)	Standard labour rate per hour	
(iv)	Standard labour hours for actual production	
(v)	Budgeted overhead absorption rate per unit	
(vi)	Overheads absorbed into actual production	

(b) Calculate the following variances for May:

	£	*F/A*
(i) Direct material price variance		
(ii) Direct material usage variance		
(iii) Direct labour rate variance		
(iv) Direct labour efficiency variance		
(v) Fixed overhead expenditure variance		
(vi) Fixed overhead volume variance.		

(c) Using the variances you have calculated, complete the operating statement for May which reconciles the standard cost of total actual production with the actual cost of total actual production.

Budgeted costs for actual production			
Variances	**Favourable**	**Adverse**	
Direct material price			
Direct material usage			
Direct labour rate			
Direct labour efficiency			
Fixed overhead expenditure			
Fixed overhead volume			
Total variance			
Actual cost of actual production			

PERFORMANCE INDICATORS CALCULATION QUESTIONS

161 BACKWARDS

A business has sales for the year of £30,000. Its financial performance indicators at the year-end include the following:

Gross profit margin	30%
Receivables collection period	30 days
Creditors payment period	48 days
Inventory	£2,100
Current ratio	2:1

Assume there are 360 days in a year.

Complete the following table:

Year-end receivables balance	
Year-end payables balance	

Calculate the business' year end cash position.

Year-end cash position	

162 REVERSE

A business has provided the following information:

Receivables collection period	45 days
Creditors payment period	64 days
Cash	£5,000
Receivables	£25,000
Payables	£18,000

All sales and purchases were on credit, cost of sales is made up entirely of credit purchases. Assume there are 360 days in a year.

Expenses were budgeted to be £80,000, split equally between fixed and variable costs. The actual fixed costs were 5% higher than expected, while the variable element was 2% higher than expected.

Complete the following table (giving all answers to the nearest £):

	£
Sales revenue	
Cost of sales	
Gross profit	
Expenses	
Net profit	

The current ratio for the business was 1.9:1.

Calculate the business' year-end inventory position, giving your answer to the nearest £.

Year-end inventory position	

163 REVENUE

What would the revenue need to have been for the total asset turnover to be 4 times if the total assets are £950,000?

164 OPERATING PROFIT

What would the operating profit need to have been for the RONA to be 25% if the net assets are £480,000?

165 GROSS PROFIT

What would the gross profit need to have been if sales revenue was £1,000,000 and the gross profit margin was 30%?

166 INVENTORY

What would the inventory value need to be if the current ratio was 2, current liabilities were £100,000, and receivables and cash totalled £120,000?

167 RECEIVABLES

What would sales revenue need to be (to the nearest £) if receivable days were 90 days and receivables were £400,000?

168 VALUE ADDED

What would be the 'value added' if sales revenue was £850,000, materials used were £300,000; labour employed was £250,000 and bought in services were £200,000?

169 PAYABLES

What would payables need to be (to the nearest £) if sales were £1,000,000, cost of sales were £700,000 and the payables days were 75 days?

170 TEES R US

Tees R Us Ltd operates a tea plantation in Kenya. The plantation produces tea for sale to Tees R Us tea bagging division and other wholesalers. The tea crop has been lower than expected due to bad weather. The actual and budgeted information is produced below.

	Actual	*Budgeted*
	£	£
Turnover	787,500	1,125,000
Cost of sales:		
Tea pickers	132,000	150,000
Tea processor operators	35,000	50,000
Depreciation of tea machines	60,000	60,000
Seeds and fertilizer	75,000	75,000
Total cost of sales	302,000	335,000
Gross profit	485,500	790,000
Administration costs	150,000	150,000
Distribution costs	300,000	350,000
Operating profit	35,500	290,000
Amount of tea in kilograms harvested and sold	1,750,000	2,500,000
Number of harvest days	100	100
Number of tea pickers	440	500
Daily cost of a tea picker	£3	£3
Net assets	£935,500	£1,190,000

Calculate the following performance indicators for the actual and budgeted information *(give answers to two decimal places)*:

	Actual	*Budgeted*
Cost of tea pickers as a % of turnover		
Cost of tea processor operators as a % of turnover		
Cost of seeds and fertilizer as a % of turnover		
Gross profit margin		
Operating profit margin		
Return on net assets		
Net asset turnover		

171 PARTY

Party Ltd has developed a skin treatment for spotty teenagers. The product competes with a dozen other companies. Topical Ltd is a major competitor and market leader with over 60% of the market. You have been given the following information about Party and Topical for the year ended 31 May 2014.

Income statement	*Party*	*Topical*
	£000	£000
Turnover	45,000	220,000
Cost of production		
Direct (raw) materials	12,000	33,000
Direct labour	7,500	22,000
Fixed production overheads	6,000	30,000
Total cost of sales	25,500	85,000
Gross profit	19,500	135,000
Selling and distribution costs	5,000	10,000
Administration costs	3,750	7,500
Advertising costs	2,500	100,000
Net profit	8,250	17,500

Other information		*Party*	*Topical*
Number of units sold (000)	Units	6,000	22,000
Net assets	(£000)	50,000	85,000

Calculate the following performance indicators for Party and Topical *(give answers to two decimal places):*

	Party	*Topical*
Selling price per unit		
Material cost per unit		
Labour cost per unit		
Fixed cost per unit		
Gross profit margin		
Net profit margin		
Advertising cost as % of turnover		
Return on net assets		

172 FUDGE

Fudge Limited has developed a new low calorie chocolate product that does not contain fat. Fudge competes with a dozen other companies making similar products. Stubbed Limited is a major competitor and has recently launched a similar product. You have been given the following information about Fudge and Stubbed for the year ended 31 July 2010.

Income statement	*Fudge*	*Stubbed*
	£m	£m
Turnover	3.2	4.0
Cost of production		
Direct (raw) materials	0.5	0.6
Direct labour	0.7	0.5
Fixed production overheads	0.3	0.1
Total cost of sales	1.5	1.2
Gross profit	1.7	2.8
Selling and distribution costs	0.5	0.5
Administration costs	0.1	0.2
Advertising costs	0.6	1.0
Net profit	0.5	1.1

Other information		*Fudge*	*Stubbed*
Number of units sold (m)	Units	6.4	6.6
Net assets	£m	10	12

Calculate the following performance indicators for Fudge and Stubbed (give answers to three decimal places:

	Fudge	*Stubbed*
Selling price per unit		
Material cost per unit		
Labour cost per unit		
Fixed production cost per unit		
Gross profit margin		
Net profit margin		
Advertising cost as % of turnover		
Return on net assets		

173 DEJAVU

You have been given the following information for the year ended 30 June 2010 for Dejavu, a CD manufacturer and distributor.

Income statement	*Budget*	*Actual*
	£000	£000
Turnover	55,000	60,000
Cost of production		
Direct materials	10,000	11,000
Direct labour	3,000	2,850
Fixed production overheads	15,000	15,000
Total cost of sales	28,000	28,850
Gross profit	27,000	31,150
Selling and distribution costs	5,000	6,500
Administration costs	3,500	4,000
Advertising costs	5,550	5,000
Net profit	12,950	15,650

Other information		*Budget*	*Actual*
Number of units sold (000)	Units	20,000	20,000
Direct labour hours worked		40,000	38,000

Calculate the following performance indicators for Budget and Actual *(give answers to two decimal places):*

	Budget	*Actual*
Selling price per unit		
Material cost per unit		
Labour cost per hour		
Fixed production cost per labour hour		
Gross profit margin		
Net profit margin		
Direct materials cost as % of turnover		

174 GRANSDEN

Gransden Ltd has two divisions, the North Division and the South Division. These are entirely retail operations. Details of their results for the year to 31 May 2010 are reproduced below

Income Statement	*North*	*South*
	£000	£000
Turnover	135,000	191,000
Cost of sales		
Opening inventory	25,000	55,000
Purchases	75,000	105,000
Closing inventory	(20,000)	(40,000)
Total cost of sales	80,000	120,000
Gross profit	55,000	71,000
Wages and salaries	10,000	12,000
Depreciation	10,000	16,000
Other costs	9,688	8,620
Operating profit for the year	25,312	34,380

Net assets	*North*	*South*
Non-current assets	100,000	160,000
Depreciation	(40,000)	(48,000)
Net book value	60,000	112,000
Inventory	20,000	40,000
Receivables	16,875	46,750
Payables	(12,500)	(8,750)
Capital employed	84,375	190,000

Calculate the following performance indicators for the two divisions *(give answers to two decimal places)*:

	North	*South*
Gross profit margin		
Operating profit margin		
Wages & salaries as a percentage of turnover		
Inventory turnover in days		
Receivable days		
Payable days (based on cost of sales)		
Return on capital employed		

BREAK EVEN ANALYSIS

175 BE

A company budgets to sell 6,000 units of a product at a selling price of £20. Variable costs are £5 per unit and fixed costs are £75,000 in total.

The contribution per unit is £ ☐

The breakeven point in units is ☐

The margin of safety in units is ☐

The margin of safety as a percentage (to 2 decimal places) is ☐

The contribution to sales (C/S) ratio (to 2 decimal places) is ☐

The break even sales are £ ☐

176 BREAKEVEN

A company budgets to sell 7,000 units of a product at a selling price of £200. Variable costs are £50 per unit and fixed costs are £750,000 in total.

The contribution per unit is £ ☐

The breakeven point in units is ☐

The margin of safety in units is ☐

The margin of safety as a percentage (to 2 decimal places) is ☐

The contribution to sales (C/S) ratio (to 2 decimal places) is ☐

The break even sales are £ ☐

177 CRAFTY

Crafty is looking to increase its sales and profits. Current figures (per annum, unless stated otherwise) are as follows:

Sales volume	100,000 units
Selling price	£2 per unit
Fixed overheads	£70,000
Labour	£0.50 per unit
Material	£0.20 per unit
Inventory levels	Nil

In order to increase sales to 110,000 units the selling price would need to fall to £1.95 per unit, the variable costs would fall by 5%, but fixed costs would rise by £5,000.

Extra investment in assets would be required of £20,000 which would be depreciated at 20% per annum.

The total annual change in profit would be:

(Negative figures should be entered using brackets.)

	Current	*Future*	*Change*
Revenue			
Material			
Labour			
Fixed overhead			
Depreciation			
Additional profit			

The return on the additional investment would be [ ] **%.**

Concerned that sales may not reach the 110,000 unit level, the Finance Director would like to know the break even volume.

Fixed costs	£
Contribution per unit	£
Break even volume (units)	

178 PIPER

Piper Limited makes bracelets.

Piper Limited has given you the following information:

The current materials cost is £25 per bracelet. Higher quality material will be used in all bracelets from January. This is expected to increase materials costs by 15%.

Selling the old inventory overseas is expected to bring in a one-off additional profit of £50k in the current accounting period to 31 December.

Current fixed production costs are £250k. As a result of new legislation, they are expected to double to £500k.

The selling price is expected to increase from £100 to £120 per bracelet.

The increased selling price is expected to cause sales volumes to drop from 20,000 units to 19,000 units

Labour is a variable cost. Labour hours are expected to be 40,000 hours for each year, and will be paid at £8 per hour.

Assume inventory levels of material are kept at zero.

All other costs will remain the same.

Calculate the total profit for the year ended 31 December by completing the table below.

(Negative figures should be preceded by a minus sign.)

	Units	*Price/cost*	*Total*
Revenue			
Materials			
Labour			
Fixed costs			
One-off profit			
Total profit			

The marketing department is concerned that the volume of sales may not reach the projected units. The finance director has asked for the break even sales volume for the year (ignoring the one-off profit).

The fixed costs are £ [ ]

The contribution per unit is £ [ ]

The break even sales volume is [ ] **units.**

179 JOYCE

Joyce Limited manufactures high-quality gates but is considering making a cheaper version in order to enter the lower end of the market. The research department has developed a suitable product, and has provided you with the following information:

Sales volume is projected to be 100,000 units per annum rising to 120,000 in the second year

Current material and labour costs per unit is £25.00 and is completely variable. In year two costs will rise to £30 per unit

Assume inventory levels are kept at zero.

Selling price will be £50 per pair of gates in the first year, rising to £60 in year 2.

Additional investment in assets will be £3,000,000 which will be depreciated at £500,000 per annum.

One-off advertising costs in the first year will be £200,000

All other costs will remain the same.

Calculate the total profit in the first year by completing the table below.

(Negative figures should be preceded by a minus sign.)

	Units	*Price*	*Total*
Revenue			
Materials and labour			
Advertising			
Depreciation			
Profit			

The return on the additional investment is ______ **%.**

The marketing department is concerned that the volume of sales may not reach the projected units. The finance director has asked for the break even sales volume for both years.

Year 1

The fixed costs are £ ______

The contribution per unit is £ ______

The break even sales volume is ______ **units.**

Year 2

The fixed costs are £ ______

The contribution per unit is £ ______

The break even sales volume is ______ **units.**

180 DAGGER

Dagger has given you the following information:

Materials currently cost £2.50 per unit. In the future, higher quality material will need to be used and this is expected to increase materials costs by 20%.

Current fixed production costs are £25,000. As a result of new legislation, they are expected to double.

The selling price is expected to increase from £10 to £12 per unit.

The increased selling price is expected to cause sales volumes to drop from 20,000 units to 18,000 units

Labour hours are expected to be 10,000 hours for each year, and will be paid at £10 per hour.

Assume inventory levels are kept at zero.

All other costs will remain the same.

Calculate the total profit for the next year by completing the table below.

(Negative figures should be entered using brackets.)

	Units	*Price/cost*	*Total*
Revenue			
Materials			
Labour			
Fixed costs			
Total profit			

The marketing department is concerned that the volume of sales may not reach the projected units. The finance director has asked for the break even sales volume for the year.

The fixed costs are £ ______

The contribution per unit (to 2 d.p.) is £ ______

The break even sales volume is ______ **units.**

181 BOSUN

Bosun has given you the following information:

The current materials cost is £250 per unit. Lower quality material will need to be used in the future and this is expected to decrease materials costs by 15%.

Current fixed production costs are £2,500,000. Cost cutting measures are expected to save fixed costs of £300,000.

The selling price is expected to decrease from £1,000 to £900 per unit.

The decreased selling price is expected to have no effect on sales volumes which are currently at 20,000 units.

Labour hours are expected to be 600,000 hours for each year, and will be paid at £8 per hour.

Assume inventory levels are kept at zero.

All other costs will remain the same.

Calculate the total profit for the second year by completing the table below.

(Negative figures should be entered using brackets.)

	Units	*Price/cost*	*Total*
Revenue			
Materials			
Labour			
Fixed costs			
Total profit			

The marketing department is concerned that the volume of sales may not reach the projected units. The finance director has asked for the break even sales volume for the year.

The fixed costs are £ [ ]

The contribution per unit is £ [ ]

The break even sales volume is [ ] **units.**

182 KEEL

Keel has given you the following information:

The current materials cost is £25 per unit. Higher quality material will need to be used in all products from next year. This is expected to increase materials costs by 15%.

Current fixed production costs are £250k. As a result of the new legislation, they are expected to double to £500k.

The selling price is expected to increase from £100 to £120 per unit.

The increased selling price is not expected to cause sales volumes to change from their current level of 20,000 units.

Labour hours are currently 35,000 hours but are expected to be 40,000 hours next year, and will be paid at £8 per hour.

Additional investment of £100,000 will be required. Depreciation will be at 20% per annum.

Assume inventory levels are kept at zero.

All other costs will remain the same.

Calculate the total annual INCREASE in profit by completing the table below.

(Negative figures should be entered using brackets.)

	Units	*Price/cost*	*Total*
Increase in revenue			
Increase in material cost			
Increase in labour cost			
Additional fixed costs			
Depreciation			
Additional profit			

The return on additional investment is [ ] **%.**

The finance director has asked for the break even sales volume for the coming year.

The fixed costs are £ [ ]

The contribution per unit is £ [ ]

The break even sales volume is [ ] **units.**

183 SAIL

Sail has given you the following information:

The current materials cost is £75 per unit. Higher quality material will need to be used in all products from next year. This is expected to increase materials costs by 10%.

Current fixed production costs are £70k. As a result of the new legislation, they are expected to double.

The selling price is expected to increase from £1,000 to £1,020 per unit.

The increased selling price is not expected to cause sales volumes to change from their current level of 20,000 units.

Labour hours are currently 395,000 hours but are expected to be 400,000 hours next year, and will be paid at £10 per hour.

Additional investment of £500,000 will be required which will be depreciated at 10% per annum.

Assume inventory levels are kept at zero.

All other costs will remain the same.

Calculate the total annual INCREASE in profit by completing the table below.

(Negative figures should be entered using brackets.)

	Units	*Price/cost*	*Total*
Increase in revenue			
Increase in material cost			
Increase in labour cost			
Additional fixed costs			
Depreciation			
Additional profit			

The return on additional investment is [ ] **%.**

The finance director has asked for the break even sales volume for the coming year.

The fixed costs are £ [ ]

The contribution per unit is £ [ ]

The break even sales volume is [ ] **units.**

184 CAFF CO

Caff Co manufactures instant coffee and is considering how it can be more environmentally friendly. Scientists have developed a new vacuum packaging which reduces the need for packaging materials by more than 50% and reduces the shelf space needed for the instant coffee packs by 60%.

You have been given the following information:

Current sales volume is 2.4 million packs per annum and this is not expected to change.

Current fixed production costs are £3.6 million.

Current labour cost per pack is £2.75 which is completely variable.

Current material cost per pack is £1.50 and is completely variable.

Assume inventory levels are kept at zero.

Variable cost of the new product will be £0.25 less per pack than the current packs.

Selling price will be increased from £7.50 to £8.25.

Fixed selling and distribution costs will reduce from £800,000 to £500,000.

Additional investment in assets will be £4 million which will be depreciated at £400,000 per annum.

All other costs will remain the same.

Calculate the total annual INCREASE in profit by completing the table below.

(Negative figures should be entered using brackets.)

	Units	*Price*	*Total*
Additional revenue			
Savings on variable costs			
Reduction in selling and distribution costs			
Additional depreciation			
Additional annual profit			

The return on the additional investment is [ ] .

The marketing department is concerned that the volume of sales may not reach 2.4 million. The finance director has asked for the break even sales volume.

The fixed costs are £ [ ]

The contribution per unit is £ [ ]

The break even sales volume is [ ] **units *(round up to the nearest whole unit).***

185 SUNSHINE

Sunshine Limited manufactures cosmetics and has recently been experimenting on the use of very fine gold dust in a new formulation for their bestselling tanning lotion. The use of this new ingredient on a mass scale requires additional investment in machinery to process the gold, however Sunshine plan to increase their selling price to offset the additional costs.

You have been given the following information.

Current sales volume is 2.4 million units per annum and this is not expected to change.

Current fixed production costs are £1.6 million.

Current labour cost per unit is £2.50 which is completely variable.

The use of the new ingredient will increase material costs from £5 to £8 per unit. Material costs are completely variable.

Assume inventory levels are kept at zero.

Selling price will be increased from £11.95 to £15.95.

The advertising costs are expected to increase by £450,000 per annum.

Additional investment in machinery will be £2 million which will be depreciated at £400,000 per annum.

All other costs will remain the same.

Calculate the total annual INCREASE in profit by completing the table below.

(Negative figures should be entered using brackets.)

	Units	*Price/cost*	*Total*
Additional revenue			
Additional materials			
Additional advertising costs			
Additional depreciation			
Additional annual profit			

The return on the additional investment is [ ] **%.**

The marketing department is concerned that the volume of sales may not reach £2.4 million despite the intense advertising campaign. The finance director has asked for the break even sales volume.

The fixed costs are £ [ ]

The contribution per unit is £ [ ]

The break even sales volume is [ ] **units.**

186 SELS AND DARLOW

A business operates two departments, Sels and Darlow. It has supplied the following information for last month.

	Sels	*Darlow*
Sales volume (units)	10,000	20,000
Selling price (£ per unit)	20	12
Variable production costs (£ per unit)	12	10
Fixed overheads (£)	60,000	10,000

The finance manager would like you to:

(a) **Calculate the contribution per unit, break-even point and margin of safety for each department**

(b) **Draft a report in which you provide an analysis of these figures as per the given section headings**

(a) Calculations:

	Sels	*Darlow*
Contribution per unit (£)		
Break-even point (units)		
Margin of safety (%)		

(b) Report:

To: Finance Manager

From: Account Technician

Subject: Sels and Darlow

Date: Today

Provide an evaluation of the differences in contribution between the two departments.

Implications of the difference in break-even point between the two departments

Which department has the better margin of safety and why?

Comment on the results from a risk perspective and suggest any potential ways of reducing it.

187 R COMPANY

R Company provides a single service to its customers. An analysis of its budget for the year ending 31 December 20X5 shows that, in Period 3, when the budgeted activity was 6,976 service units with a sales value of £62.50 each, the margin of safety was 25%.

The budgeted contribution to sales ratio of the service is 40%.

Calculate the budgeted fixed costs in period 3. £ [ ]

188 MD CO

MD Company makes and sells a single product to its customers, the CL. The budgeted sales are 10,000 units of CL per month. MD has correctly calculated the following information.

The margin of safety for the coming period is 7,000 units and fixed costs are budgeted to be £46,500.

Calculate the contribution per unit. £ [ ] per unit.

189 MULTI D

Multi D is a business that produces a single unit; it has the following output levels and costs for the last 3 months

Month	*Activity* (*units*)	*Costs* £
January	10,000	1,078,000
February	8,000	938,000
March	7,500	903,000

(a) **The fixed cost per month is £ [ ]**

The CS Ratio is budgeted to be 56.25%.

Multi D would like to maintain a minimum profit of £207,000 per month.

(b) **Complete the below sentences:**

The contribution is £ [ ] per unit.

Multi D needs to sell [ ] units to achieve the minimum profit.

(c) **Budgeted sales for April are 6,000 units. Complete the below sentences:**

With sales of 6,000 units, the contribution needs to be £ [ ] per unit to achieve the minimum profit.

This means a selling price of £ [ ] per unit.

190 BLUVAN CO

Bluvan Co makes a single product. The budgeted profit statement for next year shows that it has a margin of safety equal to 20% of budgeted sales and a unit selling price of £20. Product X has a profit volume ratio of 60% and budgeted fixed costs of £240,000 for the year.

What is the breakeven point in units? [ ] units.

What are the budgeted sales units for the period? [ ] units.

The company are concerned about potential increases in variable costs in the coming period.

By how much would the variable cost need to increase by for the company to breakeven at the current budgeted sales units.

Assume all other factors remain the same.

£ [ ] per unit.

191 SEMI

Semi has a variety of costs making up the full cost of their single product.

	£
Selling price	36
Direct material cost per unit	8
Direct labour cost per unit	10

There are 2 different overhead costs, the first is entirely fixed, and the budgeted cost are £15,000 per month.

The second has the following costs from the last 2 months:

Activity level	*Cost*
Units	£
10,000	25,000
15,000	35,000

Complete the following table:

	£
Total variable cost per unit	
Contribution per unit	

The budgeted sales for the coming month are 12,500 units.

Complete the following table:

	£
Breakeven point in units	
Margin of safety (%)	

DECISION MAKING TECHNIQUES

192 LF

LF manufactures 2 products – L and F. The following information is relevant:

	L	F
Selling price	100	200
Material requirement	4 litres	6 litres
Material price £10 per litre		
Labour requirement	2 hours	8 hours
Labour cost £8 per hour		
Maximum demand	100 units	100 units

LF has found that several of their staff have left to work for a competitor and, until they have recruited and trained new staff, they will be limited to 800 hours of labour per month.

Complete the following table:

	L	*F*
	£	£
Selling price per unit		
Material cost per unit		
Labour cost per unit		
Contribution per unit		
Contribution per limiting factor		
Rank		
Optimal production plan in units		

LF has received an important order from a regular customer requiring 78 units of each product.

The revised production plan would be [ ] units of L and [ ] units of F.

193 BQ

BQ manufactures 2 products – a B and a Q. The following information is relevant:

	B	*Q*
Selling price	100	150
Material requirement	4 kg	6 kg
Material price £10 per kg		
Labour requirement	2 hours	3 hours
Labour cost per hour	£8	£10
Maximum demand	100 units	100 units

BQ's supplier has informed them that there is a world shortage of the material they require and that that will be limited to 750 kg per month for the foreseeable future.

Complete the following table:

	B	*Q*
	£	£
Selling price per unit		
Material cost per unit		
Labour cost per unit		
Contribution per unit		
Contribution per limiting factor		
Rank		
Optimal production plan in units		

BQ has received an important order from a regular customer requiring 65 units of each product.

The revised production plan would be [ ] **units of B and** [ ] **units of Q.**

194 LEARN

Learn makes two products – A and B. The following information is available for the next month:

	A	*B*
	£ per unit	*£ per unit*
Selling price	50	60
Variable costs:		
Material cost (£5 per kg)	15	20
Labour cost	10	5
Total variable cost	25	25
Fixed costs:		
Production cost	8	8
Administration cost	12	12
Total fixed costs	20	20
Profit per unit	5	15
Monthly demand	2,000	1,800

Materials are in short supply in the coming month – only 12,000 kg are available.

Complete the table below:

	A	*B*
The contribution per unit		
The contribution per kg		

[ ] **should be made first and** [ ] **should be made second.**

The optimal production mix is:

	A	*B*
Production in units		
Workings		
Total contribution		

Learn has been approached by another material supplier who can supply 500 kg of material at a cost of £6 per kg. This is a premium of £1 above the normal cost per kg.

Should Learn purchase the additional material? YES/NO (delete as appropriate)

195 FROME

Frome makes two products – A and B. The following information is available for the next month:

	A	*B*
	£ per unit	£ per unit
Selling price	95	80
Variable costs:		
Material cost (£5 per kg)	15	20
Labour cost (£10 per hour)	30	25
Total variable cost	45	45
Fixed costs:		
Production cost	18	18
Administration cost	12	12
Total fixed costs	30	30
Profit per unit	20	5
Monthly demand	200	180

Labour is in short supply in the coming month – only 1,000 hours are available.

Complete the table below:

	A	*B*
The contribution per unit		
The contribution per hour		

[ ] **should be made first and** [ ] **should be made second.**

The optimal production mix is:

	A	*B*
Production in units		
Total contribution		

Frome has been approached by an outsourcer who has surplus labour. They can supply Frome with up to 500 hours of labour at a cost of £25 per hour. This is a premium of £15 above the normal cost per hour.

Should Learn purchase the additional hours? YES/NO (delete as appropriate)

196 US

US Limited, a printing firm, is trying to establish how it can reduce costs and increase efficiency. It has identified two machines, A1 and A2, which it could invest in to achieve these objectives. You have been asked to help US decide which of these two machines it should buy.

The following information for the next year has been forecast for the two machines.

	A1	*A2*
Machine cost	£1.1 million	£1.5 million
Sales revenue	£2.8 million	£3 million
Sales volume (units)	1 million	1.2 million
Variable cost per unit	£1.50	10 % less than A1

Fixed production overheads, currently £500,000, are expected to reduce by £50,000 if the A1 is bought and by £100,000 if the A2 is bought.

Fixed selling and distribution overheads, currently £200,000, are expected to remain the same.

Depreciation is charged at 10% per annum on a straight line basis.

The reduction in fixed production overheads is mainly due to proposed redundancies at an average cost of £20,000 per employee. US will have to make 1 person redundant if it chooses A1 and 2 if it chooses A2.

Calculate the total expected annual profit for each machine by completing the table below.

(Negative figures should be entered using brackets.)

£	*A1*	*A2*
Sales revenue		
Variable costs		
Fixed production overheads		
Fixed selling & distribution overheads		
Depreciation		
Redundancy costs		
Expected annual profit		

The expected return on investment for each machine, to the nearest whole %, is:

A1 [ ]

A2 [ ]

Which of the two machines should US buy? [ ]

197 CHATTY

Chatty Ltd (Chatty) manufactures three products I, A and IN which use the same resources (but in different amounts). Chatty also purchase a special component from an external supplier for Product A, this costs £65 per unit. The monthly demand and other financial details of the products are in the table below:

	I	A	IN
Demand (units)	4,000	2,000	6,000
	£	£	£
Selling price	100	200	50
Direct materials (£5 per kg)	10	7.50	15
Specialist labour (£10 per hour)	20	30	5
Unskilled labour (£8 per hour)	16	12	4
Variable overhead (£2 per machine hour)	10	12	2
Special component cost to buy in		65	

In addition to the above, Chatty also have fixed costs of £200,000 per month.

Machine hours limited to 30,000 hours per month, Chatty currently have an abundance of specialist labour and the other resources required. The company bases all short term decisions on profit maximisation.

Complete the table below

	I	A	IN
Contribution per unit (£ to 2DP)			
Contribution per machine hour (£ to 2DP)			
Optimum production plan (units)			

A recent addition to the production management team has suggested that Chatty could potentially make the special component in house, and has estimated the costs to do so as follows:

	£
Direct materials (£5 per kg)	17.50
Specialist labour (£10 per hour)	20
Unskilled labour (£8 per hour)	8
Variable overhead (£2 per machine hour)	4

There would be no incremental fixed costs incurred as a result of making the special component in-house.

Complete the below table to calculate the optimum production plan if Chatty were to make all the special components in house?

	I	A	IN
Contribution per unit (£ to 2DP)			
Contribution per machine hour (£ to 2DP)			
Optimum production plan (units)			

Complete the following sentences

If Chatty base their decision solely on profit maximisation they would **buy in / make** (delete as appropriate) the special component.

The difference in profit between the two options is £..

There are other factors to consider when making an outsourcing decision.

Discuss some of the other considerations that Chatty should take into account before making a final decision.

198 GRAFTERS

Grafters Ltd is a famous furniture maker known for their high quality, unique, hand crafted oak furniture.

Machinery Co, a company producing machinery, has approached Grafters Ltd about automating some of the processes currently undertaken by the craftsmen at Grafters ltd.

Below is a table with information about the current costs:

Average craftsmen salary (£)	55,000 per year
Annual tool replacement costs (£)	200,000
Number of craftsmen	20
Other variable overhead costs (£)	50,000
Oak cost (£)	600/m3
Average oak usage per year	100,000m3

Machinery Co has also supplied estimates about the impact their machines can have. These are detailed in the table below:

Rental cost per year (£)	£100,000
Reduction in tool replacement costs	50%
Reduction in workforce	70%
Reduced variable overhead cost	20%
Increase in oak usage	1%

Complete the table below estimating the current annual cost and the cost of using the machinery.

	Current cost per year £	Cost per year with machinery £
Oak costs		
Craftsmen cost		
Tool replacement cost		
Other variable overheads		
Rental cost		
Total cost		

Complete the below sentence

On financial grounds, grafters **should/should not** (delete as appropriate) agree to rent the machinery.

Using the information above. Discuss the other factors that grafters should consider regarding the production process.

Grafters have 100 years of experience producing oak furniture; the craftsmen's activities are considered a tourist attraction and people travel from miles around to see the craftsmen at work. The reputation and the distinctive handcrafting is the main reason customers pay the premium price grafters charge. If they were to go ahead with the change, Grafters do not plan to advertise it and they have also worked out a very low cost way to redesign the viewing area to make sure that the machinery was not on display.

Discuss the ethical issues of introducing the machinery to production at grafters

Machinery Co approached Grafter because they have previously worked with the new finance director at Grafters at her last employers. The finance director has a bonus incentive based on reducing costs within the organisation.

Discuss the operational and ethical issues surrounding the approach and bonus offered to the finance director.

199 CCV

CCV manufactures four products: M, D, C, and L in a single factory. Each of the products is manufactured in batches of 50 units, CCV have recently started using a just-in- time manufacturing processes and so have little or no inventory.

This batch size of 50 units cannot be changed in the short term. Despite being manufactured in batches of 50 units, they are sold as single units to CCVs customers. CCV operates in a very competitive market place and there is little differentiation available so they must accept the market price.

CCV are reviewing the profit made from each product, and for the business as a whole. The information has been set out below:

Product	*M*	*D*	*C*	*L*	*Total*
Sales units	50,000	75,000	100,000	25,000	
Direct labour hours	200,000	225,000	150,000	125,000	700,000
Machine hours	75,000	75,000	200,000	100,000	450,000
	£000	£000	£000	£000	£000
Sales revenue	1,600	1,875	2,750	2,080	8,305
Direct material	200	825	1,000	900	2,925
Direct labour	400	900	1,200	600	3,100
Overhead costs	225	225	600	300	1,350
Profit/(loss)	775	(75)	(50)	280	930

The board of CCV are concerned that two of its products are losing money and have asked for an analysis of the overhead costs to be carried out before a decision about which, if any, products are shutdown is made. This analysis shows:

(1) The sales of M, D, C & L are completely independent of each other.

(2) An overhead recovery rate of £3 per machine hour has been used to share out the overhead costs in the current analysis.

(3) The analysis of overhead costs shows that some of the overheads are product specific and would no longer be incurred if CCV stopped producing that product, while the rest of the overheads are mostly caused by one specific activity setting up the machinery. The below table shows a breakdown of the findings:

	Total	*M*	*D*	*C*	*L*
Product specific overhead	651,500	£200,000	£20,000	£10,000	£421,500
Machine set up costs	598,500				
General factory costs	100,000				
Machine set ups per batch		4	1	1	6

The general factory costs are not specific to any product and could be only be changed if the factory was closed down completely, in which case they would not be incurred.

(a) Complete the below tables to work out the cost driver rate for machine set ups:

	M	*D*	*C*	*L*	*Total*
Number of batches					
Number of machine setups					

	£
Cost driver rate- per set up	

(b) **Using the answers to a) and the other information available, complete the table below to calculate the relevant profit or loss for each product to help make a decision about shutting down any product lines:**

	M	*D*	*C*	*L*	*Total*
	£000	£000	£000	£000	£000
Sales revenue	1,600	1,875	2,750	2,080	8,305
Direct material	200	825	1,000	900	2,925
Direct labour	400	900	1,200	600	3,100
Product specific overhead					
Machine set up costs					
General factory costs					
Profit/(loss)					

(c) **Prepare a short report to CCV advising which, if any, of its four products should be discontinued in order to maximise its company profits and explain how CCV could use Value Analysis to improve its profits.**

200 WHITLEY

Whitley Co has two divisions, Sea and Bay. Division Sea produces three types of products L, E and A, using a common process. Each of the products can either be sold by Division Sea to the external market at split-off point (after the common process is complete) or can be transferred to Division Bay for individual further processing into products LS, ES and AS.

The normal monthly output from the common process is:

L 6,000 units E 5,000 units A 4,000 units

The market selling prices per unit for the products, at split-off point and after further processing, are as follows:

	£		£
L	4	*LS*	6.50
E	5	*ES*	7.50
A	6	*AS*	8.50

The specific costs for each of the individual further processes are:

	Variable cost per unit £	*Additional fixed costs per period* £
L to LS	1.20	2,000
E to ES	1.75	750
A to AS	1.50	2,250

Further processing leads to a normal loss of 10% at the beginning of the process for each of the products being processed. Whitley is considering what the most financially beneficial production plan is.

Complete the following table:

	LS £	*ES* £	*AS* £
Incremental revenue			
Incremental costs			
Net benefit/(loss)			

Complete the following sentences:

On financial grounds Whitley **should/should not** (delete as appropriate) process L further.

On financial grounds Whitley **should/should not** (delete as appropriate) process E further.

On financial grounds Whitley **should/should not** (delete as appropriate) process A further.

Currently Whitley process exactly half of the output further and sell it as LS, ES & AS. They sell the other half of the output as L, E & A.

What other considerations should Whitley take into account before making the final decision?

LIFECYCLE COSTING

201 NPV

A company is considering installing a new kitchen in which to prepare staff meals. At present, all meals are bought in from a local supplier. The kitchen equipment will cost £40,000 to buy and install and will have a useful life of 4 years with no residual value.

The company uses a discount rate of 10% to appraise all capital projects.

The cash savings from having this facility will be:

Year	*0*	*1*	*2*	*3*	*4*
£	0	15,200	14,900	13,585	11,255

Calculate the net present value of the cash flows from the project and present a recommendation as to whether the proposal should go ahead.

The relevant present value factors are:

Year	*1*	*2*	*3*	*4*
10%	0.909	0.826	0.751	0.683

Year	*0*	*1*	*2*	*3*	*4*
Cash flow £					
Discount factor					
Present value £					
				NPV	

The proposal SHOULD/SHOULD NOT go ahead. ***(Delete as appropriate.)***

202 DAFFY

Daffy will be replacing its machines in the next year and needs to decide whether to purchase or lease the machines.

The relevant discount factors are shown below.

Year	*Discount factor 10%*	*Year*	*Discount factor 10%*
0	1.000	3	0.751
1	0.909	4	0.683
2	0.826	5	0.621

(a) Calculate the discounted lifecycle cost of purchasing the machines based upon the following:

- **purchase price of £120,000**
- **annual running costs of £8,000 for the next five years, paid annually in arrears**
- **a residual value of £20,000 at the end of the five years**

Year	*0*	*1*	*2*	*3*	*4*	*5*
Cash flow						
DF						
PV						
NPC						

(b) Calculate the discounted lifecycle cost of leasing the machines for five years based upon the total annual costs of £25,000 paid annually in advance.

Year	*0*	*1*	*2*	*3*	*4*
Lease costs					
DF					
PV					
NPC					

(c) Based on the calculations it is best to [ ] **the machines. This saves £** [ ]

203 LIFECYCLE COSTING

A machine may be purchased at a cost of £30,000 and annual running costs of £2,500 per annum for the next four years paid in arrears. It would have a residual value of £5,500 at the end of the fourth year.

The company has a discount rate of 5% and the discount factors at this rate are:

Year	*1*	*2*	*3*	*4*
DF at 5%	0.952	0.907	0.864	0.823

The discounted lifecycle cost (DLC) of the machine is:

Year	*0*	*1*	*2*	*3*	*4*
Cash flow					
DF at 5%					
Present value					
DLC					

The machine could be leased for the four years instead – at an annual cost of £8,500 per annum, paid in advance.

The discounted lifecycle cost (DLC) of the lease would be:

Year	*0*	*1*	*2*	*3*	*4*
Cash flow					
DF at 5%					
Present value					
DLC					

Based on the above calculations, it would be best to [ ] the machine, as it saves £ [ ]

204 HOULTER

Houlter Ltd is considering purchasing a new machine to reduce the labour time taken to produce the X. The machine would cost £300,000. The labour time would be reduced from five hours to two hours without compromising quality and the failure rates will remain at zero.

The discount factors you will need are shown below.

Year	*Discount factor 5%*
0	1.000
1	0.952
2	0.907
3	0.864
4	0.823
5	0.784

Calculate the discounted lifecycle cost of the machine based upon the following:

(i) purchase price of £300,000

(ii) annual running costs of £30,000 for the next 5 years

(iii) a residual value of £50,000 at the end of the 5 years

Year	*0*	*1*	*2*	*3*	*4*	*5*
Cash flow						
DF						
PV						
NPC						

Calculate the discounted labour savings based upon annual production of 5,000 X, a three hour saving per unit and a labour rate of £7 per hour.

Year	*1*	*2*	*3*	*4*	*5*
Labour savings					
DF					
PV					
NPC					

Investing in the new machine saves [ ] **and is therefore financially beneficial.**

205 YANKEE (1)

Yankee Limited has discovered that instead of buying a machine outright it could lease it. You are required to complete the following tasks to establish whether the company should lease or buy the machine.

The discount factors you will need are shown below:

Year	*Discount factor 10%*	*Year*	*Discount factor 10%*
0	1.000	3	0.751
1	0.909	4	0.683
2	0.826	5	0.621

Calculate the discounted lifecycle cost of purchasing the machine based upon the following:

- **purchase price of £1,500,000**
- **annual running costs of £150,000 for the next five years, paid annually in arrears**
- **a residual value of £250,000 at the end of the five years**

Year	*0*	*1*	*2*	*3*	*4*	*5*
Cash flow						
DF						
PV						
NPC						

Calculate the discounted lifecycle cost of leasing the machine for five years based upon the total annual costs of £450,000 paid annually in advance.

Year	*0*	*1*	*2*	*3*	*4*
Lease costs					
DF					
PV					
NPC					

Based on the calculations it is best to [ ] **the machine, in order to save £** [ ]

206 BUDGE

Budge Limited will be replacing some machines in the next year and needs to decide whether to purchase or lease the machines.

The discount factors you will need are shown below.

Year	*Discount factor 10%*	*Year*	*Discount factor 10%*
0	1.00	3	0.751
1	0.909	4	0.683
2	0.826	5	0.621

Calculate the discounted lifecycle cost of purchasing the machine based upon the following:

- **purchase price of £600,000**
- **annual running costs of £45,000 for the next five years, paid annually in arrears**
- **a residual value of £220,000 at the end of the five years**

(Work to the nearest £1,000.)

Year	*0*	*1*	*2*	*3*	*4*	*5*
Cash flow						
DF						
PV						
NPC						

Calculate the discounted lifecycle cost of leasing the machine for five years based upon the total annual costs of £135,000 paid annually in advance. *(Work to the nearest £1,000.)*

Year	*0*	*1*	*2*	*3*	*4*
Lease costs					
DF					
PV					
NPC					

Based on the calculations it is best to BUY/LEASE the machine because it saves £ [ ]

207 LIFE CYCLE STATEMENTS (I)

Complete the following statements:

Lifecycle costing is a concept which traces all costs to a product over its complete lifecycle, from design through to [ ] .

sales/launch/cessation/production

One of the benefits that adopting lifecycle costing could bring is to improve decision-making and [ ] control.

production/staff/manager/cost

208 LIFE CYCLE STATEMENTS (II)

Complete the following statements:

Life cycle costing recognises that for many products there are significant costs committed by decisions in the [ ] stages of its lifecycle.

early/late/final/unit

One of the benefits of life cycle costing is the visibility of all costs is increased, rather than just costs relating to one period. This facilitates better [ ]

decision-making/maturity/variance analysis/decline

209 ABITFIT CO

Abitfit Co manufactures a small range of technologically advanced products for the fitness market. They are considering the developing a new fitness monitor, which would be the first of its kind in the market. Abitfit estimates it would take one year in the development stage, sales would commence at the beginning of the year two. The product is expected to be in the market for two years, before it will be replaced by a newer model. The following cost estimates have been made.

	Year 1	*Year 2*	*Year 3*
Units produced and sold		150,000	250,000
	£	£	£
Research and development costs	250,000		
Marketing costs	500,000	1,000,000	250,000
Administration costs	150,000	300,000	600,000
Production costs			
– Variable cost per unit		55	52
– Fixed production costs		600,000	900,000
Sales and distribution costs			
– Variable cost per unit		10	12
– Fixed sales and distribution costs		200,000	200,000

(a) Calculate the lifecycle cost in total (ignore the time value of money):

	£
Research and development costs	
Marketing costs	
Administration costs	
Total variable production cost	
Fixed production cost	
Total variable sales and distribution cost	
Fixed sales and distribution costs	
Total costs	

Based on the above, calculate the life cycle cost per unit £ [ ]

(Give you answer to 2 decimal places.)

(b) Discuss how the costs change throughout the life of a product, using the different stages of the product life cycle and examples from Abitfit.

210 LCC PLC

LCC Plc manufacture the latest in satellite navigation accessories, they are looking into developing a new product which could increase their market presence significantly. LCC believe the product will take a year to develop and then makes sales for three years then because of technological advancements it will need to be replaced by a newer model.

The following cost estimates have been made:

	Year 1	*Year 2*	*Year 3*	*Year 4*
Units produced and sold		200,000	250,000	100,000
	£	£	£	£
Research and development costs	500,000			
Marketing and Administration costs	450,000	750,000	800,000	350,000
Production costs				
– Variable cost per unit		28	25	20
– Fixed production costs		200,000	300,000	400,000
Sales and distribution costs				
– Variable cost per unit		18	16	18
– Fixed sales and distribution costs		150,000	150,000	150,000

(a) Calculate the lifecycle cost in total (ignore the time value of money):

	£
Research and development costs	
Marketing and administration costs	
Total variable production cost	
Fixed production cost	
Total variable sales and distribution cost	
Fixed sales and distribution costs	
Total costs	

Based on the above, calculate the life cycle cost per unit £ [ ]

(Give you answer to 2 decimal places.)

(b) Discuss how costs can switch between variable and fixed through the different stages of the products life cycle.

(c) Discuss how ethical considerations can be aided by the use of life cycle costing.

TARGET COSTING

211 TARGET COSTING

A new product has been developed. After extensive research it has been estimated that the future selling price will be £10 with a demand of 2,000 units.

Other useful information is given below:

Fixed costs	£1.50 per unit
Labour	4.5 hours
Profit margin required	20%
Material	2 litres at £1 per litre

Assuming no other costs arise, the target cost per hour for labour is £ ______

The labour rate is under negotiation with the union who would like an increase to £1.20 per hour. The personnel department has rejected this because the profit margin will fall to ______ %, which is unacceptable to the shareholders.

If management can agree to an increase in the labour rate but the profit margin has to stay at 20%, then material costs would need to fall by ______ %.

212 HOLDER

Holder Limited is considering designing a new product and will use target costing to arrive at the target cost of the product. You have been given the following information and asked to calculate the target cost for materials so that the purchasing manager can use this as a target in her negotiations with suppliers.

The price at which the product will be sold is £50

The company has firm orders for 36,000 units at a price of £50

The fixed costs per unit are £15.50 per unit

The labour requirement is 20 minutes at a cost of £12 per hour

The required profit margin is 20%

The material requirement is 200 grams per unit

Calculate the target cost per kilogram for the materials component of the product.

	£
Sales price per unit	
Profit margin	
Total costs	
Fixed cost per unit	
Labour cost per unit	
Maximum material cost per unit	
Target cost per kilogram	

The trade price per kilogram quoted on the supplier's price list is £120 per kilogram. The purchasing manager has negotiated a discount of 15%. The discount should be ACCEPTED/REJECTED because the £120 reduces to £ [ ] which is ABOVE/BELOW the target cost.

The minimum percentage discount needed to achieve the target cost is [ ] % (to one decimal place).

213 AKEA

Akea is a furniture manufacturer and has just received the results of a market study on the current interest in their new leather sofa range. The study indicates that the maximum price the average customer is prepared to pay for a leather sofa from Akea is £1,500. The following information is also available.

- The company estimates that 2,200 sofas can be sold in a year.
- At this level of production, the fixed overheads per sofa would be £140.
- The labour requirement per sofa is 8 hours at a cost of £25 per hour.
- The wooden frame and the stuffing material cost £110 per sofa.
- The required profit margin is 30%.
- One sofa uses 8 square metres of leather.

Calculate the target cost per square metre of leather.

	£
Sales price per sofa	
Profit margin	
Total costs	
Fixed cost per sofa	
Labour cost per sofa	
Wooden frame and stuffing material	
Maximum leather cost per sofa	
Target cost per square metre	

Akea's leather supplier quotes a list price of £100 per square metre for the grade of leather Akea needs. However, Akea has managed to negotiate a discount of 15% on this price. **The discount should be ACCEPTED/REJECTED because the £100 reduces to £ [ ] which is ABOVE/BELOW the target cost. *(Delete as appropriate.)***

The minimum percentage discount needed to achieve the target cost is [ ] %

214 SHORTY

Shorty has just received the results of a market study on the current interest in their new product range. The study indicates that the maximum price the average customer is prepared to pay for one of their products is £150. The following information is also available.

- The company estimates that 200 units can be sold in a year.
- At this level of production, the fixed overheads per unit would be £40.
- The labour requirement per unit is 4 hours at a cost of £10 per hour.
- The required profit margin is 25%.
- The material (rubber) requirement is 5 kilograms per unit.

Calculate the target cost per kg of rubber.

	£
Sales price per unit	
Profit margin	
Total costs	
Fixed cost per unit	
Labour cost per unit	
Maximum rubber cost per unit	
Target cost per kg	

Shorty's rubber supplier quotes a list price of £10 per kilogram. However, Shorty has managed to negotiate a discount of 25% on this price. **The discount should be ACCEPTED/REJECTED because the £10 reduces to £ [   ] which is ABOVE/BELOW the target cost. *(Delete as appropriate.)***

The minimum percentage discount needed to achieve the target cost is [   ] %

215 LONG

Long has designed a new product which it would like to sell for £250. It intends to use target costing to arrive at the target cost for labour. The following information is available.

- The company estimates that 20,000 units can be sold in a year.
- At this level of production, the fixed overheads per unit would be £20.
- The labour requirement per unit is 2 hours.
- The material cost is £110 per unit.
- The required profit margin is 35%.

Calculate the target cost per labour hour.

	£
Sales price per unit	
Profit margin	
Total costs	
Fixed cost per unit	
Material cost per unit	
Maximum labour cost per unit	
Target cost per labour hour	

A recruitment company quotes a rate of £20 per hour for the grade of labour Long needs. Long has managed to negotiate a discount of 15% on this price providing it recruits at least 10 workers. **The discount should be ACCEPTED/REJECTED because the £20 reduces to**

£ [ ] **which is ABOVE/BELOW the target cost.** ***(Delete as appropriate.)***

The minimum percentage discount (to 2 d.p.) needed to achieve the target cost is

[ ] **%.**

216 GRIPPIT (1)

Grippit Limited is developing a new product to monitor energy consumption. There are currently several other companies manufacturing similar products which sell for a price of £25 each. Grippit Ltd wishes to make a margin of 30%.

The target cost of the new product is £ [ ]

217 SHOCK

Shock is developing a new product. There are currently several other companies manufacturing similar products which sell for a price of £95 each. Shock wishes to make a margin of 20%.

The target cost of the new product is £ [ ]

218 TRICKY (II)

Tricky is developing a new product. There are currently several other companies manufacturing similar products which sell for a price of £205 each. Tricky wishes to make a margin of 10%.

The target cost of the new product is £ [ ]

219 TC ETHICS

TC is a company attempting to close the cost gap that exists in the target costing exercise they are doing for one of their products. They have decided to reduce the grade of labour they are using and they have also identified a cheaper material they could substitute into the product.

Write a memo to a colleague and briefly explain any ethical issues that may arise

To:	**Subject:**
From:	**Date:**
Labour	
Material	

220 TARGET COSTING STATEMENTS (I)

Complete the following statements:

To calculate the target cost, subtract the [ ] from the target price.

value analysis/target profit/value engineering/cost gap

If there is a cost gap, attempts will be made to close the gap. Techniques such as value engineering and value [ ] may be used to help close the gap.

Analysis/adding/ranging/added tax

221 TARGET COSTING STATEMENTS (II)

Complete the following statements:

The cost gap is the difference between the [ ] and the estimated product cost per unit.

original cost/value engineering/target cost/value added

Target costing works the opposite to [ ] techniques in that it starts by setting a competitive selling price first.

traditional pricing/value added/value analysis/life cycle costing

222 FORMAT

Format is developing a new product and intends to use target costing to price the product. You have been given the following information.

- The price at which the product will be sold has not yet been decided;
- It has been estimated that if the price is set at £4 the demand will be 50,000 units, and if the price is set at £5.00 the demand will be 45,000 units;
- The required profit margin is 20%;
- The variable cost per unit is £1.30 for the 45,000 unit level, and £1.20 at the 50,000 unit level.

Complete the following table:

	Sales price £4	*Sales price £5*
Target total production cost per unit		
Target fixed production cost per unit		
Total target fixed production cost		

The actual costs of production include fixed production costs of £120,000 which allow a production capacity of 50,000 units. In order to produce above this level the fixed production costs step up by £25,000.

Format should set the price at £ [ ] to achieve the target profit margin.

223 MR WYNN

Winston Wynn (Mr Wynn) runs a company that makes wedding dresses and accessories; he has recently designed a revolutionary new range of accessories. He expects the accessories to have a life cycle of two years, before fashions move on and demand will fall to zero. Mr Wynn has carried out research to determine a target selling price and expected sales units across the two years.

Expected sales volume	8,000 units
Selling price per unit	£500
Profit margin %	45%

(a) Calculate the profit per unit and target cost per unit

	£
Profit per unit (£)	
Target cost per unit	

The following information relates to the costs Mr Wynn will incur relating to the new product:

1. Direct material cost is currently £100: all of the materials in the original design for the product are luxury materials. Most of these can be replaced with lower grade material costing 60% less. However, some of the more unique features cannot be replaced, these account for 25% of the total material cost, Mr Wynn has managed to negotiate a 10% discount on the luxury material.

2. Direct labour cost: the accessories require 40 minutes of direct labour, which costs £30 per hour. The use of lower grade material, however, will mean that whilst the first unit would still be expected to take 40 minutes, but as the workers become more familiar with the process the time per unit will reduce to 30 minutes. Mr Wynn expect this to happen after 1,000 units (the first 1,000 will take 40 minutes each, every unit after that will take only 30 minutes).

3. Machining costs: the product is expected to take 2 machine hours costing £20 per hour.

4. Quality costs: It costs £40 to check a unit thoroughly to make sure it is to an acceptable standard, Mr Wynn has decided to check every 20th unit thoroughly, this means 5% of the total output will be checked in this way.

5. Remedial work: the use of lower grade material means the rate of reworks will be 15% of the total number of units and the cost of each rework will be to £40.

6. The initial design costs were in total £400,000

7. Mr Wynn expects sales and marketing costs to total £1 million across the 2 years.

(b) Complete the below table to calculate the estimated lifetime cost per unit for the new product after taking into account the points above

Ignore the time value of money. Give your answer to 2 decimal places

	Per unit cost £
Bought in material	
Direct labour	
Machining costs	
Quality costs	
Remedial work	
Initial design costs	
Sales and Marketing costs	
Estimated lifetime cost per unit	

(c) What is the cost gap, if one exists?

(d) Discuss how value analysis could be used by Mr Wynn to reduce the cost gap, giving examples specific to Mr Wynn.

224 TOPCAT

TopCat Ltd (TC) is planning to introduce a new product which is expected to have a short life. It needs to make a net profit margin of 20%.

TC has commissioned a market research company, Likely Causes & Consequences Plc (LCC) and they believe that, in total, TC will be able to sell 30,000 units of the product at £25 per unit.

The total costs which the TC expects to incur over the life of the product are shown in the table below.

Research and development £000	Market research £000	Variable manufacturing costs £000	Fixed manufacturing costs £000	Closure costs £000
150	35	300	100	75

(a) **Complete the following table to determine the target cost per unit for the new product (to the nearest penny).**

	£
Total anticipated sales revenue	
Target total net profit	
Target total costs	
Target cost per unit	

(b) Using the information above, calculate the lifecycle costs per unit (to the nearest penny) and provide a recommendation as to whether or not the product should be introduced.

	£
Total lifecycle costs	
Lifecycle cost per unit	

If a margin of 20% is required, the new product should be / should not be **(delete as appropriate) introduced.**

LCC also reported that customers would purchase more of the product if its selling price was reduced by £0.50 per unit. The company will consider making this price reduction if it can sell enough units to maintain a profit margin of 20%.

(c) Complete the table below and calculate the number of units that TC would need to sell to maintain a profit margin of 20%. Assume the lifecycle costs are expected to be as in (a) and (b) above. Enter your answers in the table below to the nearest penny

	£
Reduced selling price per unit	
Target net profit per unit	
Target total cost per unit	
Expected variable manufacturing cost per unit	
Target fixed costs per unit	

To the nearest whole unit, the required sales volume is [ ] **units.**

(d) Explain the difference between value analysis and value engineering and discuss how ethical considerations could impact the target costing process.

225 CELSIUS

Celsius is developing a new product and intends to use target costing to price the product. You have been given the following information:

- The price at which the product will be sold has not yet been decided;
- It has been estimated that if the price is set at £20 the demand will be 20,000 units, and if the price is set at £22.00 the demand will be 18,000 units;
- The required profit margin is 25%;
- The variable cost per unit is £10.50 for the 18,000 unit level, and £9.20 at the 20,000 unit level.

Complete the following table:

	Sales price £22	*Sales price £20*
Target total production cost per unit		
Target fixed production cost per unit		
Total target fixed production cost		

The actual costs of production include fixed production costs of £110,000 which allow a production capacity of 20,000 units. In order to produce above this level the fixed production costs step up by £20,000.

Celsius should set the price at £ [ ] to achieve the target profit margin.

PERFORMANCE INDICATORS WRITTEN QUESTIONS

226 PAS

Pedro's Accessory Store (PAS) is a new business, selling high quality accessories for men, from socks to ties, from laces to cuff links, all via the internet.

Pedro is the owner/manager of the company. He has no experience running a company, having become disillusioned with his old job, he decided to take a risk and set up his own business. He believes that buying high quality accessories and selling them online will grow his business very quickly from a relatively low fixed cost base.

The market for male accessories is very competitive with all the major high street clothing brands all offering their own accessories both online and in store.

Pedro expects that any business takes time to become profitable so is willing to run PAS at a loss in the short term to make sure PAS has a good foundation for future growth. One area he is particularly focussed on is that the website must be secure and be able to handle high levels of traffic. Another area he is prepared to invest in is the initial marketing effort to make sure PAS establishes a good brand image synonymous with quality products. Pedro expects that both these costs will be high initially but will not continue at that level for long.

	Year 1	*Year 2*
	£	£
Sales	2,889,598	3,635,746
Cost of sales	(1,405,331)	(2,133,296)
Gross profit	1,484,267	1,502,450
Website development and maintenance	(420,000)	(85,000)
Marketing costs	(340,500)	(170,000)
Distribution costs	(263,575)	(395,565)
Administrative costs	(300,000)	(390,000)
Other overhead costs	(268,000)	(338,000)
Profit/(loss)	(107,808)	123,885

(a) Complete the table below

	Year 1	Year 2
Revenue growth (%)		
Gross profit margin (%)		
Net profit margin (%)		

(b) Using the above information, write a report to Pedro commenting on:

(i) Revenue

(ii) Gross profit

(iii) Net profit

To:	**Subject:**
From:	**Date:**

Pedro is also very aware of not focussing solely on financial performance indicators. He believes that identifying important non-financial performance indicators and performing well against them will lead to financial success. The tables below show some of the indicators that PAS are tracking and some industry information.

	Year 1	Year 2
Number of units sold	140,956	157,870
Website visits	2,710,692	5,262,333
Sales returns	12,686	33,153
On time delivery	98%	88%
Transactions aborted due to website issues	282	7,453

Industry averages statistics are as follows:

Conversion rate for website visits to number of units sold	4.1%
Sales return rate for internet-based clothing sales	14.2%
On time delivery	95.3%

(c) Complete the following table. Give % figures to 1 decimal place and £ to 2 decimal places:

	Year 1	Year 2
Conversion rate for website visits to number of units sold (%)		
% sales returned		
Average price per sale (£ to 2 decimal places)		

(d) Using the tables above write a report to Pedro commenting on the non-financial performance of PAS over the last year, giving reasons for the changes and considering industry averages where possible.

To:	**Subject:**
From:	**Date:**

227 ARCHIMEDES

A division of Archimedes Limited is developing a new product and a colleague has prepared forecast information based upon two scenarios. The forecast income statement and statement of financial position for both scenarios is shown below:

Scenario 1 is to set the price at £7.20 per unit with sales of 120,000 units each year.

Scenario 2 is to set the price at £4.80 per unit with sales of 240,000 units each year.

Forecast Income statement	*Scenario 1*	*Scenario 2*
	£	£
Turnover	864,000	1,152,000
Cost of production		
Direct (Raw) Materials	240,000	480,000
Direct Labour	96,000	153,600
Fixed Production overheads	288,000	288,000
Total cost of sales	624,000	921,600
Gross profit	240,000	230,400
Selling and distribution costs	59,200	97,600
Administration costs	40,000	40,000
Operating profit	176,000	116,000
	Scenario 1	*Scenario 2*
Gross profit margin	27.78%	20.00%
Operating profit margin	16.30%	8.06%
Direct materials as a percentage of turnover	27.78%	41.67%
Direct materials cost per unit	£2.00	£2.00
Direct labour cost per unit	£0.80	£0.64
Fixed production cost per unit	£2.40	£1.20

Draft a report for the finance director covering the following:

(a) An explanation of why the gross profit margins are different, referring to the following.

- Sales price.
- Sales volume.
- Materials.
- Labour.
- fixed costs.

(b) An explanation of why the operating profit margins are different.

(c) A recommendation, with reasons, as to which course of action to take.

To:	**Subject:**
From:	**Date:**

(a) Why are the gross profit margins different?

Sales Price/Sales Volume

Materials

Labour

Fixed costs

(b) Why are the operating profit margins different?

(c) Recommendation, with reasons, as to which course of action to take

228 TEMPEST

Tempest plc is a large public company engaged in the running of cinemas throughout the UK. Some cinemas are very large with multiple screens. Typically these are based on large sites situated out of town, with on-site parking, and often with bar and snack facilities. Other smaller cinemas with only a few screens are typically based in city centres. They have limited parking, but similar facilities for refreshments.

Currently Tempest charges the same fee per film for both types of cinema. However the number of customers per month, and spend per customer on food and drink varies greatly at each type of cinema. The Finance Director wants to know which type of cinema is more profitable per customer.

He has prepared forecast information for both types of cinema. A typical forecast income statement and statement of financial position for both type of cinemas is shown below:

Forecast Income statement	*Out of Town*	*City Centre*
	£000	£000
Turnover	1,512	501
Cost of production		
Direct costs (90% films, 10% food)	320	108
Fixed costs	450	180
Total cost of sales	770	288
Gross profit	742	213
Administration costs (fixed)	50	50
Operating profit	692	163
Revenue from films	1,209	451
Revenue from food and drink	303	50
Gross profit margin	49%	42%
Operating profit margin	46%	32%
Number of customers per month (thousand)	150	56
Average spend per customer – Films	£8.06	£8.05
Average spend per customer – Food	£2.02	£0.89
Direct cost per customer	£2.13	£2.16
Fixed cost per customer	£3.00	£3.24

Draft a report for the Finance Director covering the following:

Explain why the gross profit margins are not significantly different using sales price, direct costs and fixed costs to illustrate your answer.

Explain why the operating profit margins are different.

Which is the most profitable type of cinema and why?

Apart from reducing fixed costs what could Tempest do to improve the profitability of the City Centre Cinemas? Use numbers to demonstrate your answer if necessary.

Tempest suspect City Centre customers are smuggling in their own sweets and snacks – give ONE way that Tempest could investigate the extent of this smuggling? What could be done to combat it?

To:	**Subject:**
From:	**Date:**

Why are the gross profit margins not significantly different?

Sales Price

Direct costs

Fixed costs

Why are the operating profit margins different?

Which is the most profitable type of cinema and why?

Apart from reducing fixed costs what could Tempest do to improve the profitability of the City Centre Cinemas?
Tempest suspect City Centre customers are smuggling in their own sweets and snacks – what could Tempest do to combat this smuggling?

229 ANIMAL

You have been provided with the information for Animal Limited:

Current position

The price is £25 per unit. At this price demand is 15,000 units each year. Advertising costs are £50,000 per year. The factory can produce a maximum of 40,000 units per year. Labour and material costs are the only variable costs.

Proposed position

The price will fall to £22 per unit. Advertising costs will increase to £75,000 per year and it is expected that this will increase demand to 30,000 units per year. The factory will still be limited to 40,000 units per year. The labour and material costs are the only variable costs.

Forecast information for each scenario is shown below.

	Current position (actual)	*Proposed position (forecast)*
Sales price per unit	£25	£22
Sales volume	15,000	30,000
	£	£
Revenue	375,000	660,000
Materials	75,000	120,000
Labour	90,000	180,000
Fixed production costs	60,000	60,000
Total cost of sales	225,000	360,000
Gross profit	150,000	300,000
Fixed advertising costs	50,000	75,000
Administration costs	30,000	40,000
Profit	70,000	185,000
Material cost per unit	£5.00	£4.00
Labour cost per unit	£6.00	£6.00
Fixed production cost per unit	£4.00	£2.00
Fixed advertising cost per unit	£3.33	£2.50
Gross profit margin	40%	45%
Profit margin	19%	28%
Inventory of finished goods	£35,000	
Trade receivables	£50,000	

Draft a report for the finance director covering the following:

(a) An explanation of why the gross profit margin for the proposed position is higher than the current position, referring to the following:

- **sales volume**
- **material cost**
- **labour cost**
- **fixed production cost**

(b) An explanation of what is likely to happen to the current asset position of the business by considering the following:

- **inventory levels (include a prediction of the proposed inventory level based upon the current holding period)**
- **trade receivable levels (include a prediction of the proposed level based upon current trade receivables collection period).**

To:	**Subject:**
From:	**Date:**

Why are the gross profit margin for the proposed position is higher than the current position:

Sales volume

Material costs

Labour costs

Fixed production cost

What is likely to happen to the current asset position:

Inventory levels

Trade receivable levels

230 FRUITY

Fruity manufactures fruit juices for sale in supermarkets. Fruity has several products including Apple fruit juice and Cranberry fruit juice. The finance department has produced the following information for each product.

Quarterly information	*Apple*	*Cranberry*
Unit information		
Sales price	£1	£1.25
Quantity of material in grams	500	550
Material cost per unit	£0.40	£0.50
Fixed production overheads	£0.20	£0.12
Full production cost per unit	£0.60	£0.62
Gross profit per unit	£0.40	£0.63
Gross profit margin	40.0%	50.4%
Volume of sales	500,000	1,000,000
Sales revenue	500,000	1,250,000
Variable production costs	200,000	500,000
Fixed production overhead	100,000	120,000
Gross profit	200,000	630,000
Marketing costs	50,000	120,000
Net profit	150,000	510,000
Net profit margin	30.0%	40.8%

A new manager has asked for your help in understanding the figures for Apple and Cranberry. He has reviewed the information and has the following questions:

1 Why is the gross profit margin of Cranberry less than 50% higher than that of Apple when the gross profit per unit is more than 50% higher?

2 I was told that the material cost is £0.80 per kilogram for Apple and £0.91 per kilogram for Cranberry. Therefore I do not understand why the material cost per unit for Apple is £0.40 and for Cranberry is £0.50. Is this correct?

3 If the fixed production overheads are constant does that mean they have no effect on the profit margin? And if the fixed production overheads increase will they affect the profit margin?

4 Can you explain why Cranberry is more profitable than Apple?

Draft an email to the new manager answering his questions.

To:	**Subject:**
From:	**Date:**

Gross profit margin

Material cost

Fixed production overheads

Profitability

231 PI ETHICS

Below are some of the results for one of the divisions of PI Ltd for the last two quarters.

Performance indicator	*Qtr 1 20X5*	*Qtr 2 20X5*
Revenue growth	9%	11%
Gross profit margin	40%	30%
Average selling price	£50	£40
Number of customers	10	9

One of the managers at PI receives a bonus based on some of the financial measures in the table above. They receive a bonus if revenue growth is over 10%.

Explain the ethical issues and any issues with goal congruence.

Ethical issues   **Goal congruence issues**

232 ZIG

Zig plc has three divisions A, B and C, whose performance is assessed on Return on Capital Employed (RoCE).

Forecast data for 20X6 is provided as follows:

	A £	B £	C £
Capital Employed	250,000	350,000	450,000
Profit	47,500	73,500	112,500

Calculate the RoCE for each division:

	A	B	C
RoCE %			

Three new proposals are being considered:

- A is considering investing £75,000 in order to increase profit by £21,000 each year.
- B is considering selling a machine, forecast to earn a profit of £25,000 in the coming year, for its net book value of £70,000.
- C is considering giving a 2.5% discount for prompt payment. This should reduce debtors by £20,000. C's sales revenue is £500,000 each year and a 50% take up of the offer is expected.

Complete the following table assuming each division proceeds with their respective proposal:

	A	B	C
Revised Capital Employed (£)			
Revised Profit (£)			
Revised RoCE (% to 1 dp)			

The managers of each division receive a bonus based on how far above the RoCE target they are, comment on the ethical implications and implications for decision making.

233 SSS

Stuart is the owner and manager of Stu's Snipping Station (SSS) which is a premium hairdressing salon in the upmarket town of Gosford; being in such a premium location, there are several similar salons trying to differentiate their service, so SSS are in a very competitive market. When Stuart first set up the salon his main focus was female clients, but he has recently turned his attention to the male market too.

The salon offers the usual range of hair services to female clients, including cuts, colouring and straightening. The male market is, overall, much simpler; usually haircuts only, so the time taken per client is much lower.

The price and mix of services provided to female clients has stayed the same over the last 4 years. Below is a table detailing the financial performance of SSS over the last 2 years:

	2015		2016	
	£	**£**	**£**	**£**
Sales		500,000		550,600
Cost of Sales:				
Stylists salaries	122,500		162,725	
Hair products	75,000		80,000	
		197,500		242,725
Gross profit		302,500		307,875
Property rental	15,000		15,000	
Administrative assistant	14,000		14,140	
Rates	8,000		9,000	
Marketing and advertising	3,000		9,000	
Total Expenses		40,000		47,140
Profit		262,500		260,735

Stuart feels the business is much busier than a year ago and is concerned that the financial results do not back this up. He has identified that the number of client visits to the salon are as follows:

	2015	2016
Female client visits	10,000	8,802
Male client visits	0	4,420

(a) Using the figures above complete the table below:

	£
Average price for hair services per female client visit in 2016 (assuming prices remained the same as 2015)	
Average price for hair services per male client visit in 2016	

Additional information:

(1) Stuart hired two stylists at the start of 2016; one was a dedicated stylist for male customers. The other was a trainee stylist on an apprentice contract and salary of £13,000.

(2) The other stylists all received a 1% pay rise at the start of 2016.

(b) Complete the following table stating your answer to 2 decimal places.

	2015	2016
Gross profit margin		
Net profit margin		

Write a report to Stuart about how the financial performance of SSS has changed over the last year.

(c) Comment on revenue, giving reasons for the change between 2015 and 2016.

(d) Comment on gross profit margin, giving reasons for the change between 2015 and 2016.

(e) Comment on net profit margin, giving reasons for the change between 2015 and 2016.

To:	**Subject:**
From:	**Date:**

Revenue

Gross profit margin

Net profit margin

Stuart is considering introducing some non-financial measures of success, the table below shows some figures that he thinks will help set up some measures.

	2015	2016
Complaints	16	176
Stylists for female clients	5	6
Stylists for male clients	0	1

The complaints related to two main factors and were from the loyal customer base that SSS had developed over the years. One of those factors was the introduction of male customers had changed the atmosphere at the salon.

(f) Complete the below table analysing the non-financial performance of the business.

	2015	2016
Customer		
% of visits that had complaints (to 2 decimal places)		
Internal business		
Number of female client visits per stylist		
Number of male client visits per stylist		
Innovation and growth		
% revenue from new male hairdressing service (to 2 decimal places)		

(g) Comment on the non-financial performance of SSS, giving reasons for the changes in the non-financial performance indicators over the last year.

234 COST REDUCTION

Distinguish between the terms 'cost reduction' and 'cost control', and outline the process of a cost reduction programme.

Cost reduction
Cost control
Outline process of a cost reduction programme

235 VALUE ANALYSIS

Value analysis is a technique widely used in cost reduction programmes. **Outline the process of value analysis.**

Value analysis

ETHICS

236 ETHICS STATEMENTS (I)

A company that takes a strong ethical stance in the way they behave will usually find their relationship with investors [ ]

improves/stays the same/gets worse/deteriorates

A worker in the accounts department who receives a profit based bonus decides to manipulate some of the expenses, artificially increasing the profits and allowing them to get a bonus has not breached the ethical principle of [ ]

professional behaviour/integrity/objectivity/confidentiality

237 ETHICS STATEMENTS (II)

Consumers may be willing to pay [ ] price for Fairtrade products, knowing that the products are grown in an ethical and sustainable fashion

a lower/a premium/a discounted/a penetration

An advantage of using life cycle costing is it could help an organisation make more [ ] decisions as they will consider all costs throughout the projects including any potential closure and clean-up costs.

sustainable/confidential/expensive/irresponsible

238 ETHICS STATEMENTS (III)

Products that have [ ] packaging could be considered unethical because they are using more of the world's resources and could potentially cost the company more money.

excess/no/sustainable/limited

Ethical actions by a business may help them achieve long term [ ] .

costs/penalties/success/expense

Section 2

ANSWERS TO PRACTICE QUESTIONS

COLLECTION OF COST INFORMATION

1 HIGH – LOW

	Units	£
High	13,100	69,750
Low	11,150	60,000
	1,950	9,750

Variable cost = £9,750/1,950 = £5 per unit

Total costs = Fixed cost + Variable cost

£69,750 = FC + (13,100 units × £5)

FC = £4,250 (in total)

2 HILOW

	Units	£
High	460	5,000
Low	410	4,500
	50	500

Variable cost = £500/50 = £10 per unit

Total costs = Fixed cost + Variable cost

£5,000 = FC + (460 units × £10)

FC = £400 (in total)

3 STEPPED

£458,750 – £418,750 = £40,000 of which £25,000 is the step up. Therefore only £15,000 is the total variable cost.

Change in output = 29,000 – 25,000 = 4,000 units.

Variable cost per unit = £15,000/4,000 units = £3.75

4 STEEPLE

£21,000 – £15,000 = £6,000 of which £5,000 is the step up. Therefore only £1,000 is the total variable cost.

Change in output = 2,400 – 2,000 = 400 units.

Variable cost per unit = £1,000/400 units = £2.50

5 PEN

£192,000 – £150,000 = £42,000 of which £25,000 is the step up. Therefore only £17,000 is the total variable cost.

Change in output = 23,400 – 20,000 = 3,400 units.

Variable cost per unit = £17,000/3,400 units = £5.00

6 POPPY

£48,750 – £38,750 = £10,000 of which £2,500 is the step up. Therefore only £7,500 is the total variable cost.

Change in output = 34,000 – 28,000 = 6,000 units.

Variable cost per unit = £7,500/6,000 units = £1.25

7 LAPEL

Units made	50,000	60,000	70,000
Costs:	£	£	£
Variable costs:			
Direct materials	5,250	6,300	7,350
Direct labour	2,250	2,700	3,150
Overheads	11,100	13,320	15,540
Fixed costs:			
Indirect labour	9,200	9,200	9,200
Overheads	15,600	15,600	15,600
Total cost	43,400	47,120	50,840
Cost per unit	0.868	0.785	0.726

	A (£)	*B* (£)	*Total* (£)
Selling price per unit	1.50	1.20	
Less: variable costs per unit			
Direct materials	0.20	0.25	
Direct labour	0.12	0.14	
Variable overheads	0.15	0.19	
Contribution per unit	1.03	0.62	
Sales volume (units)	300,000	500,000	
Total contribution	309,000	310,000	619,000
Less: fixed costs			264,020
Budgeted profit			354,980

8 SLUSH

Litres made	10,000	14,000	18,000
Costs:	£	£	£
Variable costs:			
Direct materials	1,200	1,680	2,160
Direct labour	1,000	1,400	1,800
Overheads	1,600	2,240	2,880
Fixed costs:			
Indirect labour	700	700	700
Overheads	1,600	1,600	1,600
Total cost	6,100	7,620	9,140
Cost per litre	0.61	0.54	0.51

9 THREE MONTHS

Use the two levels of production above 1,100 units per month for the high/low analysis as at these levels fixed costs are the same.

Units	*Total cost* (£)
1,400	68,200
1,200	66,600
200	1,600

Variable cost per unit = (£1,600 ÷ 200) = £8

Total fixed cost (above 1,100 units) = [£68,200 – (1,400 × £8)] = £57,000

Total cost for 1,000 units = [(£57,000 – £6,000) + (1,000 × £8)] = £59,000

10 EASTERN BUS COMPANY

Likely miles	10,000	12,000	14,000
	£	£	£
Sales revenue	100,000	120,000	140,000
Variable costs:			
Fuel	8,000	9,600	11,200
Drivers' wages and associated costs	5,000	6,000	7,000
Overheads	6,000	7,200	8,400
Fixed costs:			
Indirect labour	10,600	10,600	10,600
Overheads	25,850	25,850	25,850
Total cost	55,450	59,250	63,050
Total profit	44,550	60,750	76,950
Profit per mile	4.455	5.063	5.496

ACCOUNTING FOR OVERHEADS

11 PRODUCT R

	£
Material	22.50
Labour	17.50
Variable overhead (20,000/1,000)	20.00
Variable cost	60.00

	£
Material	22.50
Labour	17.50
Variable overhead	20.00
Fixed overhead (50,000/1,000)	50.00
Total absorption cost	110.00

		£
Change in inventory × fixed production overhead	250 × 50.00	12,500

12 PRODUCT D

	£
Material	10.60
Labour	16.40
Variable overhead (£60,000/10,000)	6.00
Variable cost	33.00

	£
Material	10.60
Labour	16.40
Variable overhead	6.00
Fixed overhead (£80,000/10,000)	8.00
Total absorption cost	41.00

13 UNDER/OVER ABSORPTION

(a)	Fixed overhead absorbed	26,500 hours × £2.50	£66,250
(b)	£66,300 – £66,250	Under absorbed	£50
(c)	Shown as a **DEBIT** in income statement		

14 BRANDED/OWN LABEL

Branded products

Rate per machine hour: £5,997,232/187,414 = £32.00

Own label products

Rate per machine hour: £2,844,968/118,540 = £24.00

Overhead absorbed	48,000 hours at £32	£1,536,000
Overhead incurred		£1,506,000
Absorption	OVER	£30,000

	Debit (£)	*Credit* (£)
Overhead absorbed	1,536,000	
Over absorption		30,000
Overhead control account		1,506,000

15 MIXING AND CANNING

The budgeted overhead recovery (absorption) rates are:

The Ingredients mixing department	£465,820/7,400 = **£62.95/machine hour**
The Canning department	£326,180/10,200 = **£31.98/direct labour hour**
Overhead absorbed	6,800 hours at £62.95 = **£428,060**
Overhead incurred	= **£450,060**
UNDER absorption	= **£22,000**

	Debit (£)	*Credit* (£)
Overhead absorbed	428,060	
Under absorption	22,000	
Overhead control account		450,060

16 AIRCRAFT

The overhead absorbed = actual miles flown × BOAR

= 6,890 × £300 = **£2,067,000**

Overhead **UNDER** absorbed = Actual overhead incurred £2,079,000

– Overhead absorbed £2,067,000

= £12,000 under absorbed

The £12,000 will be **DEBITED** to the income statement so as to increase expenses and reduce profit.

17 GARY

Fixed overhead absorption rate per hour is £120,000/(10,000 × 2 hrs) = **£6**

Marginal cost of one unit is:

	£
Material	15
Labour	8
Variable overhead	4
Marginal cost	27

Total absorption cost of one unit is:

	£
Material	15
Labour	8
Variable overhead	4
Fixed overhead (£6 × 2 hrs)	12
Total absorption cost	39

	Marginal cost		*Absorption cost*	
	£	£	£	£
Sales		450,000		450,000
Material	150,000		150,000	
Direct labour	80,000		80,000	
Variable costs	40,000		40,000	
Fixed costs	–		120,000	
Closing inventory	(27,000)		(39,000)	
	–––––––		–––––––	
		(243,000)		(351,000)
		–––––––		–––––––
Contribution/Profit		**207,000**		99,000
Fixed costs		(120,000)		–
		–––––––		–––––––
Profit		87,000		99,000
		–––––––		–––––––

		£
MAC profit		87,000
Change in inventory × fixed production overhead	1,000 units × 2 hrs × £6	12,000
TAC profit		99,000

18 CPL

	£
Selling price	12
Variable production cost (£4 + £3)	(7)
Contribution per unit	5

	£
Selling price	12
Marginal cost	(7)
Fixed production cost (£30,000/15,000)	(2)
Full absorption cost	(9)
Profit/unit	3

	£	£
Sales (12,000 units at £12)		144,000
Opening inventory (2,000 units at £7)	14,000	
Variable production costs (15,000 units at £7)	105,000	
Closing inventory (5,000 units at £7)	(35,000)	
Cost of sales (MAC basis)		84,000
Contribution		60,000
Fixed costs		(30,000)
Profit		30,000

	£	£
Sales (12,000 units at £12)		144,000
Opening inventory (2,000 units at £9)	18,000	
Production costs (15,000 units at £9)	135,000	
Closing inventory 5,000 units at £9)	(45,000)	
Cost of sales (FAC basis)		(108,000)
Profit		36,000

		£
MAC profit		30,000
Change in inventory × fixed production overhead	3,000 units × £2	6,000
FAC profit		36,000

19 TRICKY (I)

	Absorption costing			*Marginal costing*		
	Month 1 (£)	Month 2 (£)	Month 3 (£)	Month 1 (£)	Month 2 (£)	Month 3 (£)
Sales	210,000	205,400	210,000	210,000	205,400	210,000
Opening inventory	0	11,500	13,800	0	7,500	9,000
Production costs	184,000	184,000	180,000	120,000	120,000	116,000
Closing inventory	11,500	13,800	4,500	7,500	9,000	2,900
Cost of sales	172,500	181,700	189,300	112,500	118,500	122,100
Fixed overheads	0	0	0	64,000	64,000	64,000
Profit/(Loss)	37,500	23,700	20,700	33,500	22,900	23,900

Workings

Sales

Month 1 = 7,500 × £28 = 210,000; Month 2 = 7,900 × £26 = 205,400;

Month 3 = 8,400 × £25 = 210,000

Production costs (Abs)

Variable overhead cost/unit (months 1 and 2) = 24,000/8,000 = £3;

Month 3 = 20,000/8,000 = £2.50

Fixed overhead recovery rate per unit = 64,000/8,000 = £8

Month 1 and 2 = 8,000 × (7+5+3+8) = 184,000; Month 3 = 8,000 × (7+5+2.50+8) = 180,000

Closing inventory

Month 1 = (8,000 – 7,500) × 23 = 11,500; Month 2 = (500 + 8,000 -7,900) × 23 = 13,800;

Month 3 = (600 + 8,000 – 8,400) × 22.50 = 4,500

Production costs (Mar)

Month 1 and 2 = 8,000 × (7+5+3) = 120,000; Month 3 = 8,000 × (7+5+2.50) = 116,000

Closing inventory

Month 1 = 500 × 15 = 7,500; Month 2 = 600 × 15 = 9,000; Month 3 = 200 × 14.50 = 2,900

	Month 1				*Month 2*			
	Working			£	**Working**			£
MAC profit				33,500				22,900
Change in inventory × fixed production overhead recovery rate per unit.	units		ORR		units		ORR	
	+ 500	×	8	4,000	+ 100	×	8	800
TAC profit				37,500				23,700

	Month 3			
	Working			£
MAC profit				23,900
Change in inventory × fixed production overhead recovery rate per unit.	units		ORR	
	–400	×	8	–3,200
TAC profit				20,700

Month 1: £2,200 over recovered

Month 2: £2,920 under recovered

Month 3: £1,000 under recovered

Workings

	Workings	*Month 1* £	**Workings**	*Month 2* £
Fixed overhead absorbed	8,000 × 1.05 × 8	67,200	8,000 × 0.97 × 8	62,080
Fixed overhead incurred		(65,000)		(65,000)
Over/(under) absorption		2,200		(2,920)

	Workings	*Month 3* £
Fixed overhead absorbed	8,000 × 8	64,000
Fixed overhead incurred		(65,000)
Over/(under) absorption		(1,000)

20 HAIRWORKS

	£000	£000
Sales (10,000 @ £100)		1,000
Cost of sales		
Production costs (12500 unit produced at marginal cost £40)	500	
Less closing inventory (2,500 units at £40)	(100)	
		(400)
CONTRIBUTION		600
Less		
Fixed production costs		(400)
Fixed selling and admin costs		(150)
Profit for period		50

Absorption Costing Income statement		
	£000	£000
Sales (10,000@£100)		1,000
Cost of sales		
Production costs (12500 units produced at absorption cost £72)	900	
Less closing inventory (2,500 units at £72)	(180)	
		(720)
GROSS PROFIT		280
Less		
Fixed selling and admin costs		(150)
Profit for period		130

		£000
Marginal costing profit		50,000
Change in inventory × fixed production overhead	2,500 × £32	80,000
Absorption costing profit		130,000

21 RH

Marginal costing

	Six months ending		*Six months ending*	
	31 March 20X3		*30 September 20X3*	
	£000	£000	£000	£000
Sales		980		1,120
Variable cost of sales				
opening inventory	–		73.5	
production cost				
8,500 units @ £49	416.5			
7,000 units @ £49			343	
	———		———	
	416.5		416.5	
less closing inventory				
1,500 units @ £49	73.5			
500 units @ £49			24.5	
	———		———	
		343		392
		———		———
		637		728
Variable selling costs		196		224
		———		———
Contribution		441		504
Fixed production costs	155		155	
Fixed selling costs	90		90	
	———	245	———	245
		———		———
Profit		196		259
		———		———

Absorption costing

	Six months ending		*Six months ending*	
	31 March 20X3		*30 September 20X3*	
	£000	£000	£000	£000
Sales		980		1,120
Cost of sales				
opening inventory	–		103.5	
production cost				
8,500 units @ £69	586.5			
7,000 units @ £69			483	
	–––––		–––––	
	586.5		586.5	
Less closing inventory				
1,500 units @ £69	103.5			
500 units @ £69			34.5	
	–––––		–––––	
		483		552
		–––––		–––––
		497		568
(under)/over absorption (W2)		15		(15)
		–––––		–––––
Gross profit		512		553
selling costs, etc.				
variable	196		224	
fixed	90		90	
	–––––		–––––	
		286		314
		–––––		–––––
Profit		226		239
		–––––		–––––

Workings

(W1) Fixed production overhead is £20 per unit and budgeted production is 15,500 units per annum.

The budgeted overhead per annum is therefore 15,500 × 20 = £310,000. The budgeted overhead per six-month period is therefore £155,000.

(W2) Under/over-absorption is the difference between overheads incurred and overheads absorbed.

First six months	£000
Overhead incurred (W1)	155
Overhead absorbed	
8,500 units × £20/unit	170
	——
Over-absorption	15
	——

Second six months	
	£000
Overhead incurred (W1)	155
Overhead absorbed	
7,000 units × £20/unit	140
	——
Under-absorption	15
	——

Reconciliation

	First six months	*Second six months*
	£000	£000
Marginal costing profit	196	259
Increase 1,500 units × £20/unit	30	
Decrease 1,000 units × £20/unit		(20)
	——	——
Absorption costing profit	226	239
	——	——

ACTIVITY BASED COSTING

22 CAT

Machine hour absorption rate $= \dfrac{£10{,}430 + £5{,}250 + £3{,}600 + £2{,}100 + £4{,}620}{(120 \times 4) + (100 \times 3) + (80 \times 2) + (120 \times 3)}$

$= \dfrac{26{,}000}{1{,}300} = £20\text{/machine hour}$

The total costs for each product are:

	A	*B*	*C*	*D*
	£	£	£	£
Direct materials	40	50	30	60
Direct labour	28	21	14	21
Production overhead	80	60	40	60
	——	——	——	——
Per unit	148	131	84	141
	——	——	——	——
Total	17,760	13,100	6,720	16,920

Cost driver rates

Machine dept costs = 10,430/1,300 = £8.023/hr

(m/c hour basis)

Set up costs = 5,250/21 = £250/run

Stores receiving = 3,600/80 = £45/requisition

Inspection/quality control = 2,100/21 = £100/run

Material handling despatch = 4,620/42 = £110/order

Total costs	*A*	*B*	*C*	*D*
	£	£	£	£
Direct materials	4,800	5,000	2,400	7,200
Direct labour	3,360	2,100	1,120	2,520
Machine dept costs	3,851	2,407	1,284	2,888
Set up costs	1,500	1,250	1,000	1,500
Stores receiving	900	900	900	900
Inspection/quality control	600	500	400	600
Materials handling despatch	1,320	1,100	880	1,320
	——	——	——	——
	16,331	13,257	7,984	16,928
	——	——	——	——

23 SMASH-HIT

Cost centre	*Machining*	*Finishing*	*Packing*
Production overhead	£160,000	£65,000	£35,000
Direct labour hours	25,000	12,500	6,500
Recovery rate per labour hour	£6.40	£5.20	£5.38

Production cost of one unit of 'Heman 3'

	£
Direct labour 2.7 hours × £7/hour	18.90
Direct material	38.00
Production overhead	
Machining 1.5 hrs × £6.40/hr	9.60
Finishing 1.0 hrs × £5.20/hr	5.20
Packing 0.2 hrs × £5.38/hr	1.08
	——
Production cost	72.78
	——

Selling price of one unit of 'Heman 3'

	£
Production cost	72.78
Add: 15% for selling, admin and distribution	10.92
	——
	83.70
Add: 10% to cover profit	8.37
	——
Selling price	92.07
	——

Cost driver rates

Activity	*Cost pool*	*Cost driver volume*	*Cost driver rate*
Process set up	£80,000	200 set-ups	£400 per set up
Material procurement	£20,000	100 purchase orders	£200 per order
Maintenance	£25,000	20 maintenance plans	£1,250 per maintenance plan
Material handing	£50,000	4,000 material movements	£12.50 per material movement
Quality control	£45,000	500 inspections	£90 per inspection
Order processing	£40,000	600 customers	£66.67 per customer

Overhead chargeable to batch of 500 units of 'Heman 3'

	£
6 set ups × £400 per set up	2,400
6 purchase orders × £200 per order	1,200
2 maintenance plans × £1,250 per plan	2,500
150 material movements × £12.50 per material movement	1,875
75 inspections × £90 per inspection	6,750
10 sales customers × £66.67 per customer	667
	–––––
	15,392
	–––––

Tutorial note

At this point it is useful to calculate the overhead cost per unit:

$15{,}392/750$ *= £20.52)*

Production cost of one unit of Herman 3	£
Direct labour 2.7 hours × £7	18.90
Direct material	38.00
Production and other overhead	20.52
	–––––
Production cost	77.42
	–––––

24 ABC LTD

(a) OAR = (£80,000 + £40,000)/((5 × 1000) + (7×5000)) = £120,000/40,000hrs = £3/hr

DEF = £3 × 5,000 = £15,000

GHI = £3 × 35,000 = £105,000

	DEF (£)	GHI (£)
Fixed overheads	15,000	105,000

(b) Cost driver rates:

Special parts = £40,000/400 = £100 per part;

machine set ups = £80,000/200 = £400 per set up

DEF: special parts = £100 × 300 = £30,000; machine set ups = £400 × 150 = £60,000

GHI: special parts = £100 × 100 = £10,000; machine set ups = £400 × 50 = £20,000

	£	DEF (£)	GHI (£)
Cost driver rate – special parts handling	100		
Cost driver rate – machine set ups	400		
Total special parts		30,000	10,000
Total machine set ups		60,000	20,000

(c) DEF

Absorption cost = £15,000/1,000 = £15 per unit; Unit cost = £8 + £25 + £15 = £48

ABC cost = £90,000/1,000 = £90 per unit; Unit cost = £8 + £25 + £90 = £123 per unit

GHI

Absorption cost = £105,000/5,000 = £21 per unit; Unit cost = £12 + £35 + £21 = £68

ABC cost = £30,000/5,000 = £6 per unit; Unit cost = £12 + £35 + £6 = £53 per unit

	DEF	GHI
Total unit cost – Absorption costing	48.00	68.00
Total unit cost – ABC	123.00	53.00

25 FOUR LIONS LTD

(a) OAR = (£180,000 + £140,000)/((3 × 20,000) + (4 × 10,000)) = £3.20/hr

Lion = £3.20 × 60,000 = £192,000

Pride = £3.20 × 40,000 = £128,000

	Lion (£)	Pride (£)
Fixed overheads	192,000	128,000

(b) Cost driver rates:

Material movements = £180,000/2500 = £72 per movement; quality control = £140,000/100 = £1,400 per quality inspection

Lion: material movements = £72 × 2,000 = £144,000; quality control = £1,400 × 15 = £21,000

Pride: material movements = £72 × 500 = £36,000; quality control = £1,400 × 85 = £119,000

	£	Lion (£)	Pride (£)
Cost driver rate – material movements	72		
Cost driver rate – quality control	1,400		
Total material movements		144,000	36,000
Total quality control		21,000	119,000

(c) Lion

Absorption cost per unit = £192,000/20,000 = £9.60; Unit cost = 12 + 16 + 9.60 = 37.60

ABC cost per unit = £165,000/20,000 = £8.25; Unit cost = 12 + 16 + 8.25 = 36.25

Pride

Absorption cost per unit = £128,000/10,000 = £12.80; Unit cost = 20 + 24 + 12.80 = 56.80

ABC cost per unit = £155,000/10,000 = £15.50;Unit cost = 20 + 24 + 15.50 = 59.50

	Lion	Pride
Total unit cost – Absorption costing	37.60	56.80
Total unit cost – ABC	36.25	59.50

(d)

Activity Based Costing works on the premise that the volume of activities create costs and not the volume of production, so this provides a more accurate cost per unit

This more accurate cost per unit can lead to better information about pricing, sales strategy and performance management

ABC should provide Four Lions better insight into what causes (drives) overhead costs.

Overhead costs can be a significant proportion of total costs, and the management of Four Lions will be able to understand the drivers of overhead costs allowing them to manage the business properly.

ABC can be applied to all overhead costs, not just production overheads, so it could lead to savings elsewhere for Four Lions.

Research, production and sales effort at Four Lions can be directed towards those products and services which ABC has identified as offering the highest sales margins.

26 RVI

(a) OAR = (£300,000 + £500,000)/((2 × 1,000) + (1.5 × 2,000)) = £160 per surgeon hour

A = £160 × 2,000 hrs = £320,000; B = £160 × 3,000 hrs = £480,000

	A (£)	B (£)
Fixed overheads	320,000	480,000

(b) Cost driver rates:

Nursing costs = £300,000/6,000hrs = £50 per hour

Remedial costs = £500,000/5,000 visit = £100 per visit

A: nursing costs = £50 × 2,000 = £100,000; remedial costs = £100 × 2,000 = £200,000

B: nursing costs = £50 × 4,000 = £200,000; remedial costs = £100 × 3,000 = £300,000

	£	A (£)	B (£)
Cost driver rate – nurse costs	50		
Cost driver rate – remedial costs	100		
Total nursing costs		100,000	200,000
Total remedial costs		200,000	300,000

(c) A:

Absorption cost per procedure = £320,000/1,000 = £320; Procedure cost = £275 + £320 = £595

ABC cost per unit = £300,000/1,000 = £300; Procedure cost = £275 + £300 = £575

B:

Absorption cost per procedure = 480,000/2,000 = £240; Procedure cost = £235 + £240 = 475

ABC cost per unit = £500,000/2,000 = £250; Procedure cost = £235 + £250 = £485

	A	B
Total procedure cost – Absorption costing	595	475
Total procedure cost – ABC	575	485

(d)

RVI must consider if the overhead costs are primarily volume related or if the overhead is a small proportion of the overall cost, if it is ABC will be of limited benefit.

RVI could have difficulty allocating all overhead costs to specific activities.

RVI may find that in some cases the choice of both activities and cost drivers might be inappropriate.

RVI will have to take time to train staff and management how the costing exercise works.

The benefits obtained from ABC might not justify the costs.

27 ABC STATEMENTS (I)

A cost **driver** is any factor that causes a change in the cost of an activity

VPS manufactures touch screens, the most likely cost driver for the cost pool called 'quality control' is number of **inspections.**

28 ABC STATEMENTS (II)

A cost **pool** is an activity which consumes resources and for which overhead costs are identified and allocated.

F supplies pharmaceutical drugs, the most likely cost driver for the cost pool 'invoice processing costs' is the number of **invoices processed.**

STANDARD COSTING

29 BUDGIE

(a) The standard quantity of labour per unit is 30 minutes (1,750/3,500 × 60 minutes)

(b) The budgeted quantity of materials needed to produce 3,000 units of A is 6,000 litres (7,000/3,500 × 3,000)

(c) The budgeted labour hours to produce 3,600 units of A is 1,800 hours (1,750/3,500 × 3,600)

(d) The budgeted labour cost to produce 3,600 units of A is £16,200 (£15,750/3,500 × 3,600)

(e) The budgeted overhead absorption rate is £10 (£35,000/3,500)

(f) The fixed overheads were over absorbed by £1,675

Absorption rate = £43,500/4,000 units	£10.875
	£
Actual overheads	44,000
Absorbed overheads 4,200 × £10.875	45,675
Over absorbed	1,675

30 CARROT

(a) The standard quantity of labour per unit is 1.5 minutes (250/10,000 × 60 minutes)

(b) The budgeted quantity of materials needed to produce 9,950 units of B is 3,980 kg (4,000/10,000 × 9,950)

(c) The budgeted labour hours to produce 9,950 units of B is 248.75 hours (250/10,000 × 9,950)

(d) The budgeted labour cost to produce 9,950 units of B is £2,487.50 (£2,500/10,000 × 9,950)

(e) The budgeted overhead absorption rate is £0.30 (£3,000/10,000)

(f) The fixed overheads were over absorbed by £287

Absorption rate = £2,900/9,000 units	£0.322
	£
Actual overheads	3,000
Absorbed overheads 10,200 × £0.322	3,287
Over absorbed	287

31 RABBIT

(a) The standard quantity of labour per unit is 60 minutes (12,500/12,500 × 60)

(b) The budgeted quantity of materials needed to produce 12,000 units of A is 24,000 litres (25,000/12,500 × 12,000)

(c) The budgeted labour hours to produce 12,600 units of A is 12,600 hours (12,500/12,500 × 12,600)

(d) The budgeted labour cost to produce 12,600 units of A is £126,000 (£125,000/12,500 × 12,600)

(e) The budgeted overhead absorption rate is £6 (£75,000/12,500)

(f) The fixed overheads were over absorbed by £2,800

Absorption rate = £78,000/13,000 units	£6
	£
Actual overheads	74,000
Absorbed overheads 12,800 × £6	76,800
Over absorbed	2,800

32 BELLS

1 box of Bells	*Quantity*	*Cost per unit*	*Total cost*
Material	16 kg	1.50	24
Labour	3 hrs	9.00	27
Fixed overheads	1 (accept 3 hrs)	60 (20 per hr)	60
Total			111

33 TEA BAGS

1,000 tea bags		*Quantity (Units)*	*Unit price £*	*Total cost £*
Loose tea	Kilograms	3	5	15
Tea bags	Bags	1000	0.006	6
Direct labour	Hours	0.2	10	2
Fixed production overheads	Hours	0.2	50	10
				33

34 GEM

1 unit of Gem	*Quantity*	*Cost per unit*	*Total cost*
Material	5.25	7	36.75
Labour	3.5	3	10.5
Fixed overheads	3.5	15	52.5
Total			99.75

It takes a manufacturing department 750,000 hours to produce 250,000 units of Pearl. The standard hours per unit are **3 hours**.

35 BESPOKE SUIT

1 bespoke suit	*Quantity*	*Cost per unit*	*Total cost*
Material	4.50	48	216
Labour	40	15	600
Fixed overheads	40	10	400
Total			1,216

36 GARDEN SHEDS

1 Shed	*Quantity*	*Cost per unit*	*Total cost*
Material	90	6.50	585
Labour	5	10	50
Fixed overheads	5	20	100
Total			735

37 PERFORMANCE

1000 bulbs	*Quantity*	*Cost per unit*	*Total cost*
Material	40	5	£200.00
Labour	2	7	£14.00
Fixed overheads	2	15	£30.00
Total			£244.00

The standard quantity is 1,500/1,000 = **1.5 kg**.

38 DISCO

The standard machine time required for a disc is **5** hours.

39 HARRY

The standard labour time required for a unit is 2,000/500 = **4** hours.

40 OSCAR

The standard machine time required for a widget is 0.0025 hours.

41 PIZZA

The standard quantity of flour for a pizza is **0.20** kilograms.

300,000 kg/1,500,000 pizzas

MATERIAL VARIANCES

42 MAT (1)

AQ × AP

1,000 × £5 = £5,000

AQ × SP

1,000 × £5.50 = £5,500 Price variance = £500 F

SQ × SP

200 × 6 × £5.50 = £6,600 Usage variance = £1,100 F

			£
Budgeted/Standard cost of materials for actual production			6,600
Variances	**Favourable**	**Adverse**	
Direct materials price	500		
Direct materials usage	1,100		
Total variance	1,600		1,600
Actual cost of materials for actual production			5,000

43 MAT (2)

AQ × AP

12,000 × £4 = £48,000

AQ × SP

12,000 × £4.50 = £54,000 Price variance = £6,000 F

SQ × SP

2,000 × 5 × £4.50 = £45,000 Usage variance = £9,000 A

			£
Budgeted/Standard cost of materials for actual production			45,000
Variances	**Favourable**	**Adverse**	
Direct materials price	6,000		
Direct materials usage		9,000	
Total variance	6,000	9,000	3,000
Actual cost of materials for actual production			48,000

44 SMITH

AQ × SP

29,000 × 0.27 = £7,830

SQ × SP Usage variance £108 F

9,800 × 3 × 0.27 = £7,938

45 ORANGINA

AQ × AP

? × ? = ?

AQ × SP Price variance = £338 A

? × 0.50 = ?

SQ × SP Usage variance = £152 A

3,100 × 0.50 = 1,550

Many factors are unknown. Start at the bottom of the working, and work upwards.

£1,550 + £152 = £1,702 (AQ × SP)

£1,702/0.50 = 3,404 kg (AQ)

£1,702 + £338 = £2,040 (AQ × AP)

£2,040/3,404 = **0.599** (AP)

46 CUFF

AQ × AP

100 × ? =?

AQ × SP Materials price variance = £20

100 × £1 = £100

The total actual cost = £100 + £20 = £120

47 SAPPHIRE

Correct answer is 290,000 kg

145,000 units × 2 kg = 290,000 kg

48 MATERIAL

AQ × AP

60,000 × ? = £720,000

AQ × SP

60,000 × £11 = £660,000

Price variance is £60,000 A

49 KILO

AQ × AP

8,000 kg × ? = £24,000

AQ × SP

8,000 kg × £2.80 = £22,400

SQ × SP

1,800 units × 3.6 kg × £2.80 = £18,144

(W1) Standard price = £20,160/7,200 kg = £2.80 per kg

(W2) Standard quantity = 7,200 kg/2,000 units = 3.6 kg per unit

Usage variance is (£22,400 – £18,144) £4,256 A.

50 MOUSE

AQ × AP

AQ × SP

SQ × SP

2,450,000 units × 0.03 × £0.75 = £55,125

(W1) Standard quantity = 60,000 kg/2,000,000 = 0.03 kg per bottle

Correct answer **C**

51 RAW MATERIALS

AQ used × SP

2,300 kg × £0.75 = £1,725

SQ × SP

1,200 × 2kg × £0.75 = £1,800

Usage variance = £75 F

Correct answer is **D**

52 ALPHA

AQ × AP

10,000 × ? = £55,000

AQ × SP

10,000 × £5 = £50,000

Price variance = £5,000 A

Correct answer is **B**

53 BETA

AQ × AP

5,000 × ? = £27,500

AQ × SP

5,000 × £5 = £25,000

Price variance = £2,500 A

Correct answer is **C**

54 CHARLIE

AQ × SP

100,000 × £4.50 = £450,000

SQ × SP

2.50 × 42,000 × £4.50 = £472,500

Usage variance = £22,500 F

Correct answer is **D**

55 DELTA

AQ × SP

10,000 × (£28,000/8,000 kg) = £35,000

SQ × SP

1,000 units × 8 kg × £3.50 = £28,000

Usage variance = £7,000 A

Correct answer is **A**

56 EPSILON

Using the information given:

AQ × AP

1,000 kg × £? = £?

AQ × SP — Price variance = £?

1,000 kg × £3.50 = £?

SQ × SP — Usage variance = £?

(1,050 units × 0.8kg) × £3.50 = £

Total variance = £60 A

W1: SQ × SP = 1,050 × 0.8 × 3.50 = £2,940

W2: As total variance is £60 A that means AQ × AP is £60 more than SQ × SP so AQ × AP = £3,000

W3: AQ × SP = 1,000 × 3.50 = £3,500

W4: Price variance = £3,000 – £3,500 = £500 F

W5: Usage variance = £3,500 – £2,940 = £560 A

		£
Standard cost of materials for actual production		**(W1) 2,940**
Variances	**Favourable / adverse / no variance**	
Direct materials price	**Favourable**	(W4) 500
Direct materials usage	**Adverse**	(W5) 560
Actual cost of materials for actual production		**(W2) 3,000**

57 FLY

Using the information given:

AQ × AP

15,000 × ? = £450,000

AQ × SP — Price variance = £

15,000 × £32 = £

SQ × SP — Usage variance = £

(14,000 × ?) × £32 = £

Total variance = £2,000 A

W1: If the total variance is £2,000 A and AQ × AP = £450,000, then we know that SQ × SP must be £448,000

W2: AQ × SP = 15,000 × £32 = £480,000

That means:

W3: Price variance = £450,000 – £480,000 = £30,000 F

Usage variance = £480,000 – £448,000 = £32,000 A

		£
Standard cost of materials for actual production		**(W1) 448,000**
Variances	**Favourable / adverse / no variance**	
Direct materials price	**Favourable**	(W3) 30,000
Direct materials usage	**Adverse**	(W4) 32,000
Actual cost of materials for actual production		**450,000**

LABOUR VARIANCES

58 LAB (1)

AH × AR

12,000 × £8 = £96,000

AH × SR

12,000 × £8.50 = £102,000 Rate variance = £6,000 F

SH × SR

2,000 × 5 × £8.50 = £85,000 Efficiency variance = £17,000 A

			£
Budgeted/Standard cost of labour for actual production			85,000
Variances	**Favourable**	**Adverse**	
Direct labour rate	6,000		
Direct labour efficiency		17,000	
Total variance	6,000	17,000	11,000
Actual cost of labour for actual production			96,000

59 LAB (2)

AH × AR

22,000 × £10 = £220,000

AH × SR

22,000 × £9.80 = £215,600 Rate variance = £4,400 A

SH × SR

21,000 × 1 × £9.80 = £205,800 Efficiency variance = £9,800 A

			£
Budgeted/Standard cost of labour for actual production			205,800
Variances	**Favourable**	**Adverse**	
Direct labour rate		4,400	
Direct labour efficiency		9,800	
Total variance		14,200	14,200
Actual cost of labour for actual production			220,000

60 BEALE

AH × AR

340 × ? = £5,440

AH × SR Labour rate variance = £340 A

340 × £15 = £5,100

61 MY

A unit takes 0.5 hours (3,000 hours/6,000 units).

7,000 units × 0.5 hours = 3,500 hours

3,500 hours × £7 = £24,500

Correct answer is £24,500.

62 MCQ

AH × AR

12,000 hrs × = £52,800

AH × SR

12,000 hrs × £4 = £48,000

SH × SR

Rate variance is £4,800 adverse.

63 DIAMOND

AH × AR

15,000 × ? = £150,000

AH × SR

15,000 × ? = £153,750

Rate variance is £3750 F

SR = £153,750/15,000 = £10.25

Correct answer is **£10.25.**

64 JARVIS

AQ × AR

AQ × SR

18,000 hrs × £8 = £144,000

Rate variance = £7,600 A

Therefore, AQ × AR = £151,600

Correct answer is £151,600.

65 GOSSIP

140,000 units × (60,000/120,000) hours × £14 = £980,000

Correct answer is **£980,000.**

66 HIT

11,000 units × (8,000/10,000) hours × £10 = £88,000

Correct answer is **£88,000.**

67 JOY

AH × AR

3,400 × ? = £53,140

AH × SR

3,400 × £15 = £51,000

Labour rate variance = £2,140 A

Correct answer is **C**

68 KAP

AH × AR

10,000 × £?? = £55,800

AH × SR

10,000 × £5 = £50,000

Labour rate variance = £5,800 A

Correct answer is **C**

69 LEMON

AH × SR

7,000 × £9 = £63,000

SH × SR

1,000 × 6 hours × £9 = £54,000

Labour efficiency variance = £9,000 A

Correct answer is **D**

70 MUFFIN

AH × SR

16,000 × £12 = £192,000

SH × SR

10,000 × 1.5 hours × £12 = £180,000

Labour efficiency variance = £12,000 A

Correct answer is **D**

71 JAYRO

Variance		
	£	*A/F*
Direct material usage variance	Nil	N/A
Direct material price	1,100	A
Direct labour efficiency variance	4,400	A

72 PICTURE PERFECT

Variance		
	£	A/F
Direct material (wood) usage variance	112,500	A
Direct labour rate variance	10,000	F
Direct labour efficiency variance	25,000	F

73 DIVISION

W1 Standard cost of production: 0.2ltrs × 6,000 units × (£2/0.2ltrs) = **£12,000**

W2 Actual cost of materials: £12,000 – £890 = **£11,110**

11,110/£10.10 = 1,100 litres actually used.

AQ × SP = 1,100 × £10 = 11,000

Price variance = 11,110 – 11,000 = **£110 A**

Usage variance = 11,000 – 12,000 = **£1,000 F**

W3 Standard labour cost of production: 0.8 × 6,000 units × (£4/0.8hrs) = **£24,000**

W4 Actual cost of labour: £24,000 + £1,000 = £25,000

AH × SR = 4,500 × £5 = £22,500

Labour rate variance = 25,000 – 22,500 = **£2,500 A**

Efficiency variance = 22,500 – 24,000 = **£1,500 F**

Variance		£	*A/F*
Actual cost of materials	**W2**	**11,110**	
Direct material price variance		110	A
Direct material usage variance		1,000	F
Standard material cost of production	W1	**12,000**	
Actual cost of labour	W4	25,000	
Direct labour rate variance		2,500	A
Direct labour efficiency variance		1,500	F
Standard labour cost of production	W3	24,000	

74 NIGHT

W1 Standard cost of production: 1ltr × 900 units × (£20/1ltr) = **£18,000**

AQ × SP = 950 × £20 = 19,000

Usage variance = 19,000 – 18,000 = **£1,000 A**

Total material variance = 1,000 A + 100 A = **£1100 A**

Actual cost of materials = 18,000 + 1,100 = **£19,100**

W2 Standard labour cost of production: 4hrs × 900 units × (£40/4hrs) = **£36,000**

W3 Actual cost of labour: £36,000 + £2,095 = £38,095

AH × SR = 3,950 × £10 = £39,500

Labour rate variance = 38,095 – 39,500 = **£1,405 F**

Efficiency variance = 39,500 – 36,000 = **£3,500 A**

Variance		£	*A/F*
Actual cost of materials		**19,100**	
Direct material usage variance		1,000	A
Direct material total variance		1,100	A
Standard material cost of production	**W1**	**18,000**	
Actual cost of labour	W3	38,095	
Direct labour rate variance		1,405	F
Direct labour efficiency variance		3,500	A
Standard labour cost of production	W2	36,000	

75 SETTING BUDGETS

Actual results should always be compared to flexed budgets.

Correct answer is **A**

76 HINDER

The price variance will be favourable (buying at a lower price) but the usage variance will be adverse (more waste).

The correct answer is **C**

77 LABOUR VARIANCE RATIOS

Labour Activity ratio = $\frac{3,502}{3,630} \times 100 = \mathbf{96.5\%}$

Labour Efficiency ratio = $\frac{3,502}{3,471} \times 100 = \mathbf{100.9\%}$

Idle time ratio = $\frac{3,710 - 3,471}{3,710} \times 100 = \mathbf{6.4\%}$

78 LAB VAR RATIOS

Labour Activity ratio = $\frac{30,502}{29,470} \times 100 = \mathbf{103.5\%}$

Labour Efficiency ratio = $\frac{30,502}{31,630} \times 100 = \mathbf{96.4\%}$

Idle time ratio = $\frac{32,000 - 31,630}{32,000} \times 100 = \mathbf{1.2\%}$

79 LABOUR

Better quality material might enable workers to work more quickly as there might be less wastage and hence rework.

80 BASIC

Correct answer is **C**, by definition.

81 STANDARD

Ideal standards are demotivating since they expect perfect performance at all times which is not humanly possible.

Correct answer is **D**

82 TIDLE

AHp × AR

5,200 × £7.50 = £39,000

Rate variance = **£2,600 A**

AHp × SR

5,200 × £7 = £36,400

Idle time variance = **£2,100 A**

AHw × SR

4,900 × £7 = £34,300

Efficiency variance = **£1,575 F**

AP × SH × SR

41,000 × (5,000 / 40,000) × £7 = £35,875

Total variance = **£3,125 A**

83 BRIDLE

AHp × AR

5,200 × £? = £36,000

Rate variance = **£400 F**

AHp × SR

5,200 × £7 = £36,400

Idle time variance = £700 A

AHw × SR

5,100 × £7 = £35,700

Efficiency variance = **£175 F**

AP × SH × SR

4,100 × (5,000 / 4,000) × £7 = £35,875

84 SIDLE

AP × SH × SR = standard cost of labour for actual production = 9,000 pots × (5,000 hrs/10,000 pots) × £10 = **£45,000**

Actual labour cost from actual production = standard cost of labour for actual production + total labour variance = £45,000 + £4,011 adverse = **£49,011**

AHp = £49,011/£9.61 = 5,100 hrs

AHw = 5,100 – 200 = **4,900 hours**

AHp × AR

5,100 × £9.61 = £49,011

Rate variance = **£1,989 F**

AHp × SR

5,100 × £10 = £51,000

Idle time variance = **£2,000 A**

AHw × SR

4,900 × £10 = £49,000

Efficiency variance = **£4,000 A**

AP × SH × SR

9,000 × 0.5 hrs × £10 = £45,000

		£
Standard labour cost for actual production		**45,000**
Variances	**Favourable / adverse / No variance**	
Labour rate variance	**Favourable**	1,989
Idle time variance	**Adverse**	2,000
Labour efficiency variance	**Adverse**	4,000
Actual labour cost from actual production		**49,011**

VARIABLE OVERHEAD VARIANCES

85 VAR (1)

AH × AR

12,000 × £5 = £60,000

AH × SR

12,000 × £5.50 = £66,000 Expenditure variance = £6,000 F

SH × SR

2,000 × 5 × £5.50 = £55,000 Efficiency variance = £11,000 A

			£
Budgeted/Standard cost of variable overheads for actual production			55,000
Variances	**Favourable**	**Adverse**	
Variable overhead expenditure	6,000		
Variable overhead efficiency		11,000	
Total variance	6,000	11,000	5,000
Actual cost of variable overheads for actual production			60,000

86 JIF

AH × AR

3,400 × ? = £53,140

AH × SR

3,400 × £15 = £51,000

Variable overhead expenditure variance = £2,140 A

87 CALLUM

AH × SR

10,000 × £5 = £50,000

SH × SR

10,000 × 1.2 hours × £5 = £60,000

Labour efficiency variance = £10,000 F

88 VALERIE (1)

AH × AR

23,400 × ? = £103,140

AH × SR

23,400 × £5 = £117,000

Variable overhead expenditure variance = £13,860 F

Correct answer is **A**

89 VALERIE (2)

AH × SR

23,400 × £5 = £117,000

SH × SR

11,000 × 2 hours × £5 = £110,000

Variable overhead efficiency variance = £7,000 A

Correct answer is **C**

90 SHIRLEY

SH × SR

11,000 × 0.9 hours × £5 = £49,500

Total variance = £6,300 A

Actual variable overhead cost = 49,500 + 6,300 = **£55,800**

AH × AR

10,000 × ? = £55,800

AH × SR

10,000 × £5 = £50,000

Variable overhead expenditure variance = **£5,800 A**

AH × SR

10,000 × £5 = £50,000

SH × SR

11,000 × 0.9 hours × £5 = £49,500

Variable overhead efficiency variance = **£500 A**

91 VAR (2)

SH × SR

21,000 × 1 × £8.50 = **£178,500** Efficiency variance = £8,500 A

Therefore AH × SR = £178,500 +£8,500 = £187,000

AH × £8.50 = £187,000

AH = 187,000/8.50 = 22,000 hours

AH × AR = 22,000 × £8 = **£176,000**

Expenditure variance = 176,000 – 187,000 = **£11,000 F**

			£
Budgeted/Standard cost of variable overheads for actual production			178,500
Variances	**Favourable**	**Adverse**	
Variable overhead expenditure	11,000		
Variable overhead efficiency		8,500	
Total variance	11,000	8,500	2,500 F
Actual cost of variable overheads for actual production			176,000

FIXED OVERHEAD VARIANCES

92 OVERHEAD

Actual expenditure = £25,000

Budgeted expenditure = £20,000

Expenditure variance = £5,000 A

Budgeted expenditure = £20,000

SQ × SP

12,000 units × £2 per unit = £24,000

Volume variance = £4,000 F

The fixed overhead volume variance is **4,000 F**

The fixed overhead expenditure variance is **5,000 A**

93 BUDGET

OAR = £180,000/15,000 units = £12/unit

Actual expenditure = £172,000

Budgeted expenditure = £180,000

Expenditure variance = £8,000 F

Budgeted expenditure = £180,000

AP × OAR

15,600 units × £12 = £187,200

Volume variance = £7,200 F

The fixed overhead expenditure variance is **8,000 F**

The fixed overhead volume variance is **7,200 F**

94 FRANK

Actual expenditure £900,000

Budgeted expenditure £800,000

£100,000 A

Budgeted expenditure £800,000

AP × SR

42,000 × (£800,000/40,000 units) = £840,000

£40,000 F

The fixed overhead volume variance is **40,000 F**

The fixed overhead expenditure variance is **100,000 A**

95 FIXED OVERHEADS

OAR = £540,000/6,000 units = £90/unit

Actual expenditure = £600,000

Budgeted expenditure = £540,000

Expenditure variance = £60,000 A

Budgeted expenditure = £540,000

AP × OAR

7,000 units × £90 = £630,000

Volume variance = £90,000 F

The fixed overhead expenditure variance is **60,000 A**

The fixed overhead volume variance is **90,000 F**

96 TRUMPET

Budgeted production = 14,000/1.75hrs per unit = **8,000** units

Actual expenditure £209,000

Budgeted expenditure 8,000 × £25 = £200,000

Expenditure variance **£9,000 A**

Budgeted expenditure £200,000

AP × SR

6,000 × £25 = £150,000

Volume variance **£50,000 A**

97 FLOPPY

Actual expenditure £1,750,000

Budgeted expenditure 100,000 units × £15 = £1,500,000

Expenditure variance **= £250,000 A**

Budgeted expenditure £1,500,000

Actual production × Standard rate

110,000 units × 2 hrs × £7.50 = £1,650,000

Volume variance = **£150,000 F**

98 TROMBONE

Overhead absorption rate = £56,000/8,000 = **£7 per unit**

Actual output × OAR = £57,400

Total variance is £1,640 adverse

Therefore Actual expenditure £57,400 + £1,640 = **£59,040**

Budgeted expenditure £56,000

The fixed overhead expenditure variance is **£3,040 A**

Budgeted expenditure £56,000

AP × SR

8,200 × (£56,000/8,000) = £57,400

The fixed overhead volume variance is **£1,400 F**

99 VIOLIN

Budgeted expenditure £66,000

Expenditure variance is £3,040 A

Actual expenditure **£69,040**

AP × SR

10,200 × (£66,000/10,000) = £67,320

The total fixed production overhead variance is **£1,720 A**

100 HARP

AP × SR

5,200 × (£52,000/5,000) = £54,080

Total fixed overhead variance £4,960 A

Actual expenditure **£59,040**

Budgeted expenditure £52,000

£7,040 A

Budgeted expenditure £52,000

AP × SR

5,200 × (£52,000/5,000) = £54,080

£2,080 F

The fixed overhead volume variance is **£2,080 F**

The fixed overhead expenditure variance is **£7,040 A**

101 CYMBAL

Actual expenditure £49,040

Budgeted expenditure £46,000

£3,040 A

Budgeted expenditure £46,000

AP × SR

17,800 × (£46,000/18,000) = £45,489

£511 A

The fixed overhead volume variance is **£511 A**

The actual fixed overhead are **£49,040.**

102 PIANO

AP × SR

18,000 × £25 = £450,000

Actual overhead = £450,000 + £50,000 F = **£400,000**

Budgeted production = 18,000 /1.2 = 15,000

Budgeted overhead = 15,000 × £25 = **£375,000**

Actual = £400,000

Expenditure variance = **£25,000 A**

Budget = £375,000

AP × SR = £450,000

Volume variance = **£75,000 F**

103 ORGAN

OAR = £54,000/600 = £90 per unit

Actual

Budgeted = £54,000

Actual production × OAR = 700 × £90 = £63,000

Volume variance = £9,000 F

Actual Overhead = £63,000 - £3.000 F = £60,000

Expenditure variance = £60,000 - £54,000 = £6,000 A

The fixed overhead expenditure variance is **£6,000 A**

The fixed overhead volume variance is £**9,000 F**

The actual fixed overhead incurred is **£60,000**

104 FIDDLE

Budgeted expenditure £270,000

Expenditure variance is £30,000 A

Actual expenditure £300,000

Overhead absorption rate = £270,000/3,000 = £90 per unit

AP × OAR

3,500 × £90 = £315,000

The total fixed production overhead variance is £15,000 F

Budget expenditure £270,000

AP × OAR = £315,000

Volume variance is £45,000 F

Actual fixed production overheads are £**300,000**

Total fixed production overheads variance is £**15,000 F**

The overhead absorption rate is £**90** per unit

The fixed production overhead volume variance is £**45,000 F**

105 FIX (1)

Actual fixed overheads = £450,000

Budgeted fixed overheads = £400,000 Fixed overhead expenditure variance = £50,000 A

SQ × SR

21,000 × £20 = £420,000 Fixed overhead volume variance = £20,000 F

			£
Budgeted/Standard fixed cost for actual production			420,000
Variances	**Favourable**	**Adverse**	
Fixed overhead expenditure		50,000	
Fixed overhead volume	20,000		
Total variance	20,000	50,000	30,000
Actual fixed cost for actual production			450,000

106 FIX (2)

Actual fixed overheads = £245,000

Budgeted fixed overheads = £250,000

Fixed overhead expenditure variance = 5,000 F

SQ × SR

2,100 × £125 = £262,500 Fixed overhead volume variance = £12,500 F

			£
Budgeted/Standard fixed cost for actual production			262,500
Variances	**Favourable**	**Adverse**	
Fixed overhead expenditure	5,000		
Fixed overhead volume	12,500		
Total variance	17,500		17,500
Actual fixed cost for actual production			245,000

107 GOGGLE

Budgeted/standard cost for actual production (W1)			54,591
Variances	**Favourable**	**Adverse**	
Direct materials price	1,401		
Direct materials usage	390		
Direct labour rate	129		
Direct labour efficiency		208	
Variable overhead expenditure		149	
Variable overhead efficiency		1,006	
Fixed overhead expenditure	650		
Fixed overhead volume		837	
Total variance	2,570	2,200	370 F
Actual cost of actual production			54,221

(W1) £59,444 × 13,500/14,700 = £54,591

Budgeted/standard variable cost for actual production (W2)			45,178
Budgeted fixed costs			10,250
Variances	**Favourable**	**Adverse**	
Direct materials price	1,401		
Direct materials usage	390		
Direct labour rate	129		
Direct labour efficiency		208	
Variable overhead expenditure		149	
Variable overhead efficiency		1,006	
Fixed overhead expenditure	650		
Total variance	2,570	1,363	1,207 F
Actual cost of actual production			54,221

(W2) £20,520 + £24,436 + £4,238 = £49,194 × 13,500/14,700 = £45,178

108 PUG

Budgeted/standard cost for actual production (W1)			57,443
Variances	**Favourable**	**Adverse**	
Direct materials price	1,820		
Direct materials usage		390	
Direct labour rate	0	0	
Direct labour efficiency	80		
Variable overhead expenditure		2,236	
Variable overhead efficiency	465		
Fixed overhead expenditure		650	
Fixed overhead volume	910		
Total variance	3,275	3,276	1 A
Actual cost of actual production			57,444

(W1) £52,221 × 14,300/13,000 = £57,443

Budgeted/standard variable cost for actual production (W2)			47,433
Budgeted fixed costs			9,100
Variances	**Favourable**	**Adverse**	
Direct materials price	1,820		
Direct materials usage		390	
Direct labour rate	0	0	
Direct labour efficiency	80		
Variable overhead expenditure		2,236	
Variable overhead efficiency	465		
Fixed overhead expenditure		650	
Total variance	2,365	3,276	911 A
Actual cost of actual production			57,444

(W2) £19,500 + £20,150 + £3,471 = £43,121 × 14,300/13,000 = £47,433

109 TASKFORCE/OVUNABS

Materials

AQ	×	AP			
86,625 kg	×		£256,410		
AQ	×	Std P		£3,465	Favourable
86,625 kg	×	£3	£259,875		
Std Q × A Prod	×	Std P		£12,375	Adverse
2kg × 41,250	×	£3	£247,500		

Labour

AH	×	AR					
61,875 hrs	×		£173,250				
AH	×	Std R		£12,375	Adverse		
61,875 hrs	×	£2.60	£160,875			£12,375	Adverse
Std H × A Prod	×	Std R		Nil			
1.5hrs × 41,250	×	£2.60	£160,875				

Var OH

AH	×	AR			
61,875 hrs	×		£84,150		
AH	×	Std R		£2,475	Favourable
61,875 hrs	×	£1.40	£86,625		
Std H × A Prod	×	Std R		Nil	
1.5hrs × 41,250	×	£1.40	£86,625		

Fixed OH

Actual			£120,000		
			Expenditure	£2,000	Adverse
Budget			£118,000		
			Volume	£3,687.50	Favourable
AP	×	OAR			
41,250	×	£2.95	£121,687.50		

Standard absorption cost of actual production = £247,500 + £160,875 + £86,625 + £121,687.50 = £616,687.50

Standard absorption cost of actual production		616,687.50
Variance	**Favourable/ Adverse/No variance**	
Material price	Favourable	3,465.00
Material usage	Adverse	12,375.00
Direct labour rate	Adverse	12,375.00
Direct labour efficiency	No variance	0.00
Variable overhead rate	Favourable	2,475.00
Variable overhead efficiency	No variance	0.00
Fixed overheads: expenditure variance	Adverse	2,000.00
Fixed overheads: volume variance	Favourable	3,687.50
Total actual cost of actual production		633,810.00

Overhead absorbed	22,000 ×	OAR =	
Overhead incurred			180,000
Over/(under) absorption			7,000

Overhead absorbed must be 187,000, therefore the OAR is:

OAR = 187,000/22,000 = £8.50

Actual overhead			180,000	
		Expenditure variance		
Budgeted Overhead				
		Volume variance	4,250	Favourable
Actual production × OAR	22,000	× £8.50 =	187,000	

Budgeted overhead = 187,000 – 4,250 =182,750

Budgeted units = 182,750/8.50 = 21,500

Budgeted units	21,500
Budgeted overhead (£)	182,750
Overhead absorption rate (£ to 2DP)	8.50

110 BUDGETARY CONTROL REPORT

Standard cost for actual production = £586,000/4,000 × 4,200 = £615,300.

Budgeted/Standard cost for actual production	4,200	£146.50	£615,300
Variances	**Favourable**	**Adverse**	
Direct materials price		£2,300	
Direct materials usage		£5,000	
Direct labour rate	£1,760		
Direct labour efficiency		£2,800	
Variable overhead expenditure		£30,000	
Variable overhead efficiency		£12,000	
Fixed overhead expenditure		£20,000	
Fixed overhead volume	£12,000		
Total variance	£13,760	£72,100	£58,340 A
Actual cost of actual production			£673,640

111 BUDGET V ACTUAL

Budgeted/Standard cost for actual production			351,600
Variances	**Favourable**	**Adverse**	
Direct materials price		1,152	
Direct materials usage	4,080		
Direct labour rate		1,008	
Direct labour efficiency		2,880	
Fixed overhead expenditure	14,192		
Fixed overhead volume		8,000	
Total variance	18,272	13,040	5,232
Actual cost of actual production			346,368

112 OPERATING STATEMENT

Budgeted/Standard variable cost for actual production (W1)			105,600
Budgeted fixed costs			350,000
Variances	**Favourable**	**Adverse**	
Direct materials price (oranges)		6,400	
Direct materials price (cartons)		5	
Direct materials usage (oranges)	15,200		
Direct materials usage (cartons)		5	
Direct labour rate	900		
Direct labour efficiency		2,250	
Fixed overhead expenditure		15,000	
Total variance	16,100	23,660	7,560
Actual cost of actual production			463,160

(W1) £84,000 + £1,750 + £26,250 = £112,000 × 33,000/35,000 = £105,600

CONTROLLABLE AND UNCONTROLLABLE VARIANCES

113 BUGLE (1)

AQ × AP

3,500 kg × £? = £31,500

AQ × RP

3,500 × £9.50 = £33,250

Controllable price variance = £1,750 F

Correct answer is **B**

114 BUGLE (2)

AQ × RP

3,500 × £9.50 = £33,250

AQ × SP

3,500 × £10 = £35,000

Uncontrollable price variance = £1,750 F

Correct answer is **B**

115 BUGLE (3)

AQ × SP

3,500 kg × £10 = £35,000

RQ × SP

1,000 × 3.2 kg × £10 = £32,000

Controllable usage variance = £3,000 A

Correct answer is **A**

116 BUGLE (4)

RQ × SP

1,000 × 3.2 kg × £10 = £32,000

SQ × SP

1,000 × 3 kg × £10 = £30,000

Uncontrollable usage variance = £2,000 A

Correct answer is **A**

117 BUST (1)

AQ × AP

50,500 kg × £? = £350,000

AQ × RP

50,500 × £6.95 = £350,975

Controllable price variance = £975 F

Correct answer is **A**

118 BUST (2)

AQ × RP

50,500 × £6.95 = £350,975

AQ × SP

50,500 × £7 = £353,500

Uncontrollable price variance = £2,525 F

Correct answer is **D**

119 BUST (3)

AQ × SP

50,500 kg × £7 = £353,500

RQ × SP

10,000 × 4.9 kg × £7 = £343,000

Controllable usage variance = £10,500 A

Correct answer is **C**

120 BUST (4)

RQ × SP

10,000 × 4.9 kg × £7 = £343,000

SQ × SP

10,000 × 5 kg × £7 = £350,000

Uncontrollable usage variance = £7,000 F

Correct answer is **A**

121 CONTROLLABLE

Revised price = £7 × 110/100 = £7.70

Revised quantity = 5 kg × 108/90 = 6 kg

AQ × AP

50,250 kg × £? = £360,000

AQ × RP

50,250 × £7.70 = £386,925

Controllable price variance = £26,925 F

AQ × RP

50,250 × £7.70 = £386,925

AQ × SP

50,250 × £7 = £351,750

Uncontrollable price variance = £35,175 A

AQ × SP

50,250 × £7 = £351,750

RQ × SP

10,500 × 6 kg × £7 = £441,000

Controllable usage variance = £89,250 F

RQ × SP

10,500 × 6 kg × £7 = £441,000

SQ × SP

10,500 × 5 kg × £7 = £367,500

Uncontrollable usage variance = £73,500 A

122 UNCONTROLLABLE

Revised price = £10 × 115/100 = £11.50

Revised quantity = 8 kg × 105/100 = 8.4 kg

AQ × AP

9,000 kg × £? = £107,900

AQ × RP

9,000 × £11.50 = £103,500

Controllable price variance = £4,400 A

AQ × RP

9,000 × £11.50 = £103,500

AQ × SP

9,000 x £10 = £90,000

Uncontrollable price variance = £13,500 A

AQ × SP

9,000 × £10 = £90,000

RQ × SP

1,000 × 8.4 kg × £10 = £84,000

Controllable usage variance = £6,000 A

RQ × SP

1,000 × 8.4 kg × £10 = £84,000

SQ × SP

1,000 × 8 kg × £10 = £80,000

Uncontrollable usage variance = £4,000 A

TIMES SERIES, LINEAR REGRESSION AND INDEXING

123 TREND

	Q1	*Q2*	*Q3*	*Q4*
Average price	£30	£34	£54	£66
Seasonal variation	–£4	–£8	+£4	+£8
Trend	£34	£42	£50	£58

The trend in prices is an increase of **£8** per quarter.

124 RPI

	2008	*2009*	*2010*
Cost per kg of materials	£17.00	£18.60	£19.40
RPI	184	192	200
Cost/RPI × 100	£9.23913	£9.6875	£9.70

£9.70 – £9.23913/£9.23913 × 100 = 4.99 %

Correct answer is **C**

125 PRODUCT Z

		Oct	*Dec*
Cost	£30	£36	£32
Index	100		107

Index = 100/£30 × £32 = 107

Decrease = (£32 – £36)/£36 = 11.1%

Correct answer is **A**

126 TANZANITE

	Jan	*Feb*	*Mar*
Actual price	Actual price was £6.90	Actual price was £7.00	Actual price was £7.40
Seasonal variation	Seasonal variation was –10p	Seasonal variation was –15p	Seasonal variation was 10p
Trend	£7.00	£7.15	£7.30

The trend in prices is an increase of **£0.15** per month.

127 MARCH

	Jan	*Feb*	*March*
Total cost	£450,000	£500,000	£650,000
Total quantity purchased	20,000 m	25,000 m	27,500 m
Cost per m	£22.50	£20.00	£23.64
Index	100		105

£23.64/£22.50 × 100 = 105.067

Correct answer is **A**: 105

128 COST PER UNIT

	Jan	*Feb*	*Apr*
Cost	£50	£52	£56
Index	100		112

(£56 – £50)/£50 × 100 = 12% increase, and an index of 112.

Correct answer is **A**

129 PRODUCT Y

Apr	*May*	*Jun*
Actual price was £6.56	Actual price was £7.14	Actual price was £7.35
Seasonal variation was (£0.30)	Seasonal variation was £0.14	Seasonal variation was £0.21
6.86	7.00	7.14

The trend in prices is an increase of **£0.14** per month.

130 A COMPANY

	Jan	*Feb*	*March*
Total cost	£100,000	£132,000	£127,000
Total quantity purchased	10,000 kgs	12,000 kgs	11,500 kgs
Cost per kg	£10	£11	£11.04
Index	100		110 (W1)

(W1) 11.04/10 × 100 = 110

Correct answer is **B**

131 PRODUCT X

		Jan	*Apr*
Cost per unit	£42	£46	£52
Index	100		123.8 (W1)

(W1) £52/£42 × 100 = 123.8

The increase from January to April is: (52 – 46)/46 = 13%

Correct answer is **A**

132 INDEX

	Past	*May*	*July*
Cost per unit	70	82	96
Index	100	117 (W2)	137 (W1)

(W1) £96 × 100/70 = 137

(W2) £82 × 100/70 = 117

Increase from May to July: (137 – 117)/117 = 17%

Correct answer is **A**

133 DEXTER

Base	*June*	*September*
1,080	1,350	1,710
100		?

Index in September = 1,710/1,080 × 100 = 158

Increase from June to September 1,710 – 1,350/1,350 = 26.67%

The correct answer is **D**

134 WASTE

	Jan	*Feb*	*March*
Kgs	1000	1250	1100
Price per kilo	5	6	7
Total cost	£5,000	£7,500	£7,700
Index	100		?

£7/£5 × 100 = 140

The correct answer is **B**

135 FIZZ

Jan	*Feb*	*Mar*
Actual price was £550	Actual price was £675	Actual price was £650
Seasonal variation was –£50	Seasonal variation was + £50	Seasonal variation was Nil
£600	£625	£650

The trend in prices is an increase of **£25** per month.

136 ACRID

Jan	*Feb*	*Mar*
Actual price was £50	Actual price was £50	Actual price was £65
Seasonal variation was £5	Seasonal variation was – £5	Seasonal variation was Nil
£45	£55	£65

The trend in prices is an increase of **£10** per month.

137 PRODUCT J

Apr	*May*	*Jun*
Actual price was £7.20	Actual price was £7.50	Actual price was £6.90
Seasonal variation was £0.10	Seasonal variation was £0.20	Seasonal variation was (£0.60)
£7.10	£7.30	£7.50

The trend in prices is an increase of **£0.20** per month.

138 ABCO

	October	*November*	*December*
Total cost	£1,250	£1,390	£1,610
Quantity purchased	1,000 kg	1,100 kg	1,200 kg
Cost per kg	£1.25	£1.26	£1.34
Index	100		(W1) 107

The cost index for December based upon October prices is:

(W1) £1.34/£1.25 × 100 = 107

Correct answer is **B**

139 SOAP

September	= £1,200 × 126/105	£1,440
October	= £1,200 × 119/105	£1,360
November	= £1,200 × 133/105	£1,520

140 ASPHALT

June = X = 26, therefore Y = 125 + (2 × 26) = £177 per tonne

July = X = 27, therefore Y = 125 + (2 × 27) = £179 per tonne

June = 177/175 × 100 = 101.14

July = 179/175 × 100 = 102.29

141 BEST FIT

In June X = 26, therefore Y = 25.97 + (3.56 × 26) = £118.53

142 LEAST

In July X = 49, therefore Y = 105.97 + (12.56 × 49) = £721.41

143 MOST

June = X = 21, therefore Y = 15 + (4 × 21) = £99

July = X = 22, therefore Y = 15 + (4 × 22) = £103

May = X = 20, therefore Y = 15 + (4 × 20) = £95

June = 99/95 × 100 = 104.21

July = 103/95 × 100 = 108.42

144 TEA

	June X7 £	*Nov X7* £
Cost per Kg of tea	4.95	5.10
Base cost	4.80	4.80
Index	103.125	106.25

£4.80 × 108.25/100 = £5.20 or £4.80 × 108.25/100 = £5.196

£5.20/£4.80 – 1 = 8.33% or £5.196/£4.80 = 8.25%

145 FRUIT

	May X6	*June X6*	*July X6*	*Aug X6*
Cost per 1,000 kgs	£1,000	£900	£700	£800
Seasonal variation	£200	£100	–£100	£0
Trend	£800	£800	£800	£800

850/800 – 1 = 6.25% or (850 – 800)/8 = 6.25%

	May X7	*June X7*	*July X7*	*Aug X7*
Trend	£850	£850	£850	£850
Seasonal variation	£200	£100	–£100	£0
Cost per 1,000 kgs	£1,050	£950	£750	£850

146 YANKEE (2)

The seasonally adjusted sales volume for EACH of the FOUR quarters for Yankee Ltd are:

	Q1	*Q2*	*Q3*	*Q4*
Actual sales volumes	224,000	196,000	215,000	265,000
Seasonal variations	14,000	–24,000	–15,000	25,000
Trend	210,000	220,000	230,000	240,000

210,000	220,000	230,000	240,000

The seasonally adjusted growth in sales volume from Quarter 1 to Quarter 4 for Yankee Ltd is:

14%

(£240,000 – £210,000)/£210,000 × 100 = 14.28%

Should the Sales Manager be paid his bonus? **NO**

147 SEB

	Apr X3	*May X3*	*Jun X3*
Cost per litre of XYZ	£104.55	£107.70	£110.85
Increase per month		£3.15	£3.15

	July X3	*September X3*
Cost per litre of XYZ	£110.85 + £3.15 = £114.00	£114.00 + £3.15 + £3.15 = £120.30

148 TOAST

(a) Trend figures

	20X3 Qtr 1	20X3 Qtr 2	20X3 Qtr 3	20X3 Qtr 4
Actual	£3,200	£3,020	£3,320	£3,060
Seasonal variation	+£200	-£80	+£120	-£240
Trend	**£3,000**	**£3,100**	**£3,200**	**£3,300**

(b) The value of a and b in the equation Y = a + bX

b = (3300 – 3000)/(27 – 24)

a = 3300 – (27 × 100)

	£
b	**100**
a	**600**

(c) Trend for 20X7 quarter 1 and 3:

	workings	Trend (£)
20X7 Qtr 1	X = 40: y = 600 + 100 × 40 =	**4,600**
20X7 Qtr 3	X = 42: y = 600 + 100 × 42 =	**4,800**

(d) Forecast cost for 20X7 quarter 2 and 4.

	workings	Forecast (£)
20X7 Qtr 2	X= 41: y = 600 + 100 × 41 = 4,700, F = 4,700 – 80 =	**4,620**
20X7 Qtr 4	X= 43: y = 600 + 100 × 43 = 4,900, F = 4,900 – 240 =	**4,660**

(e) Quarter 1 and 2 of 20X8 expressed these as an index number with base Qtr 1 20X3.

	workings	Index number (2DP)
20X8 Qtr 1	X = 44: y = 600 + 100 × 44 = 5,000; F = 5,000 + 200 = 5,200; Index = 5,200/3,200 × 100 =	**162.50**
20X8 Qtr 2	X = 45: y = 600 + 100 × 45 = 5,100; F = 5,100 – 80 = 5,020; Index = 5,020/3,200 × 100 =	**156.88**

149 COAST

(a)

	20X2 Qtr 1	*20X2 Qtr 2*	*20X2 Qtr 3*	*20X2 Qtr 4*
Actual paid	**440,000**	418,500	**572,000**	791,000
Quantity purchased	10,000	**9,000**	11,000	**14,000**
Cost per kg	44.00	**46.50**	**52.00**	**56.50**
Seasonal variation	-5.00	-3.00	+2.00	+6.00
Trend	**49.00**	**49.50**	**50.00**	**50.50**

(b) Index = 50/44 × 100 =

114

150 STATATAC

(a)

20X6 volume of units (000)	*July*	*August*	*September*
Trend	**90**	**95**	100
Seasonal variation	10	5	**–8**
Seasonally adjusted sales	**100**	100	92

(b)

20X7 volume of units (000)	*October*	*November*	*December*
Trend	**165**	**170**	**175**
Seasonal variation	–10	–12	–15
Seasonally adjusted sales	**155**	**158**	**160**

(c) £12 × 1.12 = £**13.44**

(d) 14.50/£12 × 100 = 120.8333 ≈ **121**

151 TEX-MEX-INDEX

(a)

Year	Index	Price per kg £
20X2	105	**4.73**
20X3	**108**	4.87
20X4	110	**4.95**
20X5	**102**	4.61
20X6	**107**	4.82
20X7	115	**5.18**

(b) The percentage increase in price from 20X4 to 20X6 is **21.74** %

(140 -115)/115 × 100 = 21.74

The price in 20X7 is £**11.97**.per kg

152/127 × £10 = 11.97

(c)

20X7 volume of units (000)	*Quarter 1*	*Quarter 2*	*Quarter 3*	*Quarter 4*
Trend	100	**110**	**120**	**130**
Seasonal variation	–50	**+20**	+90	–60
Seasonally adjusted sales	**50**	130	**210**	70

VARIANCE ANALYSIS WRITTEN QUESTIONS

152 ARTETA

To: Junior accounting technician **Subject:** Material variances

From: AAT Technician **Date:** Today

Total direct material variance

The total direct material variance compares the flexed budget for materials with the actual cost incurred. The flexed budget is the budgeted cost of materials for the actual production level – 11,000 units in this example. It is incorrect to calculate the variance as £33,500 – £30,000 = £3,500 as you will not be comparing like with like in terms of activity level.

The flexing of the budget calculates the quantity of materials which are expected to be used in actual production. Therefore, the expected usage of materials to produce 11,000 units is 15,000 kg/10,000 units × 11,000 units = 16,500 kg. The expected cost would be 16,500 kg x the standard price per kg of £2 (£30,000/15,000 kg) = £33,000.

This flexed budget can now be compared with the actual costs to produce a total material variance of £500 (£33,500 – £33,000).

This variance is adverse because the actual cost was greater than the flexed budgeted cost.

This total variance can now be split into two elements:

- The variance due to the price being different from that expected – called the material price variance
- The variance due to the quantity of material used being different from that expected – called the material usage variance.

The expected price was £2 per kg and therefore the expected cost of 16,000 kg would be 16,000 × £2 = £32,000.

The price variance can now be calculated by comparing the actual cost of £33,500 with the expected cost of £32,000. This gives a variance of £1,500 which is adverse because the actual cost is greater than the expected cost.

The material usage variance is calculated by taking the quantity of materials which would be expected to be used to produce the actual volume of production. In this case 11,000 units were produced and the expected quantity of material for each unit was 1.5 kg (15,000 kg/10,000 units). Therefore, to produce 11,000 units requires 11,000 × 1.5 kg = 16,500 kg. Comparing this to the actual quantity used (only 16,000 kg) produces a variance of 500 kg. This needs to be valued at the expected cost of £2 per kg giving a favourable variance of £1,000.

The usage variance is always valued at standard cost (expected cost or budgeted cost) because the price variance has already been isolated, If both variances have been calculated correctly they should reconcile back to the total materials variance. In this example:

Price variance 1,500 A + Usage variance 1000 F = Total variance 500 A

153 MERTESACKER

To:	Junior accounting technician	**Subject:**	Labour variances
From:	AAT Technician	**Date:**	Today

Total direct labour variance

The total direct labour variance compares the flexed budget for labour with the actual cost incurred. The flexed budget is the budgeted cost of labour for the actual production level – 95 units in this example. It is incorrect to calculate the variance as £31,500 – £30,000 = £1,500 as you will not be comparing like with like in terms of activity level.

The flexing of the budget calculates the amount of labour hours which are expected to be used in actual production. Therefore, the expected hours to produce 95 units is 1,500 hours/100 units × 95 units = 1,425 hours. The expected cost would be 1,425 hours × the standard rate per hour of £20 (£30,000/1,500 hrs) = £28,500.

This flexed budget can now be compared with the actual costs to produce a total labour variance of £3,000 (£28,500 – £31,500).

This variance is adverse because the actual cost was greater than the flexed budgeted cost.

This total variance can now be split into two elements:

- The variance due to the rate being different from that expected – called the labour rate variance
- The variance due to the hours of labour used being different from that expected – called the labour efficiency variance.

The expected rate was £20 per hour and therefore the expected cost of 1,600 hours would be 1,600 × £20 = £32,000.

The rate variance can now be calculated by comparing the actual cost of £31,500 with the expected cost of £32,000. This gives a variance of £500 which is favourable because the actual cost is less than the expected cost.

The labour efficiency variance is calculated by taking the hours of labour which would be expected to be used to produce the actual volume of production. In this case 95 units were produced and the expected labour hours for each unit were 15 hours (1,500 hrs/100 units). Therefore, to produce 95 units requires 95 × 15 hrs = 1,425 hrs. Comparing this to the actual hours used (1,600 hours) produces a variance of 175 hrs. This needs to be valued at the expected rate of £20 per hour giving an adverse variance of £3,500.

The efficiency variance is always valued at standard rate (expected rate or budgeted rate) because the rate variance has already been isolated, If both variances have been calculated correctly they should reconcile back to the total labour variance. In this example:

Rate variance 500 F + Efficiency variance 3,500 A = Total variance 3,000 A

154 TOP DOG

To:	Managing Director	**Subject:**	Analysis of variances
From:	AAT student	**Date:**	1 May 2012

Direct materials price variance – £1,152 A

The direct material price variance is adverse which means that Top Dog has spent more on materials than expected. i.e. the material cost per kilogram was higher than expected.

This may have arisen due to the purchaser buying better quality materials which were more expensive.

The purchaser might want to consider other suppliers in the future so as to reduce the price. (Alternatively, they may want to update their standard for the increased price if it is going to be permanent.)

Direct materials usage variance – £4,080 F

The direct material usage variance is favourable which means that Top Dog has used fewer materials than expected during production.

This may have arisen due to better quality materials being bought which reduced the possible wastage, or it may have enabled the workers to work more quickly. i.e. less rework.

The material price and usage variance are often linked in that a price increase (adverse variance) will often lead to a usage decrease (favourable variance) and vice versa.

Top Dog has overspent on materials by £1,152 but then used fewer materials by £4,080. This leads to a possible net saving of £2,928. Top dog may want to consider continuing this strategy. They should investigate whether it is possible every period.

The wage rate may have risen with inflation which would cause the adverse variance. (Or more experienced staff could have been used who are paid a higher rate.)

Labour rate variance – £1,008 A

The labour rate variance is adverse which means that Top Dog has spent more on wages than expected. i.e. the wage rate was higher than expected.

If the wage rate rose due to inflation, and this was to remain stable, Top Dog may wish to revise their standard. Alternatively, if more experienced staff were used they may want to look at this variance in conjunction with the labour efficiency variance (less efficient) which might mean that the more experienced staff are not worth the extra cost. On the other hand, linking it to the favourable material usage variance also, overall Top Dog is slightly better off by employing more expensive, more experienced staff.

Labour efficiency variance – £2,880 A

The labour efficiency variance is adverse which means that Top Dog has spent longer on production than expected.

This could be due to a machine breakdown, where idle time might be included in the efficiency variance. (Or expensive staff may have been used who were not familiar with Top Dog's processes and therefore took longer.)

If the inefficiency was due to a machine breakdown and idle time, then maintenance of the machines might need to be improved.

Fixed overhead expenditure variance – £14,192 F

The fixed overhead expenditure variance is favourable which means that Top Dog has actually spent less on fixed overheads than budgeted.

Fixed overheads might include rent of the factory. The rent may have been reduced by the landlord.

Future negotiations with their landlord might secure further low rents.

Fixed overhead volume variance – £8,000 A

The fixed overhead volume variance is adverse which means that Top Dog has under absorbed their fixed overhead.

This has arisen due to actual production being only 2,400 units whereas the budget was to produce 2,500 units.

Training of the workforce may be necessary to improve the speed of output. Alternatively, a customer may have been lost and production was scaled down during the period since fewer barrels were required.

Note: Only one reason was required for each variance. Several have been given in this answer to aid learning.

155 OPSTAT

To:	Managing Director	**Subject:**	Analysis of variances
From:	AAT student	**Date:**	1 June 2012

Direct materials (oranges) price variance – £6,400 A

The direct material price variance is adverse which means that Opstat has spent more on oranges than expected.

This may have arisen due to the purchaser buying better quality oranges which were more expensive.

The purchaser might want to consider other suppliers in the future so as to reduce the price. (Alternatively, they may want to update their standard for the increased price if it is going to be permanent.)

Direct materials (oranges) usage variance – £15,200 F

The direct material (oranges) usage variance is favourable which means that Opstat has used fewer oranges than expected during production.

This may have arisen due to better quality/stronger tasting oranges being bought which reduced the possible quantity needed, or it may be that fewer oranges have been wasted.

The material price and usage variance are often linked in that a price increase (adverse variance) will often lead to a usage decrease (favourable variance) and vice versa.

Opstat has overspent on oranges by £6,400 but then used fewer oranges by £15,200. This leads to a net saving of £8,800. Opstat may want to consider continuing this strategy. They should investigate whether it is possible every period.

Direct materials (cartons) price variance – £5 A

This variance is adverse by only a very small amount.

It has arisen by spending slightly more on the cartons than expected.

This may not be worth investigating by management.

Direct materials (cartons) usage variance – £5 A

This variance is adverse by only a very small amount and may not be worth investigating by management.

It has arisen by using slightly more cartons than expected i.e. 100 cartons look to have been wasted (33,100 cartons used for 33,000 units).

A small number of cartons may have been lost or been identified as soiled leading to them being discarded.

Control over the cartons should be improved by keeping them clean and in an orderly manner.

Labour rate variance – £900 F

The labour rate variance is favourable which means that Opstat has spent less on wages than expected i.e. the wage rate was lower than expected.

The wage rate may have fallen due to employing less experienced staff who would have been paid a lower rate.

Opstat might consider doing this in the future which might improve their profits.

Labour efficiency variance – £2,250 A

The labour efficiency variance is adverse which means that Opstat has spent longer on production than expected.

This could be due to using cheaper staff who are less experienced or it could be due to a machine breakdown, where idle time might be included in the efficiency variance.

If the wage rate fell Opstat may wish to look at this variance in conjunction with the labour efficiency variance (less efficient) which might mean that the less experienced staff are not worth the lower cost i.e. the adverse efficiency variance outweighs the favourable rate variance.

If the inefficiency was due to a machine breakdown and idle time, then maintenance of the machines might need to be improved.

Fixed overhead expenditure variance – £15,000 A

The fixed overhead expenditure variance is adverse which means that Opstat has actually spent more on fixed overheads than budgeted.

Fixed overheads might include rent of the factory. The rent may have been increased by the landlord.

Opstat may need to revise their budget for fixed overheads. Alternatively they could investigate which cost, such as rent, might have risen and look for ways to reduce it .e.g. discussions with their landlord might secure a lower rent.

Fixed overhead volume variance – £20,000 A

The fixed overhead volume variance is adverse which means that Opstat has under absorbed their fixed overhead.

This has arisen due to actual production being only 33,000 units whereas the budget was to produce 35,000 units.

A customer may have been lost and production scaled down during the period since fewer cartons of orange were now required. A new customer could be found.

Training of the workforce may be necessary to improve the speed of output.

Note: Only one reason was required for each variance. Several have been given in this answer to aid learning.

156 DIXON

To:	Production Director	**Subject:**	Variances
From:	Accounting Technician	**Date:**	XX/XX/20XX

TR13 price variance

The TR13 price variance is likely to be favourable.

This is due to a reduction in price of 10% during the month, resulting in the actual price being lower than the standard price.

The quality of the latest batch of TR13 is higher than expected even though the price is lower, which may lead to a favourable TR13 usage variance.

TR13 usage variance

The TR13 usage variance is likely to be favourable.

The purchase of a higher quality product would usually be expected to result in less wastage, and therefore the actual quantity used would be lower than the standard usage.

The usage and price variances are often linked when a higher priced and therefore higher quality product may reduce wastage costs, however in this case the higher quality is probably due to the advances in production of TR13 and so is unlikely to be linked with the TR13 price variance.

Also employees may be demotivated by the lack of pay rise but the new material usage control policy recently implemented should keep material usage favourable.

Direct labour efficiency variance

The direct labour efficiency variance is likely to be adverse, with each unit taking more hours to manufacture than expected. Efficiency will be affected by the demotivation caused by the suspension of the pay rise.

In addition the cancelled order means that production will be lower by 33% during the month and there is likely to be idle time for employees which will have an adverse effect on the labour efficiency.

Fixed overhead expenditure variance

The fixed overhead expenditure variance is likely to be adverse, due to costs of resetting the machine and the repair of the defective machine. Therefore the actual fixed overheads will be higher than expected.

Fixed overhead volume variance

The fixed overhead volume variance is likely to be adverse because the actual volume produced is likely to be 33% lower than the forecast volume due to the cancellation of the order for 500 units. Therefore overheads are likely to be under-absorbed.

157 GRIPPIT (2)

(a) (i) Standard labour rate per hour

£4,800, budgeted cost/600, budgeted labour hours = **£8 per hour**

(ii) Standard labour hours for actual production

600hours/200 tonnes × 210 tonnes = **630 hours**

(iii) Budgeted cost per tonne of Crumb

£94,800 total budgeted cost/200 tonnes, the budgeted output = **£474**

(iv) Budgeted overhead absorption rate per tonne

£90,000, fixed overheads/200 tonnes, the budgeted output = **£450**

(v) Overheads absorbed into actual production

210 units produced × £450, the absorption rate = **£94,500**

(vi) The total standard cost of actual production

£474 (94,800/200 tonnes), standard cost per tonne × 210 tonnes

Actual output = **£99,540**

(b) (i) Direct labour rate variance

AH × AR

600 hrs × = £5,100

AH × SR

600 hrs × £8 = £4,800

(Standard rate = £4,800/600 hrs = £8)

=> **£300 (A)**

(ii) Direct labour efficiency variance

AH × SR

600 hrs × £8 = £4,800

SH × SR

210 tonnes × 3 × £8 = £5,040

(Standard hours per tonne = 600 hrs/200 tonnes = 3 hrs per tonne)

=> **£240 (F)**

(iii) Fixed overhead expenditure variance

Actual expenditure £95,000

Budgeted expenditure £90,000

=> **£5,000 (A)**

(iv) Fixed overhead volume variance

Budgeted expenditure £90,000

AP × SH × SR

210 tonnes × 3 hrs × £150 per hr = £94,500

£4,500 (F)

(c) Standard cost for actual production = £94,800 × 210/200 = **£99,540**

Budgeted/Standard cost for actual production	210 units	× £474	£99,540
Variances	**Favourable**	**Adverse**	
Direct labour rate		£300	
Direct labour efficiency	£240		
Fixed overhead expenditure		£5,000	
Fixed overhead volume	£4,500		
Total variance	£4,740	£5,300	£560
Actual cost of actual production			£100,100

To: Finance Director **Subject:** Reason for variances

From: AAT student **Date:** 16 June 2008

(i) **Direct labour rate variance**

The variance was £300 adverse. The actual cost of labour was £8.50 compared to the expected cost of £8. The Production Director has stated that a 25p per hour pay rise was awarded after the standard had been set, this therefore accounts for half of the variance. The other half of the variance must have been caused by some other reason such as overtime.

(ii) **Direct labour efficiency variance**

The variance was £240 favourable. The software upgrade is said to reduce the standard time to 2.7 hours per tonne, the actual labour time was 2.86 hours per tonne (actual hours of 600/ actual output of 210). Therefore the expected efficiency reduction was not achieved. The upgrade has improved efficiency but perhaps it will take time for the full 10% effect to be realised. There may be initial teething problems.

(iii) **Fixed overhead expenditure variance**

The variance was £5,000 adverse. The IT upgrade cost £120,000 for a 2-year licence which equates to £5,000 per month. Therefore the £5,000 expenditure variance is due to this upgrade.

(iv) **Fixed overhead volume variance**

This variance was £4,500 favourable. The expected volume of output was 200 tonnes, while the actual output was 210 tonnes. This could be due to the software upgrade improving labour efficiency which in turn produced more output per hour and hence increased the volume.

158 VARIANCE ETHICS

Ethical issues

The bonus structure at Variance Ltd could lead to problems with the production manager's integrity and objectivity.

The objectivity issue is caused by the self interest in the bonus, that the manager may make decision to ensure favourable labour variances to the detriment of Variance Ltd as a whole.

Integrity issues could be around the way she manages the employees, the materials usage variance does not impact the bonus so she could unfairly treat staff who are considerate of material waste to encourage speed.

Goal congruence issues

In terms of goal congruence, the ultimate aim should be the long term success of Variance Ltd.

The way the bonus is currently structured the manager will not be worried about the material price variance, the £6,000 adverse variance, could be an overspend on materials to get superior quality for the workers so they can do their work quicker.

Similarly, the £10,000 adverse materials usage variance could be because the manager encourages speed and a favourable labour efficiency variance over good use of the quality materials purchased.

159 WOODEN SPOON

(a)

To: Manager	**Subject:** Standard setting at Wooden Spoon
From: Accounting Technician	**Date:** 24/3/20X7

(i) **Types of standard**

Wood and treatment – the volumes appear to be based on a basic standard as they have remained unchanged since the company began.

There have been changes in design over the years which have not been reflected in the standard.

The standard appears to be too easy to achieve.

Labour – It appears the labour time is based on an ideal standard as it is based on no wastage, but the rate is based on a basic standard.

It appears unlikely that anyone could achieve this standard.

(ii) **Behavioural implications**

Note – as you've been asked to evaluate try to include positive and negatives for each standard used.

Wood and treatment

The positive here is that a comparison to the standard will give an indication as to how much material efficiency has improved over the years at Wooden Spoon, but the management are already aware of this so it is not that meaningful.

The negative is that given the standard is far too easy to achieve now, the workers will not have anything to strive for, as they could be inefficient based on current expectations and still post a favourable variance against this standard.

It is out of date and needs to be revised.

Labour

The positive of an ideal standard is that it could encourage workers to improve as they aim to achieve the target set.

The negative and more likely response in a situation like this, where on average 4% of time is non-productive during a year, is that a worker will feel that the standard time is unachievable and become demotivated.

The labour efficiency variance will have been adverse every single year that wooden spoon have used this standard and they could well have lost good employees who felt criticised in spite of working hard.

The labour rate variance would suffer similar issues to the materials usage based on the basic standard, which will compensate somewhat for the adverse labour efficiency variance when consulting the total variance.

Overall – the standards being used currently are not really suitable and need to be revised.

(iii) Revised standards and justification

Wood and treatment

They can produce 15% more spoons per batch than originally expected, so £3.45 will make 1.15 wooden spoons.

So the cost for one wooden spoon would now be: £3.45/1.15 = £3.00

Treatment: £0.46/1.15 = £0.40

Labour

An attainable standard would be more motivating and would include an allowance for non-productive time. If on average last year 4% of time was non-productive then it would be reasonable to assume that the productive time makes up 96% of the time allowed meaning that the new standard labour cost would be:

£4.80 × 100/96 = £5.00

This then needs to be adjusted for the higher wages:

£5.00 × 1.1 = £5.50

Overall prime cost would now be: 3.00 + 0.40 + 5.00 + 2.50 = £10.90

(assuming variable overhead varies with labour time: 2.40 × 100/96 = 2.50)

(b)

Goal Congruence

The issue highlights the problem with too much focus on financial measures.

Manager v business – the manager's decision while helping them achieve their bonus could have an adverse impact on the overall business should the delayed maintenance result in any machinery malfunction stopping production or even injuring an employee.

Short v long term – the manager is making a decision that will help hit a short term financial target, but through stoppages/delays could harm the long term survival of the business by failing to fulfil an order.

Ethics

The bonus creates a self-interest threat for the manager, which could impact their objectivity. The manager stands to benefit personally from actions they take which could have a detrimental impact on the business overall and potentially the health of the people working there.

160 FOODRINK

(a) (i) Standard price of materials per kilogram

£5,400/450 = **£12 per kg**

(ii) Standard usage of materials for actual production

9,900 × (450/9,000) = **495 kgs**

(iii) Standard labour rate per hour

4,500/300 = **£15**

(iv) Standard labour hours for actual production

9,900 × (300/9,000) = **330 hours**

(v) Budgeted overhead absorption rate per unit

18,000/9,000 = **£2**

(vi) Overheads absorbed into actual production

9,900 × £2 = **£19,800**

(b) (i) Direct material price variance

AQ × AP

5,014 × = £6,534

AQ × SP

594 × £12 = £7,128

= **£594 (F)**

(ii) Direct material usage variance

AQ × SP

5,014 × £12 = £7,128

SQ × SP

9,900 × (450/9,000) × £12 = £5,940

= **£1,188 (A)**

(iii) Direct labour rate variance

AH × AR

325 × = £4,225

AH × SR

325 × £15 = £4,875

= **£650 (F)**

(iv) Direct labour efficiency variance

AH × SR

325 × £15 = £4,875

SH × SR

9,900 × 300/9,000 × £15 = £4,950

= **£75 (F)**

(v) Fixed overhead expenditure variance

Actual expenditure £19,000

Budgeted expenditure £18,000

= £1,000 A

(vi) Fixed overhead volume variance

Budgeted expenditure £18,000

AP × SR

9,900 × (18,000/9,000) = £19,800

= **£1,800 (F)**

(c) Budgeted costs for actual production = £27,900 × 9,900/9,000 = **£30,690.**

Budgeted costs for actual production	9,900 units	× £3.10	£30,690
Variances	**Favourable**	**Adverse**	
Direct material price	£594		
Direct material usage		£1,188	
Direct labour rate	£650		
Direct labour efficiency	£75		
Fixed overhead expenditure		£1,000	
Fixed overhead volume	£1,800		
Total variance	£3,119	£2,188	–£931
Actual cost of actual production			£29,759

PERFORMANCE INDICATORS CALCULATIONS

161 BACKWARDS

Rec balance:

Rec days = Receivables/Revenue × 360

30 days = Receivables/30,000 × 360

(30 × 30,000)/360 = Receivables

£2,500 = Receivables

Pay balance:

Pay days = Payables/Cost of sales × 360

GP Margin = 30% so Cost of sales = 70% of revenue

48 days = Payables/(30,000 × 70%) × 360

(48 × 30,000 × 70%)/360 = Payables

£2,800 = Payables

Cash position:

Current ratio = Current assets/current liabilities

2 = (2,100 + 2,500 + cash)/2,800

2 × 2800 = 4,600 + cash

1,000 = cash

162 REVERSE

Sales Revenue

Rec days = Receivables/Revenue × 360

45 days = 25,000/Revenue × 360

Revenue = (25,000 × 360)/45

Revenue = 200,000

Cost of sales

Pay days = Payables/Cost of sales × 360

64 days = 18,000/Cost of sales × 360

Cost of sales = (18,000 × 360)/64

Cost of sales = 101,250

Expenses

80,000/2 = 40,000

Fixed = 40,000 × 1.05 = 42,000

Variables = 40,000 × 1.02 = £40,800

Expenses = 42,000 + 40,800 = 82,800

	£
Sales revenue	**200,000**
Cost of sales	**101,250**
Gross profit	**98,750**
Expenses	**82,800**
Net profit	**15,950**

Inventory position:

Current ratio = Current assets/current liabilities

1.9 = (5,000 + 25,000 + Inventory)/18,000

1.9 × 18,000 = 30,000 + Inventory

34,200 – 30,000 = inventory

4,200 = inventory

Year-end inventory position	**£4,200**

163 REVENUE

4 × £950,000 = £3,800,000

164 OPERATING PROFIT

RONA = Operating profit/Net assets × 100%

25% = Operating profit/£480,000 × 100%

Operating profit = £120,000

165 GROSS PROFIT

Gross profit margin = Gross profit/Sales revenue × 100

30 = Gross profit/£1,000,000 × 100

Gross profit = £300,000

166 INVENTORY

Current ratio = Current assets/Current liabilities

2 = (Inventory + £120,000)/£100,000

Inventory = £80,000

167 RECEIVABLES

Receivable days = Receivables/Sales revenue × 365

90 = £400,000/Sales revenue × 365

Sales revenue = £1,622,222

168 VALUE ADDED

Value added = Sales revenue – Cost of materials used and bought in services

Value added = £850,000 – £300,000 – £200,000

Value added = £350,000

169 PAYABLES

Payable days = Payables/Cost of sales x 365

75 = Payables/£700,000 × 365

Payables = £143,836

170 TEES R US

	Actual	*Budgeted*
Cost of tea pickers as a % of turnover	16.76%	13.33%
Cost of tea processor operators as a % of turnover	4.44%	4.44%
Cost of seeds and fertilizer as a % of turnover	9.52%	6.67%
Gross profit margin	61.65%	70.22%
Operating profit margin	4.51%	25.78%
Return on net assets	3.79%	24.37%
Net asset turnover	0.84	0.95

171 PARTY

	Party	*Topical*
Selling price per unit	7.50	10.00
Material cost per unit	2.00	1.50
Labour cost per unit	1.25	1.00
Fixed cost per unit	1.00	1.36
Gross profit margin	43.33%	61.36%
Net profit margin	18.33%	7.95%
Advertising cost as % of turnover	5.56%	45.45%
Return on net assets	16.50%	20.59%

172 FUDGE

	Fudge	*Stubbed*
Selling price per unit (£)	0.500	0.606
Material cost per unit (£)	0.078	0.091
Labour cost per unit (£)	0.109	0.076
Fixed production cost per unit (£)	0.047	0.015
Gross profit margin	53.125%	70.000%
Net profit margin	15.625%	27.500%
Advertising cost as % of turnover	18.750%	25.000%
Return on net assets	5.000%	9.167%

173 DEJAVU

	Budgeted	*Actual*
Selling price per unit	2.75	3.00
Material cost per unit	0.50	0.55
Labour cost per hour	75.00	75.00
Fixed production cost per labour hour	375.00	394.74
Gross profit margin	49.09%	51.92%
Net profit margin	23.55%	26.08%
Direct materials cost as % of turnover	18.18%	18.33%

174 GRANSDEN

	North	*South*
Gross profit margin	40.74%	37.17%
Operating profit margin	18.75%	18.00%
Wages and salaries as a percentage of turnover	7.41%	6.28%
Inventory turnover in days	91.25	121.67
Receivable collection period in days	45.63	89.34
Payable days	57.03	26.61
Return on capital employed	30.00%	18.09%

BREAK EVEN ANALYSIS

175 BE

The contribution per unit is selling price – variable costs = £20 – £5 = £15

The breakeven point in units is fixed costs/contribution per unit = £75,000/£15 = 5,000

The margin of safety in units is budgeted sales – break even sales = 6,000 – 5,000 = 1,000

The margin of safety as a percentage (to 2 decimal places) is 1,000/6,000 × 100% = 16.67%

The contribution to sales (C/S) ratio is £15/£20 = 0.75

The break even sales is fixed costs/c/s ratio = £75,000/0.75 = £100,000

(Check this by taking break even units × selling price: 5,000 units × £20 = £100,000)

176 BREAKEVEN

The contribution per unit is selling price – variable costs = £200 – £50 = £150

The breakeven point in units is fixed costs/contribution per unit = £750,000/£150 = 5,000

The margin of safety in units is budgeted sales – break even sales = 7,000 – 5,000 = 2,000

The margin of safety as a percentage (to 2 decimal places) is 2,000/7,000 × 100% = 28.57%

The contribution to sales (C/S) ratio is £150/£200 = 0.75

The break even sales is fixed costs/c/s ratio = £750,000/0.75 = £1,000,000

(Check this by taking break even units × selling price: 5,000 units × £200 = £1,000,000)

177 CRAFTY

	Current	*Future*	*Change*
Revenue	200,000	214,500	14,500
Material	(20,000)	(20,900)	(900)
Labour	(50,000)	(52,250)	(2,250)
Fixed overhead	(70,000)	(75,000)	(5,000)
Depreciation		(4,000)	(4,000)
Additional profit			2,350

The return on the additional investment would be **11.75%** (2,350/20,000 × 100).

Fixed costs (75,000 + 4,000)	£79,000
Contribution per unit [(214,500 – 20,900 – 52,250)/110,000]	£1.285
Break even volume (units)	61,479

178 PIPER

	Units	*Price/cost*	*Total*
Revenue	19,000	£120.00	2,280,000
Materials	19,000	£28.75	–546,250
Labour			–320,000
Fixed costs			–500,000
One-off profit			50,000
Total profit			963,750

The fixed costs are **£500,000**

The contribution per unit is £120 – £28.75 – £16.84 = **£74.41 per unit**

The break even sales volume is £500,000/£74.41 **= 6,720 units**

179 JOYCE

	Units	*Price/cost*	*Total*
Revenue	100,000	£50	5,000,000
Materials and labour	100,000	£25	–2,500,000
Advertising			–200,000
Depreciation			–500,000
Profit			1,800,000

Additional investment/additional assets = £1,800,000/£3,000,000 = **60%**

Year 1

The fixed costs are £500,000 plus £200,000 (year 1) = **£700,000**

The contribution per unit is £50 less £25 = **£25 per unit**

The break even sales volume is (700,000/25) **28,000 units.**

Year 2

The fixed costs are **£500,000**

The contribution per unit is £60 less £30 = **£30 per unit**

The break even sales volume is **16,667 units.**

180 DAGGER

	Units	*Price/cost*	*Total*
Revenue	18,000	12	216,000
Materials	18,000	3	(54,000)
Labour			(100,000)
Fixed costs			(50,000)
Total profit			12,000

The fixed costs are **£50,000**

The contribution per unit is **£3.44** (62,000/18,000)

The break even sales volume is **14,535 units.**

181 BOSUN

	Units	*Price/cost*	*Total*
Revenue	20,000	900	18,000,000
Materials	20,000	212.50	(4,250,000)
Labour			(4,800,000)
Fixed costs			(2,200,000)
Total profit			6,750,000

The fixed costs are **£2,200,000**

The contribution per unit is **£447.50** (8,950,000/20,000)

The break even sales volume is **4,917 units**.

182 KEEL

	Units	*Price/cost*	*Total*
Increase in revenue	20,000	20	400,000
Increase in material cost	20,000	3.75	(75,000)
Increase in labour cost			(40,000)
Additional fixed costs			(250,000)
Depreciation			(20,000)
Additional profit			15,000

The return on additional investment is 15%.

The fixed costs are **£520,000**

The contribution per unit is £120 – 28.75 – 16 = **£75.25**

The break even sales volume is **6,911 units**.

183 SAIL

	Units	*Price/cost*	*Total*
Increase in revenue	20,000	20	400,000
Increase in material cost	20,000	7.50	(150,000)
Increase in labour cost			(50,000)
Additional fixed costs			(70,000)
Depreciation			(50,000)
Additional profit			80,000

The return on additional investment is 16%.

The fixed costs are **£190,000**

The contribution per unit is £1,020 – 82.50 – 200 = **£737.50**

The break even sales volume is **258 units.**

184 CAFF CO

	Units	*Price/cost*	*Total*
Additional revenue	2,400,000	0.75	1,800,000
Savings on variable costs	2,400,000	0.25	600,000
Reduction in selling and distribution costs			300,000
Additional depreciation			(400,000)
Additional annual profit			2,300,000

Additional profit/additional assets = £2,300,000/£4,000,000 = **57.50%**

The fixed costs are £3.6 million plus £500,000 plus additional depreciation of £400,000 = **£4.5 million.**

The contribution per unit is £8.25 less (1.50 – 0.25) = 7 – 2.75 = **£4.25 per unit**

The break even sales volume is **1,058,824 units.**

185 SUNSHINE

	Units	*Price/cost*	*Total £*
Additional revenue	2.4 m	£4	9.60 m
Additional materials	2.4 m	£3	(7.20 m)
Additional advertising costs			(0.45 m)
Additional depreciation			(0.40 m)
Additional annual profit			1.55 m

Additional profit/additional assets = £1,550,000/£2,000,000 = **77.50%**

The fixed costs are £1.6 million plus advertising costs of £450,000 plus additional depreciation of £400,000 = **£2.45 million.**

The contribution per unit is £15.95 less (2.50 + 8) = 15.95 – 10.50 = **£5.45 per unit**

The break even sales volume is **449,542 units.**

186 SELS AND DARLOW

(a)

	Sels	*Darlow*
Contribution per unit (£)	8	2
Break-even point (units)	7,500	5,000
Margin of safety (%)	25	75

Workings

Contribution per unit: Sels = 20 – 12 = 8; Darlow = 12 – 10 = 2

Breakeven point (units):

Sels = £60,000/£8 per unit = 7,500 units; Darlow = £10,000/£2 per unit = 5,000 units

Margin of Safety:

Sels = (10,000 – 7,500)/10,000 × 100 = 25%; Darlow = (20,000 – 5,000)/20,000 × 100 = 75%

(b) Note: Make sure you start basic and build up your answer, don't be afraid to state the obvious, if you don't tell the marker that you know it, the marker can't give you credit.

Provide an evaluation of the differences in contribution between the two departments.

On first glance, Sels looks better as it has the higher contribution. The main reason for Sels better contribution per unit is the higher selling price it has in comparison to Darlow. The variable cost is very similar between the 2 products so has little impact on the contribution per unit.

Sels has a higher operating gearing as while the variable costs are similar, Sels fixed costs are much higher.

Implications of the difference in break-even point between the two departments

Darlow has the lower breakeven point of the two.

Despite the lower contribution per unit, the fixed costs in Darlow are significantly lower reducing the breakeven point in comparison to Sels significantly.

The implications of this difference are that Darlow will breakeven at a lower volume of sales.

Sels will have to sell 50% more units to breakeven than Darlow.

Which department has the better margin of safety and why?

Darlow has the better margin of safety.

The reasons for the difference are:

(1) The sales volume is double that of Sels

(2) The fixed costs are significantly lower leading to the lower breakeven point.

If Sels sales fell by only 2,500 units they would not be making a profit.

Comment on the results from a risk perspective and suggest any potential ways of reducing it.

Darlow is overall a safer option; sales could fall by up to 75% before there are any issues covering all the costs.

Care must be taken to maintain the variable cost of Darlow as a 10% increase would change the MoS to 50% & a 20% rise would mean it no longer generated a positive contribution.

Sels is riskier; however, as is often the case with higher risk they can lead to higher rewards. If sales volumes increased significantly so would rewards due to the higher contribution per unit.

Reducing risk:

- Risk could be reduced by lowering the operating gearing of Sels, i.e. reducing the fixed cost in proportion to the variable costs.
- If budgeted sales volume increased then the safety buffer before they breakeven would also be increased.
- Variable costs could be reduced, increasing the contribution and therefore reducing breakeven point.
- The selling price could be increased to increase contribution per unit, although consideration must be given to the impact that this could have on demand.

187 R COMPANY

MofS = (BS – BEP)/BS × 100

25% = (6,976 – BEP)/6,976 × 100

BEP = 6,976 – (0.25 × 6976) = 5,232 units

C/S Ratio = (Contribution per unit / Selling price) × 100

40% = (contribution per unit / 62.50) ×100

Contribution per unit = 0.4 × 62.50 = £25

At the BEP, contribution is equal to the level of fixed costs.

Remember: **BEP (units) = Fixed costs/Contribution per unit**

Contribution at this volume is:

5,232 × £25 = £130,800

So the fixed costs are **£130,800**.

188 MD CO

MofS (units) = BS – BEP

7,000 units = 10,000 units – BEP

BEP = 10,000 – 7,000 = 3,000 units

BEP = Fixed costs/contribution per unit

3,000 = 46,500/contribution per unit

Contribution per unit = £46,500/3,000 units = **£15.50**

189 MULTI D

(a) Using the high-low method

Var cost = (1,078,000 – 903,000)/(10,000 – 7,500) = 175,000/2,500 = £70 per unit.

Fixed cost = 1,078,000 – (10,000 × £70) = **£378,000**

(b) As the variable cost is £70 per unit and the CS ratio is 56.25%

	£	%
Selling price		100
Variable cost	70	43.75
		56.25

Selling price = 70/0.4375 = £160 so the contribution = 160 – 70 = **£90 per unit.**

Units to achieve a target profit = (FC + Target profit)/contribution per unit

Units to achieve a target profit = (378000 + 207000)/90 = 585000/90 = **6,500 units.**

(c) Rearranging the target profit equation:

Contribution per unit = (FC + target profit)/number of units

= (378,000 + 207,000)/6,000

= **£97.50**

Contribution per unit = SP – var cost per unit

97.50 = SP – 70

SP = £167.50 per unit.

190 BLUVAN

Contribution per unit is £20 × 60% = £12. Hence variable cost is £8.

Breakeven point is £240,000 ÷ £12 = **20,000 units.**

With a safety margin of 20% the budget was **25,000 units.**

Keeping all variables fixed, except the variable cost per unit, we can now find the new variable cost per unit.

If the company is to breakeven at 25,000 units then: Contribution = Fixed costs

Therefore the contribution per unit must be FC/Budgeted sales units.

Contribution per unit = 240,000/25,000 = £9.60 per unit.

The selling price is £20 per unit, so the variable cost would be: 20 – 9.60 = £10.40 per unit.

The variable cost would have to increase to £10.40 per unit.

This is **£2.40** higher than the original cost, i.e. 30% higher

191 SEMI

Using the high low method:

Variable cost per unit = (35,000 – 25,000)/(15,000 – 10,000) = 10,000/5,000 = £2

Total variable cost per unit = 8 + 10 +2 = £20

Contribution per unit = 36 – 20 = £15

	£
Total variable cost per unit	20
Contribution per unit	16

Fixed costs:

Fixed part of the semi variable cost = £35,000 – (15,000 × £2) = £5,000

Total Fixed cost = £15,000 + £5,000 = £20,000

BEP (units) = £20,000/£16 = 1,250 units

MofS = (12,500 –1,250)/12,500 × 100 = 90%

Breakeven point in units	1,250
Margin of safety (%)	90

DECISION MAKING TECHNIQUES

192 LF

	L	*F*
	£	£
Selling price per unit	100	200
Material cost per unit	(40)	(60)
Labour cost per unit	(16)	(64)
Contribution per unit	44	76
Contribution per limiting factor	22	9.50
Rank	1	2
Optimal production plan in units (W1)	100	75

(W1) 100 units of L × 2 hours = 200 hours, leaving 600 hours for F. At 8 hrs per F this produces 75 F.

The revised production plan would be 88 units of L and 78 units of F. (W2)

(W2) (78 × 2 hours) + (78 × 8 hours) = 780 hours

20 hours spare to make more L, at 2 hours each = 10 more L (78 + 10 = 88)

193 BQ

	B	*Q*
	£	£
Selling price per unit	100	150
Material cost per unit	(40)	(60)
Labour cost per unit	(16)	(30)
Contribution per unit	44	60
Contribution per limiting factor	11	10
Rank	1	2
Optimal production plan in units (W1)	100	58

(W1) 100 units of B × 4 kg = 400 kg, leaving 350 kg for Q. At 6 kg per Q this produces 58 Q.

The revised production plan would be 90 units of B and 65 units of Q. (W2)

(W2) (65 × 4 kg) + (65 × 6 kg) = 650 kg

100 kg spare to make more B, at 4 kg each = 25 more B (65 + 25 = 90)

194 LEARN

	A	B
The contribution per unit	25	35
The contribution per kg	8.33	8.75

B should be made first and **A** should be made second.

	A	B
Production in units	1,600	1,800 (1,800 × 4 = 7,200)
	(12,000 – 7,200 = 4,800 left)	
Total contribution	1,600 × 25 = 40,000	1,800 × 35 = 63,000

Should Learn purchase the additional material? **YES** (The additional cost per kilogram is less than the contribution earned per kilogram.)

195 FROME

	A	B
The contribution per unit	50	35
The contribution per hour	16.67	14

A should be made first and **B** should be made second.

	A	B
Production in units	200	160
	(200 × 3 = 600 hours)	(1,000 hours – 600 hours = 400 hours) (400/2.5 hours each = 160)
Total contribution	200 × 50 = 10,000	160 × 35 = 5,600

Should Learn purchase the additional hours? **NO** (The additional cost per hour is more than the contribution earned per hour.)

196 US

£	*A1*	*A2*
Sales revenue	2,800,000	3,000,000
Variable costs	(1,500,0000	(1,620,000)
Fixed production overheads	(450,000)	(400,000)
Fixed selling & distribution overheads	(200,000)	(200,000)
Depreciation	(110,000)	(150,000)
Redundancy costs	(20,000)	(40,000)
Expected annual profit	520,000	590,000

The expected return on investment for each machine, to the nearest whole %, is:

A1 **47%** (520,000/1,100,000 × 100)

A2 **39%** (590,000/1,500,000 × 100)

US should buy machine **A1** (as it has a higher expected return on investment).

197 CHATTY

Workings:

	I	A	IN
	£	£	£
Selling price	100	200	50
Direct materials (£5 per kg)	10	7.50	15
Specialist labour (£10 per hour)	20	30	5
Unskilled labour (£8 per hour)	16	12	4
Variable overhead (£2 per machine hour)	10	12	2
Special component cost to buy in		65	
Contribution per unit	44	73.50	24
Contribution per machine hour	8.80	12.25	24
Ranking	3	2	1

Product	Units	Hrs/unit	Hrs used	Hrs left
IN	6,000	1	6,000	24,000
A	2,000	6	12,000	12,000
I	2,400	5	12,000	–

	I	A	IN
Contribution per unit (£ to 2DP)	44.00	73.50	24.00
Contribution per machine hour (£ to 2DP)	8.80	12.25	24.00
Optimum production plan (units)	2,400	2,000	6,000

There is no change for I & IN, but the estimated cost to make the special component is £15.50 cheaper than buying it in so the contribution per unit of A is now:

73.50 + 15.50 = £89

It takes 2 machine hours to make the special component so it would now take in total 8 machine hours to make a unit of A (2 hours for the special component plus 6 hours normally), so the contribution per machine hour is now:

89/8 = 11.125

The ranking doesn't change, but the production plan would now be:

Product	Units	Hrs/unit	Hrs used	Hrs left
IN	6,000	1	6,000	24,000
A	2,000	8	16,000	8,000
I	1,600	5	8,000	–

	I	A	IN
Contribution per unit (£ to 2DP)	44.00	89.00	24.00
Contribution per machine hour (£ to 2DP)	8.80	11.13	24.00
Optimum production plan (units)	1,600	2,000	6,000

Workings:

Original profit

	Units	*Contribution per unit* £	*Total* £
IN	6,000	24	144,000
A	2,000	73.5	147,000
I	2,400	44	105,600
Total contribution			396,600
Less fixed cost			(200,000)
Profit			196,600

Revised profit

	Units	*Contribution per unit* £	*Total* £
IN	6,000	24	144,000
A	2,000	89	178,000
I	1,600	44	70,400
Total contribution			392,400
Less fixed cost			(200,000)
Profit			192,400

If Chatty base their decision solely on profit maximisation they would **buy in** the special component.

The difference in profit between the two options is £**4,200**

Considerations could include:

Quality – the quality of either making or buying the component may be superior, doing the cheapest option could compromise the quality of the special component and therefore product A, which would be an issue as it commands a premium price.

Use of spare capacity – Chatty has an abundance of both specialist labour and materials, what will they do with this, could the decision they make lead to redundancies. The staff could be on fixed wages and therefore be paid for idle time.

Impact on customers – in house production would reduce availability of machine hours to make product I, therefore disappointing customers who would like to buy I.

Ethics – would decision be considered fair to customers/staff if it is purely financially driven either deliberately reducing the quality or putting jobs at risk.

198 GRAFTERS

	Current cost per year £	*Cost per year with machinery* £
Oak costs	60,000,000	60,600,000
Craftsmen cost	1,100,000	330,000
Tool replacement cost	200,000	100,000
Other variable overheads	50,000	40,000
Rental cost	–	100,000
Total cost	61,350,000	61,170,000

On financial grounds, grafters **should** agree to rent the machinery.

Other factors:

Quality – The machinery may compromise the quality of the product, it already leads to increased materials cost which suggests an increase in wastage.

Morale of workforce – those that remain will not have the same loyalty to Grafters.

Reliability of machinery – if the machines breakdown, with a reduced workforce Grafters may struggle to meet customer orders on time.

Reliability of estimates – approached by Machinery Co, they may not know the full extent of the work and veracity of the savings they suggest.

Ethical

Integrity – not mentioning change, trading on reputation of handcrafted even though it is not transparent and many people will continue to buy under the assumption the item is handcrafted.

Integrity – Hiding change in viewing gallery is another example of not being open and honest with their customers.

Professional behaviour – with so many of the workforce being made redundant, it seems difficult to believe that those that remain will be happy with their positions and the level of work they do may well drop.

Approach

The saving is £180,000 which is a relatively small amount (less than 1%) of the total costs.

Once committed and dependent on the machinery the cost could rise.

Familiarity threat given that the FD has a previous relationship with Machinery Co, which may lead to her trusting that their machines are going to save them all these costs even if they are actually substandard.

Bonus

A bonus based on one financial measure is very short term.

The finance directors objectivity will be compromised as they stand to benefit from the decision so may not act in the best interests of the company.

199 CCV

(a)

	M	*D*	*C*	*L*	*Total*
Number of batches	1,000	1,500	2,000	500	5,000
Number of machine setups	4,000	1,500	2,000	3,000	10,500

Workings:

Number of batches: M = 50,000/50 = 1,000; D = 75,000/50 = 1,500; C = 100,000/50 = 2,000; L = 25,000/50 = 500

Number of machine set ups: M = 1,000 × 4 = 4,000; D = 1,500 × 1 = 1,500; C = 2,000 × 1 = 2,000; L = 500 × 6 = 3,000

	£
Cost driver rate- per set up	57

Working: 598,500/10,500 = £57

(b)

	M	*D*	*C*	*L*	*Total*
	£000	£000	£000	£000	£000
Sales revenue	1,600	1,875	2,750	2,080	8,305
Direct material	200	825	1,000	900	2,925
Direct labour	400	900	1,200	600	3,100
Product specific overhead	200	20	10	421.5	651.5
Machine set up costs	228	85.5	114	171	598.5
General factory costs					100
Profit/(loss)	572	44.5	426	(12.5)	930

Workings:

M = 4,000 × 57 = 228,000; D = 1,500 × 57 = 85,500; C = 2,000 × 57 = 114,000; L = 3,000 × 57 = 171,000

The profit statement shows that Product L is now loss making and therefore from a financial perspective it should be discontinued as this would increase the company's profits by £12,500.

This is in contrast to the original profit statement which showed that products M and L were profitable and products D and C were loss making.

Products M, D and C should be continued because they all have a positive profit. The discontinuance of product L will release resources that were previously used by that product. If there is sufficient demand for products M, D, or C then CCV may be able to increase its output of these other products and increase its profits by even more than £12,500.

Value Analysis is a technique that improves the processes of production so as to achieve a reduction in cost without compromising the quality or usefulness of the product.

CCV would need to compare its products with those provided by its competitors to see if their products offer features that are not found in the products of their competitors. CCV would then have to determine whether these features are important to their customers. If they are not important then these features could be removed without affecting the value of the product.

Alternatively, CCV should review the design of its products as it may be able to produce them using different, lower cost, materials without affecting the customer's perception of the product. This would enable CCV to reduce its costs and thereby increase its profit.

200 WHITLEY

	LS £	ES £	AS £
Incremental revenue	11,100	8,750	6,600
Incremental costs	8,480	8,625	7,650
Net benefit/(loss)	2,620	125	(1,050)

Workings:

Incremental revenue

LS:

Rev from L = 6,000 units @ £4 = 24,000

Rev from LS = (6,000 × 0.9) × £6.50 = 35,100

Incremental rev = 35,100 – 24,000 = 11,100

ES:

Rev from E = 5,000 units @ £5 = 25,000

Rev from ES = (5,000 × 0.9) × £7.50 = 33,750

Incremental rev = 33,750 – 25,000 = 8,750

AS:

Rev from A = 4,000 units @ £6 = 24,000

Rev from AS = (4,000 × 0.9) × £8.50 = 30,600

Incremental rev = 30,600 – 24,000 = 6,600

Incremental costs

LS = (6,000 × 0.9) × 1.20 + 2,000 = 8,480

ES = (5,000 × 0.9) × 1.75 + 750 = 8,625

AS = (4,000 × 0.9) × 1.50 + 2,250 = 7,+650

On financial grounds Whitley should process L further.

On financial grounds Whitley should process E further.

On financial grounds Whitley should not process A further.

Sales independent, i.e. but not producing AS will there still be a demand for LS & ES. Or by not producing L & E will customers still want A

Demand, there may not be a demand in the market place for all the output at the prices specified and so Whitley may not be able to sell everything they make.

Impact on customers, some customer may be upset that the product they normally buy is no longer made.

LIFECYCLE COSTING

201 NPV

Year	*0*	*1*	*2*	*3*	*4*
Cash flow	(40,000)	15,200	14,900	13,585	11,255
DF	1.000	0.909	0.826	0.751	0.683
PV	(40,000)	13,817	12,307	10,202	7,687
				NPV	£4,013

The proposal **SHOULD** go ahead.

202 DAFFY

Year	*0*	*1*	*2*	*3*	*4*	*5*
Cash flow	(£120,000)	(£8,000)	(£8,000)	(£8,000)	(£8,000)	£12,000
DF	1.000	0.909	0.826	0.751	0.683	0.621
PV	(£120,000)	(£7,272)	(£6,608)	(£6,008)	(£5,464)	£7,452
NPV	(£137,900)					

Year	*0*	*1*	*2*	*3*	*4*
Lease costs	(£25,000)	(£25,000)	(£25,000)	(£25,000)	(£25,000)
DF	1.000	0.909	0.826	0.751	0.683
PV	(£25,000)	(£22,725)	(£20,650)	(£18,775)	(£17,075)
NPV	(£104,225)				

Based on the calculations it is best to LEASE the machines. This saves £33,675.

203 LIFECYCLE COSTING

Year	*0*	*1*	*2*	*3*	*4*
Cash flow	(30,000)	(2,500)	(2,500)	(2,500)	3,000
DF at 5%	1.000	0.952	0.907	0.864	0.823
Present value	(30,000)	(2,380)	(2,268)	(2,160)	2,469
NPV	(34,339)				

Year	*0*	*1*	*2*	*3*	*4*
Cash flow	(8,500)	(8,500)	(8,500)	(8,500)	–
DF at 5%	1.000	0.952	0.907	0.864	0.823
Present value	(8,500)	(8,092)	(7,710)	(7,344)	–
NPV	(31,646)				

Based on the above calculations, it would be best to **LEASE** the machine, because it saves **£2,693** (£34,339 – £31,646).

204 HOULTER

Year	*0*	*1*	*2*	*3*	*4*	*5*
Cash flow ('000)	(£300)	(£30)	(£30)	(£30)	(£30)	£20
DF	1.000	0.952	0.907	0.864	0.823	0.784
PV	(£300)	(£28.56)	(£27.21)	(£25.92)	(£24.69)	£15.68
NPV (£000)	(£390.70)					

Year	*1*	*2*	*3*	*4*	*5*
Labour savings in '000 (3 × 5,000 × £7 per year)	£105	£105	£105	£105	£105
DF	0.952	0.907	0.864	0.823	0.784
PV (£000)	£99.960	£95.235	£90.720	£86.415	£82.320
NPV (£000)	£454.650				

Investing in the new machine saves **£63,950** and is therefore financially beneficial.

205 YANKEE (1)

Year	*0*	*1*	*2*	*3*	*4*	*5*
Cash flow	(£1,500,000)	(£150,000)	(£150,000)	(£150,000)	(£150,000)	£100,000
DF	1.000	0.909	0.826	0.751	0.683	0.621
PV	(£1,500,000)	(£136,350)	(£123,900)	(£112,650)	(£102,450)	£62,100
NPV	(£1,913,250)					

Year	*0*	*1*	*2*	*3*	*4*
Lease costs	(£450,000)	(£450,000)	(£450,000)	(£450,000)	(£450,000)
DF	1.000	0.909	0.826	0.751	0.683
PV	(£450,000)	(£409,050)	(£371,700)	(£337,950)	(£307,350)
NPV	(£1,876,050)				

Based on the calculations it is best to **LEASE** the machine, to save **£37,200**.

206 BUDGE

£000

Year	*0*	*1*	*2*	*3*	*4*	*5*
Cash flow	(£600)	(£45)	(£45)	(£45)	(£45)	£175
DF	1.000	0.909	0.826	0.751	0.683	0.621
PV	(£600)	(£41)	(£37)	(£34)	(£31)	£109
NPV	(£634)					

£000

Year	*0*	*1*	*2*	*3*	*4*
Lease costs	(£135)	(£135)	(£135)	(£135)	(£135)
DF	1.000	0.909	0.826	0.751	0.683
PV	(£135)	(£123)	(£112)	(£101)	(£92)
NPV	(£563)				

Based on the calculations it is best to **LEASE** the machine because it saves **£71,000**.

207 LIFE CYCLE STATEMENTS (I)

Lifecycle costing is a concept which traces all costs to a product over its complete lifecycle, from design through to **cessation**.

One of the benefits that adopting lifecycle costing could bring is to improve decision-making and **cost** control.

208 LIFE CYCLE STATEMENTS (II)

Life cycle costing recognises that for many products there are significant costs committed by decisions in the **early** stages of its lifecycle.

One of the benefits of life cycle costing is the visibility of all costs is increased, rather than just costs relating to one period. This facilitates better **decision-making**.

209 ABITFIT CO

(a) The total life cycle cost is all the costs across the products life added together

	£
Research and development costs	250,000
Marketing costs = 500,000 + 1,000,000 + 250,000	1,750,000
Administration costs = 150,000 + 300,000 + 600,000	1,050,000
Total variable production cost = (£55 × 150,000) + (£52 × 250,000)	21,250,000
Fixed production cost = 600,000 + 900,000	1,500,000
Total variable sales and distribution cost = (£10 × 150,000) + (£12 × 250,000)	4,500,000
Fixed sales and distribution costs	400,000
Total costs	30,700,000

The life cycle cost per unit is then the total cost divided by the total number of units:

Life cycle cost per unit = £30,700,000/400,000 = £76.75

(b)

Intro

At this stage the R&D cost (to create the product) and marketing (to create awareness of the product) will be the most significant. Looking at Abitfit in Yr1 almost 90% of the costs are from these two areas.

Growth

Marketing expense is still vital at this stage, but production costs will also be increasing in significance. Looking at Abitfit marketing costs doubled in the second year.

Maturity

Here production costs will be the most significant, although there will be economies of scale and learning effects that will reduce the costs. Looking at Abitfit the production cost per unit falls from £55 per unit to £52 per unit.

Decline

As sales and production start to fall a company could lose some of the economies of scale at this stage. There are likely to costs associated with decommissioning/clean up at the end of the products life. Looking at Abitfit the increase in administration costs could be associated with the decommissioning/clean-up.

210 LCC PLC

(a) The total life cycle cost is all the costs across the products life added together

	£
Research and development costs	500,000
Marketing and administration costs = 450,000 + 750,000 + 800,000 + 350,000	2,350,000
Total variable production cost = (£28 × 200,000) + (£25 × 250,000) + (£20 × 100,000)	13,850,000
Fixed production cost = 200,000 + 300,000 + 400,000	900,000
Total variable sales and distribution cost = (£18 × 200,000) + (£16 × 250,000) + (£18 × 100,000)	9,400,000
Fixed sales and distribution costs	450,000
Total costs	27,450,000

The life cycle cost per unit is then the total cost divided by the total number of units:

Life cycle cost per unit = £27,450,000/550,000 = 49.91

(b)

Production costs

One of the key areas likely to experience this change is the production cost. During the growth phase production costs are likely to be variable and increase in line with production, but in the maturity phase due to economies of scale like bulk buying and the learning effect the production costs may remain fairly constant regardless of the production levels.

Then moving into decline they may well revert back to variable as economies of scale are lost.

(c)

Life cycle costing is the accumulation of costs throughout a products life, from inception to abandonment. It can often highlight costs that have previously been overlooked and also can lead to greater focus on costs in the design phase.

This can aid ethical considerations by highlighting the costs associated with the clean-up/decommissioning of a product or site that could lead to more environmentally friendly practices throughout the life of the product reducing the final clean-up cost.

The focus of cost in the design phase could also have benefits as companies give careful consideration to the resources or amount of resources required for a product and features/processes that consume significant resources/costs but add little value could be removed.

TARGET COSTING

211 TARGET COSTING

	£
Selling price	10
Profit margin at 20%	(2)
Total costs	8
Fixed costs	(1.50)
Material cost	(2)
Maximum labour cost	4.50
Target cost per hour (£4.50/4.5 hours)	1

Extra labour cost = £0.20 × 4.5 hours = £0.90

New total cost = £2 + £4.50 + £0.90 + £1.50 = £8.90

Profit = £10 – £8.90 = £1.10

Profit margin = 11%

If labour cost increases by £0.90, material costs will need to fall by £0.90, for the margin to remain the same.

Therefore material costs will need to fall by £0.90/£2 = 45%

212 HOLDER

	£
Sales price per unit	£50.00
Profit margin (20% of sales)	£10.00
Total costs	£40.00
Fixed cost per unit	£15.50
Labour cost per unit	£4.00
Maximum material cost per unit	£20.50
Target cost per kilogram	£102.50

The discount should **ACCEPTED** because the £120 reduces to **£102** which is **BELOW** the target cost.

The minimum percentage discount needed to achieve the target cost is **14.6%**.

213 AKEA

	£
Sales price per sofa	1,500
Profit margin @ 30%	(450)
Total costs	1,050
Fixed cost per sofa	(140)
Labour cost per sofa 8 hrs × £25	(200)
Wooden frame and stuffing material	(110)
Maximum leather cost per sofa	600
Target cost per square metre (£600/8m)	75

Akea's leather supplier quotes a list price of £100 per square metre for the grade of leather Akea needs. However, Akea has managed to negotiate a discount of 15% on this price. The discount should be **REJECTED** because the £100 reduces to **£85** which is **ABOVE** the target cost.

The minimum percentage discount needed to achieve the target cost is **25%** (£25/£100)

214 SHORTY

	£
Sales price per unit	150.00
Profit margin	(37.50)
Total costs	112.50
Fixed cost per unit	(40.00)
Labour cost per unit	(40.00)
Maximum rubber cost per unit	32.50
Target cost per kg	6.50

The discount should be REJECTED because the £10 reduces to £7.50 which is ABOVE the target cost.

The minimum percentage discount needed to achieve the target cost is **35%** (£3.50/£10)

215 LONG

	£
Sales price per unit	250.00
Profit margin	(87.50)
Total costs	162.50
Fixed cost per unit	(20.00)
Material cost per unit	(110.00)
Maximum labour cost per unit	32.50
Target cost per labour hour	16.25

The discount should be REJECTED because the £20 reduces to

£17 which is ABOVE the target cost.

The minimum percentage discount needed to achieve the target cost is **18.75%** (£3.75/£20)

216 GRIPPIT (1)

	£
Selling price	25.00
Profit margin at 30%	(7.50)
Target cost	17.50

217 SHOCK

	£
Selling price	95
Profit margin at 20%	(19)
Target cost	76

218 TRICKY (II)

	£
Selling price	205.00
Profit margin at 10%	(20.50)
Target cost	184.50

219 TC ETHICS

To: TC Colleague	**Subject:** Ethics and Target Costing
From: AAT Student	**Date:** Today

Labour

Reducing the skill level of labour used is fine from a product cost point of view; a key consideration is how the current grade of labour will be used in future. If they are to be made redundant, that could not only cost the company more in the short term, but also have a detrimental effect on the long term success of the workforce.

Then there is the impact on the members of staff made redundant, which could impact the morale of those that remain, while the job losses could have an adverse impact on the local community.

Another consideration is that the product should not lose any value to the customer, value analysis is about reducing cost without reducing the value of the product to the consumer.

If TC are putting pressure on the managers, or awarding a bonus linked to achieving the target cost then their objectivity may be compromised and make a decision which is not goal congruent with the long term company aims.

Material

A consideration is confidentiality, should TC disclose to the public the change in materials. The material could be unethically sourced. Another issue would be around the quality of the material and the impact on the final product. As with the labour, if the end product is inferior then the customer should be informed, if there is no adverse impact on the product or the health of the consumer from using the product then TC do not need to disclose it to the customer.

220 TARGET COSTING STATEMENTS (I)

To calculate the target cost, subtract the **target profit** from the target price.

If there is a cost gap, attempts will be made to close the gap. Techniques such as value engineering and value **analysis** may be used to help close the gap.

221 TARGET COSTING STATEMENTS (II)

The cost gap is the difference between the **target cost** and the estimated product cost per unit.

Target costing works the opposite to **traditional pricing** techniques in that it starts by setting a competitive selling price first.

222 FORMAT

	Sales price £4	**Sales price £5**
Target total production cost per unit	£4 × 80% = £3.20	£5 × 80% = £4.00
Target fixed production cost per unit	£3.20 – £1.20 = £2.00	£4.00 – £1.30 = £2.70
Total target fixed production cost	£2.00 × 50,000 = £100,000	£2.70 × 45,000 = £121,500

Format should set the price at £5 to achieve the target profit margin.

223 MR WYNN

(a)

	workings	**£**
Profit per unit	45% × 500 =	225
Target cost per unit	500 – 225 =	275

(b)

	workings	**£**
Bought in material	(£100 × 25% × 90%) + (£100 × 75% × 40%)	52.50
Direct labour	W1	15.63
Machining costs	2 × 20 = 40	40.00
Quality costs	((8,000 × 5%) × 40)/8,000	2.00
Remedial work	((8,000 × 15%) × £40)/8,000	6.00
Initial design costs	400,000/8,000	50.00
Sales and Marketing costs	£1,000,000/8,000	125.00
Estimated lifetime cost per unit		291.13

W1

First 1,000:

40/60hrs × 1,000 units @ £30 per hour = £20,000

Rest: 8,000 – 1,000 = 7,000 units

30/60hrs × 7,000 units @ £30 per hour = £105,000

Labour cost = 20,000 + 105,000 = £125,000

(c) There is a cost gap of **£16.13** per unit as it stands.

(d)

Material

Mr Wynn could see if he can negotiate discounts on the lower grade materials as well as the luxury materials.

Labour

Mr Wynn could look into training the workers to try to speed up the familiarisation or to decrease the time below the 30 minutes.

Machine costs

Mr Wynn should look into different machines that could do the work faster than the 2 hours it currently takes, or cheaper than the current cost of £20 per hour.

Quality costs

The additional training could reduce the need for inspections below the current 5% level.

Remedial work

Training could also help reduce the amount of remedial work required as the workers may become more proficient with the materials/processes used.

Sales and marketing

Mr Wynn could look into alternative marketing tools or distribution networks that could reduce the cost below current expectation of £1 million for the 2 year period.

224 TOPCAT

(a)

		£
Total anticipated sales revenue	30,000 × 25	750,000.00
Target total net profit	750,000 × 20%	150,000.00
Target total costs	750,000 – 150,000	600,000.00
Target cost per unit	600,000/30,000	20.00

(b)

		£
Total lifecycle costs	150 + 35 + 300 + 100 + 75 =	660,000.00
Lifecycle cost per unit	660,000/30,000	22.00

If a margin of 20% is required, the new product **should not be** introduced.

(c)

		£
Reduced selling price per unit	25 – 0.50	24.50
Target net profit per unit	24.50 × 20%	4.90
Target total cost per unit	24.50 × 80%	19.60
Expected variable manufacturing cost per unit	£300,000/30,000 units	10.00
Target fixed costs per unit	19.60 – 10	9.60

To the nearest whole unit, the required sales volume is **37,500** units.

Total life cycle fixed costs = 150,000 + 35,000 + 100,000 + 75,000 = £360,000

Units required to produce to have a fixed cost per unit of 9.60 = 360,000/9.60 = 37,500 units

(d)

Value engineering

Value engineering is a philosophy of designing products which meet customer needs at the lowest cost while assuring the required standard of quality and reliability.

Value analysis

Value analysis relates to existing products. A company may sell a product with a feature that they discover adds no value to the customer, but incurs cost to include in the product. Using value analysis they would remove this feature, thus saving money, without harming the value of the product to the customer.

Ethics

Focus on reducing cost while good for the profitability of the company, careful thought must be given to maintaining the value of the end product to the customer. The whole point of target costing is that costs are reduced without reducing the performance of the product, it certainly should not compromise the safety of the workers or the consumers. Consideration must be given to suppliers too, pushing the supplier to provide components at a cheaper price could lead to poor working conditions at the supplier or even put them out of business.

225 CELSIUS

	Sales price £22	**Sales price £20**
Target total production cost per unit	£22 × 75% = £16.50	£20 × 75% = £15
Target fixed production cost per unit	£16.50 – £10.50 = £6.00	£15 – £9.20 = £5.80
Total target fixed production cost	£6.00 × 18,000 = £108,000	£5.80 × 20,000 = £116,000

Celsius should set the price at £20 to achieve the target profit margin.

PERFORMANCE INDICATORS WRITTEN QUESTIONS

226 PAS

(a)

	Year 1	Year 2
Revenue growth (%)		25.8
Gross profit margin (%)	51.4	41.3
Net profit margin (%)	–3.7	3.4

(b)

Report

To: Pedro	**Subject:** Financial performance of PAS
From: Accounting Technician	**Date:** Today

Revenue

Almost £2.9 million revenue in the first year of a new business seems very good, but to have revenue growth in the second year of almost 26% in a competitive market place appears to be a fantastic performance by PAS.

Revenue growth can come from growing sales volume, increasing the selling price or a combination of the two; it would be interesting to know how PAS have achieved this growth.

Gross profit

A first year gross profit margin of over 50% looks like an excellent start to business for PAS, the high percentage appears to back up the premium image that PAS are trying to achieve.

Gross profit growth of only 1.2% in the second year is slightly disappointing after such strong sales revenue growth, it suggests that either PAS has bought sales by discounting the prices or that there are cost control issues to consider.

The gross profit margin falling to 41.3% backs up this concern, and it would be interesting to be able to find out why the gross profit margin has fallen so much.

Net profit

A loss in year one is disappointing, but as PAS seem to be taking a long term view it is not unexpected. Especially as some initial set up costs such as the website and marketing costs are so high as predicted by Pedro, if these were at the level of year 2 in year 1 then PAS would have returned a very healthy net profit.

The profit, even though it is small in year 2 is very encouraging. If the initial costs continue to fall, although not at the same rate, this should help increase the profit for the company.

The distribution costs appear high, having increased by over 50%, twice the rate of the revenue growth and could be a cause for concern. This could be down to establishing a good reputation for on time delivery or rising fuel costs.

Administrative costs and other overhead heads have also increased although this is more in line with the revenue growth, PAS should be looking for economies of scale in these areas as they continue to grow.

(c)

	Year 1	*Year 2*
Conversion rate for website visits to number of units sold (%)	5.2	3.0
% sales returned	9.0	21.0
Average price per sale (£ to 2 decimal places)	20.50	23.03

(d) **Report**

To:	Pedro	**Subject:**	Non-financial performance of PAS
From:	Accounting Technician	**Date:**	Today

Average selling price

The average selling price per unit has increased in year 2, which answers one of the queries after reviewing the financials, sales revenue has grown through both increased prices and higher volume, while the decline in gross profit is down to escalating cost of sales

Conversion rate

After a fantastic start in year 1 where the conversion rate is well above the industry average, the performance here has dropped well below industry average in year 2. This is a cause for concern for PAS, and could be linked to the increased prices charged discouraging customers from making a purchase.

PAS need to look to understand where the cost increases are coming from and control these so they do not lose more customers in coming years.

It could also be linked to poor internet reviews as returns have increased and there have been fewer deliveries on time.

It could also be due to technical issues with the website, as these have increased this could have put customers off or prevented them from buying the products.

Sales returns

The percentage of sales returns has increased dramatically in the 2nd year and is a real cause for concern for PAS, it is now 50% higher than the industry average, for a company looking to get a reputation for quality this is not the way to go.

PAS need to look at the reasons for the returns and look to rectify them.

On time delivery

One of the factors influencing sales returns in year 2 could be the poor performance against on time delivery. Having been well above industry averages in year 1, PAS have again fallen below.

It could be that the accessories were purchased for a special event, but arrived late and so the customer had been out and purchased from an alternative source.

The drop in on time delivery is despite the increasing distribution costs; in fact the returns could well be a factor in the increased distribution costs as a company striving for differentiation would probably pay for the returns costs.

Website performance

One final cause for concern is the number of transactions that were aborted due to website issues. PAS invested heavily in the website in year 1 and for it to be struggling already is not good. Internet security is a key issue for users and they may well be put off buying from the site in the future if a transaction fails.

PAS should go back to the developers to address this issue as there may well be within warranty period.

227 ARCHIMEDES

To:	Finance director	**Subject:**	Various
From:	Accounting technician	**Date:**	Today

(a) Why are the gross profit margins different

Sales Price/Sales Volume

The sales price is higher under Scenario 1 which will result in an increase in the gross profit margin, however the sales volume is half that of Scenario 2, which will reduce the margin because the fixed cost per unit will be higher.

Materials

The materials cost per unit is constant and therefore does not affect the gross profit margin. There is no economy of scale.

Labour

Labour cost per unit is £0.80 for Scenario 1 decreasing to £0.64 for Scenario 2. The more units that are produced the lower the labour cost per unit. This will improve the margin for Scenario 2. It may be because of economies of scale in production or the learning effect.

Fixed costs

Fixed costs are constant in total therefore as the volume of production increases the fixed cost per unit reduces and this will increase the margin.

(b) Why are the operating profit margins different

The operating profit margins are different due in part to the reduction in gross profit for Scenario 2 and in part due to the increased sales and distribution costs in Scenario 2.

(c) Recommendation, with reasons, as to which course of action to take

Based purely on the forecast information Scenario 1 is the best option creating the largest profit. However, the sales volume is lower than Scenario 2 and therefore the market share is lower. It may be worth setting the price lower to gain market share.

228 TEMPEST

To:	Finance director	**Subject:**	Profitability
From:	Accounting technician	**Date:**	Today

Why are the gross profit margins not significantly different?

Sales Price

The Sales price in each cinema is the same and therefore the revenue earned per customer does not have any effect on the gross profit margin.

Direct costs

The direct cost per customer is slightly higher at the City centre cinemas (£2.16 versus £2.13 at the out of town sites). This only has a small effect on the gross profit margin.

Fixed costs

The fixed costs per customer are higher per customer at the City Centre cinemas (£3.24 per customer versus £3.00 per customer). This explains the majority of the difference in the gross profit margin.

Why are the operating profit margins different?

Both cinemas have the same administrative costs despite having a different number of customers – this works out at £0.33 per customer at the out of town cinemas and £0.89 at the city centre cinemas. This cost is fixed, and accounts for the difference in operating profit margins.

Which is the most profitable type of cinema and why? (Many different answers could be given.)

The Out of Town sites earn £4.61 per customer and the City Centre sites earn £2.90 per customer. This can mostly be explained by the increased admin costs at the city centre cinemas.

Apart from reducing fixed costs what could Tempest do to improve the profitability of the City Centre Cinemas? (Use numbers to demonstrate your answer if necessary.)

The average spend on food per customer is much lower at the City Centre cinemas – only £0.89. If customers could be persuaded to spend an extra £1.00 when the variable cost of food is only 10% then this would result in an extra £0.90 per customer per visit.

We could try to increase the numbers attending the City Centre cinemas – this would spread the fixed admin cost over more customers increasing profit per customer.

Tempest suspect City Centre customers are smuggling in their own sweets and snacks – give ONE way that Tempest could combat it?

Market research – ask the customers – are food prices at the cinema too high?

Look for evidence of food wrappers that aren't sold in cinemas

Tactic to combat smuggling – Offer promotions e.g. 2 for 1.

229 ANIMAL

To:	Finance Director	**Subject:**	Profit and current assets
From:	Accounting Technician	**Date:**	XX/XX/20XX

Why are the gross profit margin for the proposed position is higher than the current position:

Sales volume

The sales volume is expected to increase by 100% .i.e. it is forecast to double.

The volume increase will increase the profit margin if the fixed costs remain constant.

In this case the fixed production costs remain unchanged at £60,000 and therefore the increased volume will improve the gross profit margin because the fixed production costs are spread across more units thereby lowering the total unit cost and increasing the profit per unit. This is the principle of 'economies of scale'.

Material cost

The material cost per unit reduces by 20%, from £5.00 to £4.00 per unit, which will also improve the margin for the proposed position. The doubling of the volume is likely to allow the company to purchase in greater quantities and access additional discounts (economies of scale).

Labour cost

The labour cost per unit is unchanged at £6.00 and therefore would have no effect on the margin if the selling price remained constant. However, the selling price has fallen which makes the labour cost proportionately larger in percentage terms, which will reduce the gross profit margin.

There do not appear to have been any economies of scale or any learning effect.

Fixed production costs

The fixed production costs are constant in total at £60,000 but the important point is that they are spread over more units. The proposed position increases the volume by 100% which reduces the fixed production cost per unit. Fixed production costs reduce by 50% from £4.00 to £2.00. This will improve the margin for the proposed position.

What is likely to happen to the current asset position:

Inventory levels

Inventory levels are likely to increase significantly because the volume of demand is expected to be higher and therefore higher inventory levels will be needed to fulfil orders. Based upon the current inventory level in relation to cost of sales the forecast position will be that inventory levels may increase to around £56,000.

(Current inventory days = Inventory/Cost of sales × 365 = 35,000/225,000 × 365 = 56.78 days

Proposed inventory level = £360,000 × 56.78 days/365 days = £56,002)

Trade receivable levels

Trade receivables' levels are likely to increase because the turnover increases – increased sales will likely lead to increased receivables. The current position is that trade receivable days are 48.67 days (50,000/375,000 × 365).

Therefore, assuming a similar profile, trade receivables will increase to around £88,000.

(660,000 × 48.67/365 = £88,006).

230 FRUITY

To:	Manager	**Subject:**	Profitability
From:	Accounting Technician	**Date:**	XX/XX/20XX

1 Why is the gross profit margin of Cranberry less than 50% higher than that of Apple when the gross profit per unit is more than 50% higher?

The gross profit per unit of Cranberry is 57.5% higher than Apple. While the gross profit margin of Cranberry is only 26% higher than Apple.

The reason for this apparent anomaly is due to the sales price per unit of Cranberry being 25% higher than Apple.

Therefore the calculation of the gross profit margin for Cranberry results in a larger denominator, and therefore 63p per unit as a percentage of £1.25 (50.4%) is not over 50% higher than the calculation of the gross profit margin for Apple (40%).

2 I was told that the material cost is £0.80 per kilogram for Apple and £0.91 per kilogram for Cranberry. Therefore I do not understand why the material cost per unit for Apple is £0.40 and for Cranberry is £0.50. Is this correct?

The cost per kilogram is correct at £0.80 for Apple and £0.91 for Cranberry. Apple requires 500 grams (0.5 kilograms) of material per unit, which is why the cost per unit is £0.40 (0.5 × £0.80).

Cranberry requires 550 grams (0.55 kilograms) of material per unit, which is why the cost per unit is £0.50 (0.55 × £0.91).

3 If the fixed production overheads are constant does that mean they have no effect on the profit margin? And if the fixed production overheads increase will they affect the profit margin?

If the fixed production overheads were constant in total, because the production volume of Cranberry is 500,000 units greater than Apple this will result in the fixed production overhead per unit being lower. This is because the fixed production overheads are spread over more units, which reduces the cost per unit of Cranberry and therefore the profit margin will be improved.

However, in this scenario, the total costs have increased by 20% (from £100k to £120k), and thus the unit cost is 20% higher than might have been expected (at £0.12/unit and not £0.10/unit).

The impact this has on the gross profit margin depends on sales. If sales reduce, then the cost as a percentage of sales will increase; if sales increase, then the cost as a percentage of sales will reduce, improving the margin.

Comparing Cranberry to Apple, the fixed cost per unit is lower for Cranberry, whilst the sales price is higher, both of which help to reduce cost as a % of sales, and thus improve the margin.

Even if the fixed costs had remained constant, there could still have been an impact on profit margin if the sales had changed.

4 Can you explain why Cranberry is more profitable than Apple?

The reasons that Cranberry is more profitable than Apple are as follows:

- Sales price per unit of Cranberry is higher than Apple by 25% which will improve the profit
- The sales volume is much higher for Cranberry which means that fixed costs per unit are lower than Apple again improving the profit
- The variable cost (material) per unit is higher for Cranberry which will have a negative effect and decrease the actual profit for Cranberry
- The fixed production cost per unit is lower for Cranberry due to the volume being greater than Apple which improves the profit for Cranberry
- The marketing costs for Cranberry are 140% (£120,000 – £50,000/£50,000 × 100%) higher than Apple which will result in a higher marketing cost per unit (£0.10 (£50,000/500,000) v £0.12 (£120,000/1,000,000)). This will reduce the net profit for Cranberry. However, since the price of Cranberry is much higher, the marketing costs are only 9.6% of sales (£0.12/£1.25). Apple's marketing costs are 10% of sales (£0.10/£1). This 0.4% difference helps to improve Cranberry's profit margin.
- There are two main reasons that Cranberry is more profitable – the greater sales price and the greater sales volume. These, in combination, outweigh the increased marketing costs and the increased material costs for Cranberry.

231 PI ETHICS

Ethical issues

The manager has clearly received their bonus in qtr 2 having missed out in qtr 1. It appears their objectivity may have been impaired by the bonus and a potential personal need to receive that bonus.

Other financial and non-financial measures have deteriorated, the managers integrity could be called into question about why the selling price has dropped so much in the last quarter. A clear reason could be buying sales through discounts.

To counter this, the manager may well have compromised on quality or service as the number of customers is decreasing, a sign of poor service. This could lead to people questioning the managers professional competence and due care.

Goal congruence issues

In terms of goal congruence, the overall profitability of the company of the company would help here, but the manager looks to have made short term decisions to achieve their bonus which could lead to adverse long term consequences for the company.

Acting in their own self-interest could lead to the company's reputation being damaged and more customers could be lost in future quarters.

232 ZIG

	A	*B*	*C*
RoCE %	19	21	25

	A	*B*	*C (W)*
Revised Capital Employed (£)	325,000	280,000	430,000
Revised Profit (£)	68,500	48,500	106,250
Revised RoCE (% to 1 dp	21.1	17.3	24.7

(W)

As C's working capital is reduced by 20,000, so is the capital employed.

£450,000 – £20,000 = £430,000

Discount given = £500,000 × 0.5 × 0.025 = £6,250.

Profit will now be: £112,500 – £6,250 = £106,250

Ethics

Objectivity – As the managers stand to benefit from the decision they make, they may prioritise their personal financial benefit ahead of the companies benefit.

For example the managers of division B and C may be reluctant to proceed with the proposals or even reject them as it reduces the RoCE of their divisions.

Decision making implications

In this particular case it would depend on the target set, for example if the target was 20% then the manager of A would be keen to proceed with the proposal to achieve the target and receive their bonus. The manager of division B would reject the proposal to maintain their bonus.

233 SSS

(a)

	£ per visit
Average price for hair services per female client in 2016	50
Average price for hair services per male client in 2016	25

There were no price changes for female clients between 2015 and 2016, so using the 2015 figures:

Ave price in 2015 = 500,000/10,000 = £50 per visit

If that's the average price for female clients in 2016, then the male price is:

Ave price per visit = (550,600 – (£50 × 8,802))/4,420

= 110,500/4,420

= £25 per visit

(b)

	2015	*2016*
Gross profit margin (% to 2 DP)	60.50	55.92
Net profit margin (% to 2 DP)	52.50	47.35

To: Stuart	**Subject:** Financial performance of SSS
From: Accounting Technician	**Date: Today**

(a) Revenue

Revenue has grown by 10.12% in the last year, which in tough economic conditions and a competitive market place is a good performance.

Of more concern for SSS is that the core customer base (and more lucrative at £50 per visit) customer base is in decline. There has been a 12% fall in visits from female clients. This could be linked to the trainee stylist not performing very well; customers may have chosen to go to one of the competitors leading to a decline in revenue.

The growth is entirely down to the launch of the new male services, with £110,500 revenue being generated from the new services

(b) Gross profit margin

Gross profit has grown by just under 2% in 2016, which is disappointing given a revenue growth of over 10%.

The reason for this decline is that Cost of Sales has increased at a higher rate than 10%, this is mainly down to stylist salaries, who all received pay rises and two new stylists were recruited.

The main issue is the additional female trainee stylist, as the arrival increases the cost of sales and coincides with the decline in female clients, making the additional stylist unnecessary.

It would appear that male services command a lower gross profit margin. With further analysis this is not the case. The stylist for male clients is paid £26,000.

This one stylist is generating revenue of £110,500 (4,420 visits × £25 per visit), which is pretty impressive.

(c) Net profit margin

The net profit for the period has fallen by almost 1%, which is another disappointment for SSS given both the revenue growth and growth in gross profit. This led to a decline on Net profit margin from 52.50% to 47.35%.

Total expenses were up almost 18% in 2016 in comparison to 2015.

The main issue is the increase marketing and advertising spend, which has increased by £6,000 – a 200% rise on 2015. While this is a lot, it is quite normal for businesses launching a new product or service to increase this type of spend and it would be expected to reduce in 2017.

Also, the additional £6,000 may have contributed to the £110,500 revenue generated by the new service, so SSS may consider it to have been worthwhile.

A lot of these expenses are outside of the control of SSS in the short term, for example property rental and rates, combined these have only increased by just over 4%.

The administrative assistant has also had a 1% pay rise in line with the rest of the staff who were present in 2015.

(c)

	2015	*2016*
Customer		
% of visits that had complaints (2dp)	0.16	1.33
Internal business		
Number of female client visits per stylist	2,000	1,467
Number of male client visits per stylist		4,420
Innovation and growth		
% revenue from new male hairdressing service (to 2 decimal places)		20.07

% revenue from new male hairdressing service = 110,500/550,600 × 100 = 20.07

(d)

Customer

The number of complaints has increased dramatically, a major factor is the new service being offered has upset a lot of the core customer base.

The new trainee stylist may not yet be as good as the experienced stylists leading to further complaints.

Internal business

A business will often look at utilisation of assets, and while Stuart is correct that overall the premises themselves have more client visits, the appointments per female stylist is down over 25%. This will be partly due to the number of female visits being lower but also the increase in number of stylists for female clients.

The male stylist appears to be well utilised although we do not have any comparative numbers here from either prior year or industry averages. It is unfair to compare the number of appointments per male stylist to the number of appointments per female stylist as the service provided to male clients is much quicker.

Innovation and growth

Over 20% of revenue has come from the new service SSS have offered, which suggests the new service has been well received.

The concern is that it has led to a decline in core services of 12%.

SSS need to decide how to continue this new venture; it may be beneficial to set up another salon for male services.

234 COST REDUCTION

Cost reduction is action taken to reduce the cost of goods or services without impairing suitability for the use intended, whereas cost control involves the use of control methods, such as budgetary control and standard costing, to determine whether action is required.

Cost reduction is a technique which has the objective of reducing costs to some predetermined accepted norm or standard, but at the same time maintaining the desired quality of the product or service.

It is a concept which attempts to extract more 'value added' from the resources without loss of effectiveness.

Cost reduction programmes require the support of the senior management team and should embrace the full range of the firm's value adding activities and products.

Focus on a number of issues should be considered.

- Reduction of waste.
- Streamlining activities.
- Product improvement.

Cost reduction compels planning and good practice and benchmarks for achievement may be set.

Some formal management techniques can be used to implement cost reduction programmes, including:

- variety reduction
- value analysis
- work study
- organisation and method study.

All members of the management team should have a clear perception of cost reduction and its benefits in contributing, other things being equal, to improved profitability.

235 VALUE ANALYSIS

Value analysis is an assessment process underpinning the cost reduction technique. It is usually undertaken by a quality team during the design stages of the product or delivery of a service. The team would comprise a number of managers including technical and production personnel together with finance staff.

The task the team undertakes is to design the product, or plan the service, at minimum cost, but meeting the quality standard required.

The assessment is a systematic attempt to eliminate unnecessary cost on every aspect of the product's functions, methods of production and components.

The process involves asking a series of questions which may include the following.

- Can the function of the product be achieved in an alternative way?
- Are all the product functions essential?
- Can the product be made more compact and from alternative, cheaper material?
- Can we standardise components, e.g. some components on the Mercedes 'C' class are also on the 'S' class?
- Can the design or process be modified so that the product or service can be supplied more easily and at less cost?

This is an ongoing process where each of the company's products or services should come under regular scrutiny.

ETHICS

236 ETHICS STATEMENTS (I)

A company that takes a strong ethical stance in the way they behave will usually find their relationship with investors **improves**.

A worker in the accounts department who receives a profit based bonus decides to manipulate some of the expenses, artificially increasing the profits and allowing them to get a bonus has not breached the ethical principle of **confidentiality**.

237 ETHICS STATEMENTS (II)

Consumers may be willing to pay *a* **premium** price for Fairtrade products, knowing that the products are grown in an ethical and sustainable fashion

An advantage of using life cycle costing is it could help an organisation make more **sustainable** decisions as they will consider all costs throughout the projects including any potential closure and clean-up costs.

238 ETHICS STATEMENTS (III)

Products that have **excess** packaging could be considered unethical because they are using more of the world's resources and could potentially cost the company more money.

Ethical actions by a business may help them achieve long term **success**.

Section 3

MOCK ASSESSMENT QUESTIONS

TASK 1 **(12 MARKS)**

The following is the budget information for a typical month at Stew Ltd who make a single product:

Expense	
Direct material	10 litres at £2 per litre
Direct labour	1 hours at £8 per hour
Monthly salary of supervisor	£2,500
Monthly property rental costs	£8,000
Machine rental costs	£3,000 per month, plus £1.25 per unit
Machine maintenance	£2,000 per 2,500 units produced

Calculate the budgeted monthly cost of production for each of the activity levels to the nearest £ and classify each cost as variable, semi variable, stepped fixed or fixed.

Cost	*Monthly production*		*Cost classification*
	5,200 units	*12,000 units*	
	£	£	
Direct material			
Direct labour			
Supervisor salary			
Property rental costs			
Machine rental costs			
Machine maintenance			

TASK 2 **(15 MARKS)**

A company provides you with the following budget and actual information:

Standard cost information

Direct material	10 litres @ £7.50
Direct labour	2 hours @ £6.00
Fixed overheads	2 hours @ £8.00

Actual information

Output 2,400 litres

		£
Direct material	24,550 litres	184,616
Direct labour	5,040 hours	30,492
Fixed overheads		38,500

Additional information

Budgeted fixed overhead for the year is £38,400.

Overheads are recovered on the basis of direct labour hours.

Production is anticipated to be evenly spread throughout the year.

(a) Calculate the following information relating to the new unit: **(5 marks)**

Budgeted production	
Budgeted labour hours	
Actual price of the direct material per litre	
Actual direct labour rate per hour	

Another company makes two products, the flock and the crock.

They have 2 overhead activities special parts handling and machine set ups, the budgeted costs for each are £350,000 and £120,000 respectively.

	Flock	*Crock*
Direct materials – £ per unit	6	8
Direct labour – £ per unit	7.50	10
Number of special parts	200	300
Number of machine set ups	50	250
Budgeted production units	10,000	20,000

(b) Complete the table below using Activity Based Costing (ABC) principles. (8 marks)

	£	*Flock* (£)	*Crock* (£)
Cost driver rate – special parts handling			
Cost driver rate – machine set ups			
Total special parts			
Total machine set ups			

(c) Using the information from (b) calculate the total cost per unit using ABC. Give your answers to two decimal places. (2 marks)

	Flock	*Crock*
Total unit cost – ABC		

TASK 3 (15 MARKS)

You are a management accounting technician at Stewart Chemicals which produce a range of products, one of which is 'Stew 2'. It is packed in 10 litre drums.

One of your responsibilities is the preparation of a monthly performance report using standard costing and variance analysis.

The following information relates to the financial performance for June 20XX.

			Budget		*Actual*	
Drums of 'Stew 2'			5,000		4,800	
Costs	*Units of input*	*Standard cost per unit of input*	*Standard cost per drum*	*Standard cost of budgeted production*	*Actual cost per unit of input*	*Actual cost*
Direct material	10 litres	£2	£20	£100,000	£2.05	£105,000
Direct labour	1 hour	£8	£8	£40,000	£8.20	£41,820
Fixed overhead	1 hour	£15	£15	£75,000		£80,000
			£43	£215,000		£226,820

Calculate the following variances and prepare a statement reconciling the standard cost of actual production to the actual cost of production for June 20XX.

Reconciliation of standard cost of actual production to actual cost of production for June 20XX.

	£	F/A	£
Standard cost of actual production			
Direct labour rate			
Direct labour efficiency			
Direct material price			
Direct material usage			
Fixed overhead expenditure			
Fixed overhead volume			
Total variance			
Actual cost			

TASK 4 **(12 MARKS)**

Materials have been priced as follows for the past four years:

	£
20X0	1.57
20X1	1.73
20X2	1.84
20X3	2.05

(a) Convert the price of the materials for the four years to index numbers using 20X0 as the base year. Give your answers to TWO decimal places. **(2 marks)**

Year	*Price (£)*	*Index number*
20X0	1.57	
20X1	1.73	
20X2	1.84	
20X3	2.05	

(b) The total price increase over the four years expressed as a percentage (to 2 decimal places) is [ ] % **(1 mark)**

(c) If the price increase for 20X4 is 9% compared to 20X3, **(1 mark)**

(i) The price in 20X4 is £ [ ]

(ii) The index number for the 20X4 price is [ ]

A business has costs which follow the linear regression equation Y = a + bX, where X is the output volume.

The following data has been gathered about the costs for the last 2 months:

Output (units)	*Total costs (£)*
500	4,600
900	7,000

(d) calculate the values of a and b. **(2 marks)**

a = ☐

b = ☐

(e) Insert the three month moving averages into the table below: **(5 marks)**

Month	*Sales (units)*	*Three month moving average (units)*
July	2,320	
August	2,400	
September	2,420	
October	2,520	
November	2,660	
December	3,000	
January	2,540	

(f) Complete the following sentences **(1 mark)**

Prediction of a figure that lies within a range of data that has previously been observed is referred to as ☐

random variations/trend/interpolation/extrapolation

The observation that sales of a particular item are usually higher during the run up to Christmas is an example of ☐

underlying trend/residual variation/cyclical variation/seasonal variation

TASK 5 **(18 MARKS)**

On producing your usual monthly variance analysis report, the Production Manager informs you that of the total hours worked in the period, 200 hours was 'down time' as there had been a major breakdown of plant and this had resulted in 2,000 litres of raw material being wasted. The remuneration package for the Production Manager includes a bonus which is linked to linked having net favourable variances on the areas they can control.

Write a memo to the Finance Director explaining the possible effect of these factors on the variances for labour efficiency and material usage, and make any recommendations you feel may be appropriate. (12 marks)

Comment on the ethical issues the bonus measure could cause. (6 marks)

MEMO
To: **From:** **Date:** **Subject:**

TASK 6 **(15 MARKS)**

A Ltd has developed an updated product. The product competes with a dozen other companies. B Ltd is a major competitor and market leader with over 60% of the market. You have been given the following information about A and B for the year ended 31 May 2012.

Income statement	*A*	*B*
	£000	£000
Turnover	35,000	200,000
Cost of production		
Direct (raw) materials	12,000	33,000
Direct labour	7,500	22,000
Fixed production overheads	6,000	30,000
Total cost of sales	25,500	85,000
Gross profit	9,500	115,000
Selling and distribution costs	1,000	10,000
Administration costs	3,750	7,500
Advertising costs	2,500	50,000
Net profit	2,250	47,500

Other information		*A*	*B*
Number of units sold	Units	6,000,000	22,000,000
Net assets	£	50,000,000	85,000,000

Calculate the following performance indicators for A and B *(give answers to two decimal places):*

	A	*B*
Selling price per unit		
Material cost per unit		
Labour cost per unit		
Fixed cost per unit		
Gross profit margin %		
Net profit margin %		
Advertising cost as % of turnover		
Return on net assets		

TASK 7 **(18 MARKS)**

The current materials cost is £80 per unit. Higher quality material will need to be used in all products from next year. This is expected to increase materials costs by 10%.

Current fixed production costs are £70k. As a result of the new legislation, they are expected to increase to £100,000.

The selling price is expected to increase from £800 to £820 per unit.

The increased selling price is not expected to cause sales volumes to change from their current level of 20,000 units.

Labour hours are currently 195,000 hours but are expected to be 200,000 hours next year, and will be paid at £15 per hour.

Additional investment of £500,000 will be required which will be depreciated at 20% per annum.

Assume inventory levels are kept at zero.

All other costs will remain the same.

Calculate the total annual INCREASE in profit by completing the table below. **(10 marks)**

	Units	*Price/cost*	*Total*
Increase in revenue			
Increase in material cost			
Increase in labour cost			
Additional fixed costs			
Depreciation			
Additional profit			

The return on additional investment is [ ] **%.** **(1 mark)**

The finance director has asked for the break even sales volume for the coming year. **(3 marks)**

The contribution per unit is £ [ ]

The break even sales volume is [ ] **units**

The margin of safety is [ ] **%**

Explain how the break-even point and margin of safety can help companies make decisions and deal with risk. **(4 marks)**

TASK 8 **(15 MARKS)**

SCL is a furniture manufacturer and has just received the results of a study on the current interest in their new leather sofa range. The study indicates that the maximum price the average customer is prepared to pay for a leather sofa is £1,000.

The company estimates that 1,200 sofas can be sold in a year.

At this level of production, the fixed overheads per sofa would be £240.

The labour requirement per sofa is 8 hours at a cost of £15 per hour.

The wooden frame and the stuffing material cost £90 per sofa.

The required profit margin is 30%.

One sofa uses 10 square metres of leather.

Calculate the target cost per square metre of leather. **(8 marks)**

	£
Sales price per sofa	
Profit margin	
Total costs	
Fixed cost per sofa	
Labour cost per sofa	
Wooden frame and stuffing material	
Maximum leather cost per sofa	
Target cost per square metre	

SCL's leather supplier quotes a list price of £30 per square metre for the grade of leather SCL needs. However, SCL has managed to negotiate a discount of 15% on this price.

The discount should be ACCEPTED/REJECTED because the £30 reduces to £ [ ]

(to the nearest pence) which is ABOVE/BELOW the target cost. ***(Delete as appropriate.)***

The minimum percentage discount needed to achieve the target cost is [ ] **%**
(to 2 decimal places). **(2 marks)**

Discuss how SCL could use value analysis if they needed to further reduce the cost of the sofa in the future, identify any ethical considerations they may face. **(5 marks)**

Section 4

MOCK ASSESSMENT ANSWERS

TASK 1

Cost	*Monthly production*		*Cost classification*
	5,200 units	*12,000 units*	
	£	£	
Direct material	104,000	240,000	Variable
Direct labour	41,600	96,000	Variable
Supervisor salary	2,500	2,500	Fixed
Property rental costs	8,000	8,000	Fixed
Machine rental costs	9,500	18,000	Semi variable
Machine maintenance	6,000	10,000	Stepped fixed

TASK 2

(a)

Budgeted production £38,400/(2 hours × £8)	2,400
Budgeted labour hours 2,400 × 2 hours	4,800
Actual price of the direct material per litre used (£184,616/24,550)	£7.52
Actual direct labour rate per hour (£30,492/5,040 hours)	£6.05

(b)

	£	*Flock* (£)	*Crock* (£)
Cost driver rate – special parts handling	700		
Cost driver rate – machine set ups	400		
Total special parts		140,000	210,000
Total machine set ups		20,000	100,000

Cost driver rates:

Special parts = £350,000/(200 + 300) = £700

Machines set ups = £120,000/(50 + 150) = £400

Flock costs:

Special parts = £700 × 200 = 140,000; machine set ups = £400 × 50 = 20,000

(c)

	Flock	*Crock*
Total unit cost – ABC	29.50	33.50

Flock = 6 + 7.50 + ((140,000 + 20,000)/10,000) = 29.50

Crock = 8 + 10 + ((210,000 + 100,000)/20,000) = 33.50

TASK 3

	£	F/A
Direct material price variance AQ × AP = AQ × £2.05 = £105,000 (AQ = 51,220) AQ × SP = 51,220 × £2 = £102,440	2,560	A
Direct material usage variance AQ × SP = 51,220 × £2 = £102,440 SQ × SP = 4,800 × 10 × £2 = £96,000	6,440	A
Direct labour rate variance AQ × AP = AQ × £8.20 = £41,820 (AQ = 5,100) AQ × SP = 5,100 × £8 = £40,800	1,020	A
Direct labour efficiency variance AQ × SP = 5,100 × £8 = £40,800 SQ × SP = 4,800 × 1 × £8 = £38,400	2,400	A
Fixed overhead expenditure variance Actual = £80,000 Budget = £75,000	5,000	A
Fixed overhead volume variance Budget = 5,000 × 1 × £15 = £75,000 SQ × SP = 4,800 × 1 × £15 = £72,000	3,000	A

	£	F/A	£
Standard cost of actual production (W1)			206,400
Direct labour rate	1,020	A	
Direct labour efficiency	2,400	A	
Direct material price	2,560	A	
Direct material usage	6,440	A	
Fixed overhead expenditure	5,000	A	
Fixed overhead volume	3,000	A	
Total variance	20,420	A	20,420
Actual cost			226,820

(W1) £215,000/5,000 units × 4,800 units = £206,400

TASK 4

(a)

Year	*Price (£)*	*Workings*	*Index number*
20X0	1.57		100 (base year)
20X1	1.73	1.73/1.57 × 100	110.19
20X2	1.84	1.84/1.57 × 100	117.20
20X3	2.05	2.05/1.57 × 100	130.57

(b) £((2.05 – 1.57)/1.57) × 100 = **30.57%**

(c) (i) £2.05 × 1.09 = **£2.23**

(ii) 2.23/1.57 × 100 = **142.04**

(d) b = (£7,000 – £4,600)/(900 – 500) = **£6**

a = £4,600 – (£6 × 500) = **1,600**

(e)

Month	*Sales (units)*	*Three month moving average (units)*
July	2,320	
August	2,400	2,380 (W1)
September	2,420	2,447
October	2,520	2,533
November	2,660	2,727
December	3,000	2,733
January	2,540	

(W1) = (2320 + 2400 + 2420)/3= 2380

(f) Prediction of a figure that lies within a range of data that has previously been observed is referred to as **interpolation**.

The observation that sales of a particular item are usually higher during the run up to Christmas is an example of **seasonal variation**.

TASK 5

MEMO

To:	Finance Director	**Subject:**	Variances
From:	Accounting Technician	**Date:**	Today

Since producing my variance analysis report, I have been informed by the Production Manager of factors affecting both labour efficiency and material usage.

Direct labour efficiency variance

The workforce may have appeared to have been inefficient, taking too many hours to produce the required number of units. However, 200 of those hours were due to 'down time' arising from a plant breakdown, thus accounting for part of a possible adverse labour efficiency variance.

This efficiency variance should ideally be split into a genuine efficiency variance (controllable by the workers) and an idle time variance (caused by the plant breakdown and out of the control of the workers).

The production manager should investigate whether the plant has now been fixed so that this does not happen again.

Direct material usage variance

The breakdown in the plant caused waste of 2,000 litres of raw material. This is a related variance to the one above. The material usage variance will probably be adverse, having had to use more material to complete the required production.

Again, the wasted material might be removed from the usage variance to identify whether usage (apart from the wastage identified) was otherwise favourable or adverse.

Both the efficiency and usage variances caused by the machine breakdown should be allocated to the manager in charge of machine maintenance. He or she should explain how this has happened and explain what they intend to do to ensure that this does not happen in the future.

Ethical issues

As the production manager has a bonus linked into having net controllable favourable variances, the production manager may have their objectivity compromised.

This may lead to them trying to apportion blame to external influences for any issues. The reasons given may well be correct, but the company should verify that they really are outside of the production manager's control.

The machine breakdown could have been caused by the production manager delaying maintenance in a previous period to avoid costs.

A consideration for the likelihood of any unethical behaviour would be the size of the bonus; if it is a significant proportion of the remuneration then it will add to the pressure for the production manager to achieve the target as they may rely on the money.

TASK 6

	A	*B*
Selling price per unit	5.83	9.09
Material cost per unit	2.00	1.50
Labour cost per unit	1.25	1.00
Fixed cost per unit	1.00	1.36
Gross profit margin %	27.14	57.50
Net profit margin %	6.43	23.75
Advertising cost as % of turnover	7.14	25.00
Return on net assets	4.50	55.88

TASK 7

	Units	*Price/cost*	*Total*
Increase in revenue	20,000	20	400,000
Increase in material cost	20,000	8	(160,000)
Increase in labour cost			(75,000)
Additional fixed costs			(30,000)
Depreciation			(100,000)
Additional profit			35,000

The return on additional investment is 7%.

The fixed costs are £200,000

The contribution per unit is £820 – £88 – £150 = £582

The break even sales volume is £200,000/£582 = 344 units.

Margin of safety = (budgeted sales – breakeven point)/budgeted sales

= (20,000 – 344)/20,000 = 0.9828 or 98.28%

The breakeven point is when a company makes no profit or loss, costs equal income or more specifically contribution equals fixed costs. Being able to work out how many units would be required to be sold to breakeven can help a company decide which products to sell or which markets to sell in. If they think their sales will not be enough to breakeven they could avoid that market.

Margin of Safety considers the difference between planned sales and the breakeven point. We all know that what we plan to happen does not always work out and it gives a company the opportunity to assess the buffer they have and consider if it is enough to make sure they will turn a profit. If a margin of safety is small, say 1% or 100 units, the company could decide not to sell, or take steps to ensure sales are as close to budget as possible.

By using these criteria, companies can highlight risk areas and focus on the biggest risks, thus reducing the overall risk to the company.

TASK 8

	£
Sales price per sofa	1,000
Profit margin (30% × £1,000)	300
Total costs	700
Fixed cost per sofa	240
Labour cost per sofa (8 hours × £15)	120
Wooden frame and stuffing material	90
Maximum leather cost per sofa	250
Target cost per square metre (£250/10 metres)	25

The discount should be **REJECTED** because the £30 reduces to **£25.50** (£30 × 0.85) which is **ABOVE** the target cost.

The minimum percentage discount needed to achieve the target cost is **16.67%** (£5/£30).

Value analysis is about reducing the cost of production while maintaining the value to the customer.

SCL could look at the materials used in the construction of the frame or stuffing the cushion and see if there is a cheaper alternative that is as effective as the current material used.

They could also look at the labour used, some of the work will require skilled workers that are paid at a higher rate, but they may be able to do some of the work with lower skilled/unskilled staff.

Ethics

The decision about what labour to use or what material to use would not just be about price/cost. They would also need to consider their customers safety and the impact on the environment. Obviously they would have to comply with legal requirements about safety, but if they chose a cheaper type of material that while still safety compliant was more flammable, they would be increasing the risks to the customer.

Often manufacturing overseas can lead to a reduction in labour costs, but SCL would need to make sure that the labour force was not being exploited or treated unfairly.